THE NATO INTERNATIONAL
STAFF/SECRETARIAT: 1952-1957

Lord Ismay, KG, PC, GCB, CH, DSO

Secretary-General of NATO, 1952–1957

THE NATO INTERNATIONAL STAFF/SECRETARIAT

1952-1957

A STUDY IN INTERNATIONAL ADMINISTRATION

by

Robert S. Jordan

LONDON
OXFORD UNIVERSITY PRESS
NEW YORK   TORONTO
1967

Oxford University Press, Ely House, London, W.1

GLASGOW NEW YORK TORONTO MELBOURNE, WELLINGTON
CAPE TOWN SALISBURY IBADAN NAIROBI LUSAKA ADDIS ABABA
BOMBAY CALCUTTA MADRAS KARACHI LAHORE DACCA
KUALA LUMPUR HONG KONG TOKYO

Made in Great Britain at the Pitman Press, Bath

FOREWORD AND ACKNOWLEDGEMENT

THE North Atlantic Treaty Organization, in the public image, has represented military preparedness during the Cold War, incipient Atlantic Community, political harmony (or disharmony), and, to some extent, economic and financial co-operation. Most of these aspects of the Organization have been discussed at length both in the spoken and the written word. But one most important aspect of the Alliance has not been written about: the detailed working of the leading civilian agencies—the Council, the Office of the Secretary-General, and the International Staff/Secretariat.

These agencies have been described in general terms in journals, books, and public speeches; but they have not been treated as a self-contained area of activity within the framework of the Alliance, performing duties and fulfilling roles in some ways related to one another, and in other ways disparate. The purpose of this study, using unpublished documents and interviews, as well as published materials, is to trace the development of the role of the International Staff/Secretariat during Lord Ismay's tenure of office as first Secretary-General.

As the name 'Staff/Secretariat' implies, this central civilian body discharged a dual service. One was to perform the duties of a permanent secretariat to the Council, its committees, subcommittees, and working groups, under an Executive Secretary. The other service was to respond to the operating needs of the Alliance in political, economic, financial and logistic matters. Four functional Divisions and two Independent Offices were created to meet these needs, all reporting directly to the Secretary-General but also under the general supervision of Council Committees composed of national representatives, some of which were chaired by members of the International Staff/Secretariat.

A large part of this study is devoted to the problems encountered in the internal administration of the International Staff/Secretariat, including the employment characteristics peculiar to the so-called international civil servant. These matters are developed in detail because they bring to light important conditions bearing upon the role of the International Staff/Secretariat in the life of the Alliance and show the obstacles to, as well as the opportunities for, building an international civil service. Emoluments, recruitment and promotion procedures, although capable of being administratively organized into a uniform system, which in theory could be applied to international organizations in general, must meet the problems of diversity of fiscal responsibility and national policies. The subordination of the former to the latter still remains one of the pervasive facts of international life and should not be overlooked in contemplating the future of international administration. The principles of public personnel administration based on the merit system have never been upheld without significant qualifications when they have been applied to international organizations. For sound reasons NATO has been no exception.

The notion that a member nation's interest, if it is its true interest, should *ipso facto* also be the interest of the Alliance falls under the weight of its own contradiction. Fifteen national interests simply do not add up to one Alliance interest in every sphere of the Alliance's activity. By the same token, an international civil servant who acts in what could be considered the Organization's true interest will not, in every case, act in the interest of his own nation as that interest is interpreted by his government.

Any specific convergence of national interests in NATO was achieved through the traditional methods of negotiation, mediation, compromise, and bargaining. The unique position of the Secretary-General as both the servant of the Council (in his role as Head of the International Staff/Secretariat), and at the same time as the presiding officer of the Council (in his role as Vice-Chairman, later Chairman), gave him opportunities to exert his influence in this essential activity which were not as readily available to his forebears in the League of Nations and the United Nations Organization.

In summary, this study develops the point that NATO stands as much in the growing tradition of functional international organization as in that of military alliances. In NATO the two are intertwined to an unprecedented extent. The various Divisions and Independent Offices of the International Staff/Secretariat have been applying themselves to matters of military finance, equipment, and supply, but they have also been establishing precedents and relationships, and working out problems which can have a significant impact on the development of international administration.

The author is indebted to many persons in and out of NATO for enabling him to complete this study. He is first of all grateful to the United States Educational Commission in the United Kingdom for arranging a Fulbright grant to St. Antony's College, Oxford. He is also deeply indebted to Captain Lord Coleridge, C.B.E., Executive Secretary of NATO, who made it possible for the study to be conducted at NATO Headquarters, and to the Secretary-General for permission to quote from NATO documents.

Although singling out a few persons does not do justice to the help of many others, the author would nevertheless like to express gratitude to Mr. Eugene Merrill, former Controller for NATO Infrastructure, who encouraged him to begin the study; to Miss Lucille Peart of the International Staff/Secretariat for reviewing the manuscript on behalf of NATO Headquarters, as it was being written; to Mrs. Ruth Brosnan of the staff of The George Washington University, who assisted so generously in revising the manuscript for publication; and to Colonel Merrill G. Hatch, of the United States Army, whose consistent interest in the project provided a motivation for its completion. The two persons in the academic world to whom the author owes an unrepayable debt for their steadfast interest and support are Professor Norman H. Gibbs of All Souls College, Oxford, and Professor John B. Whitton of Princeton University.

The author had the privilege of showing the manuscript, as revised for publication, to Lord Ismay a few months before his death. He hoped that Lord Ismay would also see the published work. Since that is not possible, he would like to close this foreword by quoting a letter which Lord Ismay wrote after reading the manuscript, and which he said the author could feel free to publish. The letter reflects Lord Ismay's unfailing modesty and consideration for others:

3rd September 1965.

My dear Jordan,

I am grateful to you for letting me see your study of the creation and work of the International Staff/Secretariat of NATO during my term of office as Secretary-General: and I am glad that the fruits of your excellent research are to be placed on record by the Oxford University Press. Thus the lessons that were learned, both by our successes and our mistakes, will be available for those who may be responsible for international administration in one field or another in the days to come.

I have not of course attempted to check your study in detail, but as a general comment, I must insist, without any false modesty, that you give far too much credit to myself, and far too little credit to my advisors, particularly Lord Coleridge, for the good work done and solid reputation gained by the International Staff/Secretariat.

Yours sincerely,
Ismay

Oxford   Robert S. Jordan
September 1965

TABLE OF CONTENTS

PART IV ADMINISTRATION OF THE DIVISIONS OF THE INTERNATIONAL STAFF/SECRETARIAT

PART V CONCLUSIONS 289

TABLES

ABBREVIATIONS

AFCENT	Allied Forces Central Europe
ARQ	Annual Review Questionnaire
ASG	Assistant Secretary-General
BBC	British Broadcasting Corporation
CID	Committee of Imperial Defence
DPB	Defence Production Board
DPC	Defence Production Committee
ECA(US)	Economic Co-operation Administration
ECSA	European Crypto Security Agency
EDC	European Defence Community
ELLA	European Long Lines Agency
EMCC	European Military Communications Co-ordination Committee
ENCA	European Naval Communication Agency
EPU	European Payments Union
ERFA	European Radio Frequency Agency
EUCOM	European Command
FEB	Financial and Economic Board
FICA	Federation of International Civil Servants Associations
MAAGs(US)	Military Assistance Advisory Groups
MDAP(US)	Mutual Defence Assistance Programme
MPSB	Military Production and Supply Board
MSA(US)	Mutual Security Administration
NATO	North Atlantic Treaty Organization
OEEC	Organization for European Economic Co-operation
OSP	Off-shore Procurement
P & P	Payments and Progress
PL	Production and Logistics
POL	Petrol, Oil and Lubricants
PWS	Permanent Working Staff
SACLANT	Supreme Commander, Atlantic
SHAPE	Supreme Headquarters, Allied Powers Europe
STANAG	Standardization Agreement
TCC	Temporary Council Committee
USIS	United States Information Service
WEU	Western European Union
WUDO	Western Union Defence Organization

PART I

LORD ISMAY COMES TO NATO

'We must not underrate the contributions of personality and chance, nor must we ignore the effect of the system on the men who ran it.'

John Ehrman

'. . . although Britain was the last of the great nations to develop her own machinery for systematic defence planning, the popularity of the methods she adopted is now as great as that of the Prussian General Staff in earlier times.'

N. H. Gibbs

CHAPTER I

THE TRADITION OF
INTERNATIONAL ADMINISTRATION

WHEN Lord Ismay assumed the mantle of office as first
Secretary-General of NATO in April 1952, he was in part
assuming an entirely new role in the history of international
organizations, and in part treading the path of eminent
predecessors.

From his title, it would appear that his role was already well
defined, for many men have been called 'Secretary-General'.
The term goes back at least to 1861, when the following reference was made in a book discussing the administration of
Java: 'The Governor-General is further assisted by a Secretary-
General, who has under him three secretaries of Government
and a large staff of clerks.'[1] But the use of the term to describe the
head of an international organization began with the establishment of an international secretariat in the League of Nations.

Prior to the League, there had been nothing resembling an
international budget and civil service such as is known today—
they were unthinkable in the days when national sovereignty
was the first rule of international life. In the periodic conferences
held to work out procedures for the peaceful settlement of
international disputes, mainly through arbitration or mediation or 'good offices', *ad hoc* secretariats were used. It remained
for the League of Nations to introduce into international
relations the political and administrative significance which is
now attached to the office of Secretary-General.[2] The example

---

[1] The quotation appears in the *Oxford English Dictionary* (1933), IX.

[2] The Head of the British Secretariat to the Paris Peace Conference
(1919) recalled that he first met the term 'Secretary-General' as it applies to
international organizations at the Conference. The secretariat to the Conference had a secretary-general and a committee composed of a secretary
from each of the Inviting Powers. Lord Hankey commented: 'The "donkey-
work" was done in the Quai d'Orsay in principle, but in practice the most

set by Sir Eric Drummond, the first Secretary-General of the League, has had a direct influence on all later attempts at international administration. It is therefore appropriate to examine in detail both the source of his powers and how he exercised them.

His powers derived from three specific grants in the League Covenant. A general grant of power was contained in Article II, which stated that 'the action of the League under this covenant shall be effected through the instrumentality of an Assembly and of a Council, with a permanent Secretariat'.

The Secretariat itself was defined in Article VI as comprising 'a Secretary-General and such secretaries and staff as may be required'. As to the specific role of the Secretary-General, Article VI provided that 'the Secretary-General shall act in that capacity at all meetings of the assembly and of the Council'. From the records of the Peace Conference, it can be inferred that the phrase 'in that capacity' meant, at the very least, that the Secretary-General carried responsibilities similar to those of a British Cabinet Committee secretary.

The most important political power conferred on the Secretary-General was that of summoning a meeting of the Council if, after having been notified by a government of the existence of a dispute which threatened peace, he and the President of the Council considered that the dispute warranted such action, or if he had been requested to do so by a member State. He was responsible for making 'all necessary arrangements for a full investigation and consideration thereof' (Articles XI and XV).

In his position as administrative head of the League Secretariat, no limitation was placed upon the Secretary-General. Decisions as to the type of staff, its composition and functions, were left to him. He was subject only to the limits imposed by the nature of the work, the position itself, and, of

---

important part was done in the British Secretariat in the Villa Majestic which I had reinforced from the Secretariat of the Supreme War Council at Versailles which was still in existence. . . .' (Private memorandum, The Rt. Hon. Lord Hankey, P.C., G.C.B., G.C.V.O., to Robert Jordan, 31 Aug. 1959. Lord Hankey was also Secretary to the British Cabinet and the Committee of Imperial Defence.)

course, the budget. His authority for his actions was unquestioned.[3]

Within this constitutional framework, Sir Eric Drummond left his mark in two important respects: first, in the type of Secretariat he established; and second, in his personal role both within the League and before the world. He discussed his contribution in the first respect in a journal article written in March 1924:

Two theories were prevalent [at the Peace Conference]. The first was that the Secretariat should be composed of national delegations of the various members of the League. Each delegation would be paid for by the Government of the country from which it came, and be responsible solely to that Government. The practice which had prevailed at the international conferences previous to the foundation of the League of Nations would thus be continued, while the duties of the Secretary-General would be largely confined to the co-ordination on special occasions of the services of the national delegations of the Secretariat, and to the centralization of administrative functions.

Those who advocated the second theory held that the Secretariat should form, as far as was practicable, an international Civil Service, in which men and women of various nationalities might unite in preparing and presenting to the members of the League an objective and common basis of discussion. They would also be entrusted, it was proposed, with the execution of any decisions ultimately taken by the Governments. Under this scheme the Secretary-General would not only be the co-ordination centre of the activities of the Secretariat, but its members would be responsible to him alone, and not to the Governments of the countries of which they were nationals, and would be remunerated from the general funds of the League.

The old system had not given altogether satisfactory results; and when the members of a committee set up by the Plenary Peace Conference met to consider the matter of organization, I strongly urged that the second plan should be adopted.[4]

Sir Eric then went on to give his reasons for supporting the second plan:

[3] Egon F. Ranshofen-Wertheimer, *The International Secretariat* (Washington, 1945), p. 44.

[4] Article in *The World Today*, March 1924, as quoted in C. Howard-Ellis, *The Origin Structure and Working of the League of Nations* (London, 1928), pp. 171–2.

2

International conferences in the past had often suffered from the lack of any organized international preparatory work and we felt that it was exactly in this domain that a new system was required if the League were to fulfil the purposes for which it had been founded. It seemed to us that it would be of great value if an expert and impartial organization existed which, before discussion by the national representatives took place, could draw up objective statements of the problems to be discussed, and indicate those points on which it seemed that the Governments were generally in accord. If this could be done, we held that discussion by the Government representatives would be automatically limited to matters where divergence of view really existed—and all who have had experience of international affairs know how much this increases the chances of reaching a definite and successful result. Furthermore, we maintained that the execution of decisions should be entrusted to people who, being the servants of all the States Members of the League, could be relied upon to carry them out with complete freedom from national bias.[5]

Drummond's ideas were adopted and he successfully created the first truly international civil service, based upon the principle of loyalty to the organization rather than to the country of national origin.[6] As a former member of the League Secretariat observed, he 'ensured the Secretary-General of the League becoming a new and unprecedented institution in the history of the world'.[7] The testimony of the first Secretary-General of the United Nations also paid tribute to this innovation of Drummond's: 'His decision to create the first truly international secretariat was a decision of profound significance —surely one of the most important and promising political developments of the twentieth century. His place in history is secure.'[8]

As a public international figure, the Secretary-General's

---

[5] Ibid.

[6] The International Institute of Agriculture, with headquarters at Rome, in theory had an international civil service prior to the League of Nations, but in practice the staff was entirely Italian because the salaries were too low to attract other nationalities. (Interview with Dr. A. Loveday, former Director of the Economic, Financial and Transit Dept. of the League of Nations, and former Warden of Nuffield College, Oxford, 15 Oct. 1959.)

[7] Howard-Ellis, p. 172.

[8] Trygve Lie, *In the Cause of Peace* (New York, 1954), p. 41.

place in history is less secure. He did not enter the debates of the League organs unless it was absolutely necessary, and these occasions usually concerned personnel or budgetary matters. He did not utilize his annual report either to dramatize his own role or to forward his own views.[9] He did not regard himself as an independent innovator in the political workings of the League. He was an organizer and administrator; at most, a negotiator and mediator.[10] It is possible that if Drummond had attempted to formulate an independent programme, he might have aroused the League to more energetic decisions. On the other hand, the resistance of the member States to such a positive role might have thwarted him and redounded adversely on his office.

This is not to say that Drummond never engaged in political activity. Quite the contrary. He was widely reputed to be an excellent behind-the-scenes man. Speculating upon the nature of the first Secretary-General of the United Nations, a former personal assistant to Drummond made this observation: 'The new international institution will be fortunate if it secures the services of one who was as gifted a moderator, as impartial a negotiator, as trusted and well-informed a political confessor

[9] The annual reports, however, according to a Chatham House Study Group headed by Sir Eric Drummond (then the Rt. Hon. the Earl of Perth), 'provided the text of the chief debates in each body, and furnished delegates with all the material they required for the discussion of past and future policy'. *The International Secretariat of the Future* (London, 1944), p. 8.

[10] Mr. Ranshofen-Wertheimer had a definite opinion about this. He said: 'All things considered, it can be stated that it was a mistake on the part of the statesmen responsible for establishing the League to choose an administrator. . . . Experience proves that it is a statesman who must be chosen as head of a political agency. He must be an international leader. Unless he is that, no international agency can exhaust the possibilities inherent in its mission. The lesson of the League in this respect is as clear as possible, hardly open to contention, and absolutely convincing' (p. 49). A former Director of the League of Nations disagreed with this observation; he felt that Sir Eric Drummond should not have been characterized as an administrator but rather as a skilful diplomat. To set the extreme of administrator *v.* international leader, he felt, leaves out the very valuable role of skilled diplomatist and negotiator, which Sir Eric Drummond was. (Interview with Dr. A. Loveday, 15 Oct. 1959.)

. . . as Sir Eric Drummond.'[11] However, these attributes are not those characteristic of dynamic, positive, public leadership.

Perhaps one of the reasons Drummond did not expand his public functions was that he was a poor speaker and found this sort of work personally uncongenial. Although he travelled a lot he was not widely known to the general public and made little attempt at a direct appeal to it. As he said himself: 'Behind-the-scenes activities suited my temperament and previous experience. I was neither a Parliamentarian nor a politician and totally unaccustomed to making speeches in public.'[12] Lord Ismay, by contrast, found his public functions more agreeable, and believed them to be essential (*below* Chapter IX).

Drummond's successor, M. Avenol, a Frenchman, did not extend the outlines of the office beyond its initial scope. Reflecting upon his role, he observed:

> According to the Covenant, the Secretary-General was quite a 'personage'. There was nothing which said he could not take important political initiative . . . I favoured an active role for the Secretary-General . . . but there was the respected example of Sir Eric. He was, you know, very respected. I could not easily change this tradition. . . . The role of the Secretary-General depends upon the man. And upon the circumstances. . . .[13]

Administratively, Avenol altered the structure and relationships of the Secretariat so that it favoured the Continental rather than the British administrative concept. He installed a strong *chef de cabinet* who pulled together the strings of internal administration more firmly into the Secretary-General's office.[14] This development was paralleled to some extent in

---

[11] J. V. Wilson, 'Problem of an International Secretariat', *International Affairs*, XX (1944), as quoted in Stephen M. Schwebel, *The Secretary-General of the United Nations* (Cambridge, 1952), pp. 6–7.

[12] ibid. p. 7.   [13] ibid. pp. 8–9.

[14] In Dr. Loveday's opinion the opponents of the shift made too much of it. He believed that it was very useful to have a responsible officer in the Secretary-General's office who co-ordinated the various departmental papers, rather than, as previously, leaving it to the Directors themselves to do this. (Interview with Dr. A. Loveday, 15 Oct. 1959.)

NATO by M. Paul-Henri Spaak, Lord Ismay's successor. After Avenol's resignation at the outbreak of World War II, the League Secretariat and Secretary-General's office became a caretaker operation, and had little influence on the course of world events.

When time came for the drafters of the Charter of the United Nations to consider the type of leadership for it, opposition developed to the use of the title 'Secretary-General'. This opposition is interesting in view of the fact that apparently the drafters of the League Covenant had also not been entirely satisfied with the restrictive implications of the title. According to the British draft of the Covenant, which was the basis of the finished document, the chief officer of the League was to be called 'Chancellor'. This would have made his organization a 'chancellery' instead of a 'secretariat'.[15] The Chancellor would have had far more discretionary powers than were given to the Secretary-General. During the United Nations Charter-drafting days, when it was announced that the title 'Secretary-General' had been agreed upon, some of the people who had been intimately connected with the League protested that this title had been too restricting for the head of the League of Nations administration and would therefore be even more inappropriate for the head of the much larger administration of the United Nations. Even President Roosevelt found the title inadequate: he suggested the 'World's Moderator'.[16]

[15] For a discussion of the contemplated powers of the Secretary-General of the League, see Ranshofen-Wertheimer, Ch. IV. Here is one explanation why the title 'Chancellor' was suggested: 'The intention was to make M. Venizelos the first Chancellor, and give him the power to summon meetings of the Council on his own initiative. When Venizelos refused, and it was decided to put a civil servant instead of what was at the time considered a great statesman at the head of the Secretariat, the name was changed, and Articles XI and XV slightly altered so as to make it clear that the Council could be summoned only on the initiative of some government member of the League.' (Howard-Ellis, p. 163.) Lord Hankey has written: 'There was great and prolonged discussion on the term "Chancellor". I resisted on the ground that "the tail must not appear to wag the dog", which would happen for certain by the adoption of so pompous a title as "Chancellor" and eventually I got my way.' (Private memorandum from Lord Hankey to Robert Jordan, 31 Aug. 1959.)

[16] Schwebel, p. 18.

Mr. Trygve Lie, the first occupant of the office of Secretary-General of the United Nations Organization, also clearly did not subscribe to the limited concept of the office as it had existed under his League predecessors. He commented: 'In my view it was clearly not the intention of the Charter that the limited concept of the office of Secretary-General which Sir Eric evolved in the League should be perpetuated in the United Nations.'[17]

In fact the wording of the Charter's and the Covenant's provisions for their secretariats was similar. Article 97 of the Charter stated that 'the Secretariat shall comprise a Secretary-General and such staff as the Organization shall require. . . . He shall be the chief administrative officer of the Organization.' Article VI of the Covenant said much the same. The Secretary-General of the League was 'appointed by the Council with the approval of the majority of the Assembly' (Article VI); Article 97 of the Charter said that the Secretary-General 'shall be appointed by the General Assembly upon the recommendation of the Security Council'. The essential ingredient in both was the concurrence of the Great Powers.[18]

---

[17] Lie, pp. 41–42.

[18] The variation in the method of renewal of Mr. Lie's appointment—the extension of his first term rather than a fresh appointment to a second five-year term—in the face of Soviet opposition to his taking a second term, did not mitigate the original intent of the Charter; in fact, if anything, it affirmed the necessity for the concurrence of permanent members of the Security Council if the Secretary-General was to provide effective leadership. In this sense the U.N.'s experience was not very far removed from the workings of traditional coalition diplomacy. The Council of Europe also had difficulty in ascertaining who should be consulted in making the nomination for their Secretary-General. The Consultative Assembly wanted it firmly established that the Council of Ministers should consult with the Consultative Assembly before coming to a final decision on any specific candidate (see Article 36 of the Statute of the Council of Europe). After the first appointment the Assembly made the following recommendation to the Council of Ministers: '. . . that in future, before making recommendations concerning the appointment of the Secretary-General or of a Deputy Secretary-General, it should consult the representatives of the Assembly on the Joint Committee, the creation of which was approved by the Committee of Ministers in May, 1951. . . .' (Council of Europe, 'Report on the Appointment of the Secretary-General and on the Appointment and

The chief difference between the two offices was that the Secretary-General of the United Nations could make recommendations directly to the organs of the United Nations on his own initiative. He could place items on the provisional agenda for meetings of the General Assembly, and, more important, under Article 99 he could bring to the attention of the Security Council 'any matter which in his opinion may threaten the maintenance of international peace and security'. As the Preparatory Commission of the United Nations pointed out, Article 99 gave the Secretary-General 'a quite special right which goes beyond any power previously accorded to the head of an international organization'.[19]

Article 99 opened up possibilities for an active political role which under the Covenant had not been constitutionally open to Sir Eric Drummond. The Secretary-General of the United Nations had been clothed with powers of initiative until then reserved exclusively to member States in their sovereign entities. It is conceivable that the negative example of the League prompted the positive approach of the United Nations.

Mr. Lie did not hesitate to adopt the 'expansive' approach to his office. In his submission of unsolicited memoranda to the United Nations organs and in his use of the annual report as a kind of 'State of the Union' message, he acted according to a broad conception of his office. He was also not as reluctant as Sir Eric Drummond to attribute world-wide significance to his public role. As he said:

The Secretary-General might be the symbol of the Organization as a whole—the symbol, in other words, of the international spirit. This, and his strategic situation at the very centre of international affairs as confidant of the world's statesmen and as spokesman to the world's peoples, attached significant influence to his position. . . . I was determined that the Secretary-General should be a force for peace.[20]

Promotion of the Staff of the Council of Europe', Fifth Ordinary Session, 20 Sept. 1953. Recommendation 49 of the Fifth Ordinary Session of the Consultative Assembly, 21 Sept. 1953.)

[19] Schwebel, p. 21.
[20] Lie, p. 42.

To be 'a force for peace' implied more than the role of a semi-anonymous 'civil-servant-type' official. To interpret the position as a symbol of the 'international spirit' gave an aura of ubiquity to it not claimed by Drummond. Even if the Secretary-General of the United Nations has perhaps not been able to operate in complete conformity with these assertions of Trygve Lie, the personalities of the two men who held the post while Lord Ismay was Secretary-General of NATO and the interests they served gave the idea of their symbolic function a plausibility not possible for the League.

The United Nations Charter granted that, in his secretariat role 'the Secretary-General shall act in that capacity in all meetings of the General Assembly, of the Security Council, of the Economic and Social Council, and of the Trusteeship Council. . . .' (Article 98.) The question again arises as to what was meant by the phrase 'in that capacity'. But by the time the Charter was drawn up the meaning had been affected not only by international and national traditions and by the legal provisions of the office itself, but also by the accrual of experience from the League. Most important for this study, Sir Eric Drummond's forthright advocacy of a truly international secretariat made a similar conception for the United Nations Secretariat virtually unassailable.[21]

It should be noted here that Sir Eric Drummond and Lord Ismay were to a large extent the products of the national administrative background from which they came. The kind of international secretariat which Drummond advocated, and which Lord Ismay was later to lead, was one which could serve a multitude of Committees. In Britain it is said that the process of governing is by committees—from the myriad interdepartmental committees at all levels to the biggest committee of them all, the House of Commons. Lord Ismay's career in government had been in the area of military planning, and this area, no less than any other in the British Government, conducted its business through committees.

---

[21] The idea of an international secretariat performing secretarial duties for a governing council of member governments has been generally accepted; but the idea that an international staff should engage in activities of a technical or 'operational' nature, has not received universal acceptance. For Lord Ismay's views on the subject see Ch. VI of this study.

The first permanent Cabinet-level committee which engaged in over-all defence planning was the Committee of Imperial Defence (CID). It was formed in 1902 and by a Cabinet Minute of 1904 became a permanent committee under the chairmanship of the Prime Minister.[22] The committee was charged to advise the Prime Minister on defence matters, and through a series of subcommittees to draw up plans for execution if Britain should become involved in a major war.

It soon became apparent to the Prime Minister and his colleagues that it was of little use to appoint a committee, to charge them with specific responsibilities, and then not to know what decisions had been taken, to whom they applied, or whether they had been carried out. When such a committee operated within a complex governing organization, the need for co-ordination and cross-communication became imperative. To deal with this problem a secretariat system was established which developed hand-in-hand with the growth of the military planning function. The first Secretary to the CID, Lord Sydenham, served from 1904 to 1907. He organized a central secretariat through which the various subcommittees of the CID functioned, and which came to be characterized as 'the cornerstone of the whole edifice'.[23]

Lord Sydenham was succeeded by Rear-Admiral Sir Charles Ottley, who served until 1912, and was in turn succeeded by Sir Maurice Hankey (later Lord Hankey).[24] Under Lord

[22] N. H. Gibbs, *The Origins of Imperial Defence*, Inaugural lecture delivered before the University of Oxford (Oxford 1955), p. 22; private memorandum, from Lord Hankey to Robert Jordan, 31 Aug. 1959. Being a Prime Ministerial—and not a Cabinet—Committee, records could be taken of the meetings. The Cabinet was still acting under the tradition that no record should be taken of proceedings at its meetings.

[23] Quoted in Lord Hankey, *Diplomacy by Conference* (London, 1946), p. 84. To be precise, a secretariat was first used in the subcommittee on Colonial and Coastal Defence, whose procedures were adopted in part by the entire CID under a recommendation of the War Office (Reconstitution) Committee—the Esher Committee—made in Jan. 1904. The following May and July, Treasury Minutes to this effect were published. John Ehrman, *Cabinet Government and War, 1890–1940* (Cambridge, 1958), p. 31.

[24] *Diplomacy*, p. 87. Sir Charles Ottley became unpopular because, rather than remain a passive secretary who synthesized other people's

Hankey, the secretariat of the CID came to play a significant role in the affairs of the nation, for during World War I the secretariat, along with the CID itself was incorporated into the Cabinet and the Imperial War Cabinet. This was the first time that the British Cabinet had used a professional secretariat.[25]

In tribute to the work of Lord Hankey and his secretariat, the Machinery of Government Committee which met in 1918 to consider post-war governmental organization, made this recommendation:

> . . . we think that there is one feature in the procedure of the War Cabinet which may well assume a permanent form, namely, the appointment of a Secretary to the Cabinet charged with the duty of collecting and putting into shape its agenda, of providing the information and material necessary for its deliberations, and of drawing up records of the results for communication to the Departments concerned.[26]

---

thinking, he preferred to advance his own ideas as well. Apparently it was considered important that the secretary should not compromise his posture of impartiality. (Interview with Lord Ismay, 28 May 1959.)

[25] The CID Secretariat was used by the Prime Minister, Mr. H. H. Asquith in his War Council, Dardanelles Committee, and War Committee, and then by Lloyd George in his War Cabinet and Imperial War Cabinet. Asquith said: 'We established the War Committee . . . which took over to a large extent the functions of the Committee of Imperial Defence. Experts were present and we always had the leading representatives of the Army and Navy present, and a record was kept of their proceedings.' (*Diplomacy*, p. 72.) Lord Hankey traced the development thus: 'As I always picture this story, it begins with Balfour's creation of the CID in 1904; the first phase of establishing principles for coordination of defence forces by Balfour; the successive stages of policy, plans and preparations by Asquith (the four Ps); and after the outbreak of war, the adaptation of the system by trial and error to the running of the war; that is to say first Asquith's War Council, then the first coalition's . . . stupid Dardanelles Committee, followed by the War Committee; and finally, after Lloyd George became PM the War Cabinet. But under Lloyd George the system was extended to the coordination of the British Empire forces by the Imperial War Cabinet, and, after the Italian defeat at Caporetto the Supreme War Council of the Allies with a joint Secretariat, where the British section (a branch of my Cabinet office), took and held the lead.' (Unpub. letter to Professor N. H. Gibbs, 31 Aug. 1959.)

[26] Ministry of Reconstruction, *Report of the Machinery of Government Committee* (London, 1918), p. 6.

In 1921 the CID was reconstituted, with Lord Hankey as head of a secretariat serving both the CID and the Cabinet. He filled this dual role until his retirement in 1938 when Sir Edward Bridges became Secretary to the Cabinet and Colonel Hastings Ismay became Secretary to the CID.

Ismay came to this position with extensive experience. From 1926 to 1930 he had been an Assistant Secretary to the CID, and from 1936 to 1938 Deputy-Secretary.[27] When World War II began the CID was once again integrated into the Cabinet, with Sir Edward Bridges as Secretary to the War Cabinet. Ismay became chief-of-staff to the Prime Minister, Mr. Winston Churchill, in Churchill's capacity as Minister of Defence, and his representative on the Chiefs-of-Staff Committee. The CID-Cabinet structure was thus converted into an organization called the 'Offices of the War Cabinet and of the Minister of Defence'.

The exact role of Lord Ismay during the war has been clearly explained. A White Paper of 1942 outlined Britain's war leadership structure:

> The ultimate responsibility for the conduct of the war rests with the War Cabinet, the Chiefs of Staff being their professional advisers. The Prime Minister and Minister of Defence [both Mr. Churchill] superintends on behalf of the War Cabinet, the work of the Chiefs of Staff committee.[28]

Churchill himself said: '. . . the formulation of strategic plans and the day-to-day conduct of operations . . . were

---

[27] *Who's Who, 1956*, p. 1532. Lord Hankey said of his thoughts concerning the recalling of Lord Ismay to the CID in 1938: 'When I was nearing the age of retirement I brought Ismay back as head of the CID branch of the Cabinet Secretariat. My idea was that he should take over, on my retirement, two, and, if possible all three of the posts I then held, namely Secretary to the Cabinet, and to the CID (including Chiefs-of-Staffs Sub-Committee), and perhaps the Clerkship of the Privy Council. But Ismay would not take more than the CID; Bridges took the Cabinet; and Howarth (my Deputy for the Cabinet) took over the Privy Council. In retrospect I think that was right at the time with a war approaching—but, in the long run, after the war and after Ismay had left that office, the division went far towards spoiling the efficiency of the Cabinet organization—but that is another story.' (Private memorandum to Robert Jordan, 31 Aug. 1959.)

[28] Quoted in John Ehrman, *Grand Strategy* (London, 1956), VI, p. 322.

settled by the Chiefs-of-Staff Committee acting directly under
the Minister of Defence'.[29] According to Churchill, Lord
Ismay fitted into the picture in this way:

> For the purpose of maintaining general supervision over the con-
> duct of the War, which I do under the authority of the War Cabinet
> and the Defence Committee, I have at my disposal a small staff,
> headed by Major-General Ismay, which works under the long-
> established procedure and machinery of the pre-war Committee
> of Imperial Defence, and forms part of the War Cabinet secre-
> tariat.[30]

There is a significant difference between planning a war and
fighting it. Besides a qualitative difference in decision-making
itself, the co-ordination necessary to conduct the war had to be
both internal, i.e. national, and external, i.e. inter-Allied.
Decisions made by the Chiefs-of-Staff Committee might have
been in agreement with, complementary to, or contradictory
of decisions made in Washington, Moscow, or elsewhere.
There had to be some central agency or person in the British
Government through whom the war-making threads would
pass.

There was no doubt who this person was. Churchill has
stated: '. . . as confidence grew the War Cabinet intervened
less actively in operational matters, though they watched them
with close attention and full knowledge. They took almost the
whole weight of home and party affairs off my shoulders, thus
setting me free to concentrate upon the main theme.'[31]

Since Churchill kept direct control over the functions of war
planning and execution, the man who stood closest to him also
stood closest to the major decisions taken in the British share
of the war. Lord Ismay, because of his official standing and his
personal influence, occupied this position. He was the pin-
wheel in the British machinery for the conduct of the war.
This is what he did:

As Deputy Secretary (Military) of the War Cabinet, Ismay supervised the running of the military Committees and their relations

[29] Winston Churchill, *The Second World War* (London, 1950), II, p. 16.
[30] Winston S. Churchill, *The War Speeches of the Rt. Hon. Winston S.
Churchill*, comp. Charles Eade (London, 1952), II, p. 217.
[31] *The Second World War*, II, p. 18.

with other interests; as a member of the Chiefs of Staff's Committee, he took his share of responsibility in its decisions, and geared the machine to its demands; as Chief of Staff to the Minister of Defence, he acted as the link between the machine, the Committee and the Minister, and as the link for the Committee with Washington and for the Prime Minister with allies and with commanders.[32]

In recognition of his service Ismay was awarded a barony in 1947. Under the post-war Labour Government he went to India as Chief-of-Staff to Lord Mountbatten, who as the last Viceroy had the difficult task of assisting at India's transition to independence. With the return of Churchill to power, Ismay became Secretary of State for Commonwealth Affairs, which post he reluctantly relinquished in 1952 to become Secretary-General of NATO.[33]

In sum, Lord Ismay was first a military staff officer, then a highest-level aide, co-ordinator, expediter, and diplomatist (he attended the Cairo, Malta, Teheran, Quebec, Moscow, and Yalta Conferences), and then a Cabinet minister.[34] He had had dealings with the Russians, the French, and the Americans on the highest plane, yet he was one of the second layer of public men by whom and through whom the top layer accomplished their affairs. He has been described as a 'tactful go-between, as "an interpreter, one among a thousand"; he explained, he soothed, he suggested, he harmonised. . . .'[35]

[32] Ehrman, *Grand Strategy*, VI, p. 333.

[33] *Who's Who, 1956*, p. 1532.

[34] S. E. Morison, in *American Contributions to the Strategy of World War II* (London, 1958), did not mention Lord Ismay in his discussion of the British war planning system. This is unfortunate.

[35] J. R. M. Butler, *Grand Strategy* (London, 1957), II, p. 250. General Eisenhower, in his memoirs, paid this tribute to Ismay: 'Ismay's position . . . was, from the American point of view, a critical one because it was through him that any subject could at any moment be brought to the attention of the Prime Minister and his principal assistants. It was fortunate, therefore, that . . . his personality was such as to win the confidence and friendship of his American associates. He was one of those men whose great ability condemned him throughout the war to a staff position. Consequently his name may be forgotten; but the contributions he made to the winning of the war were equal to those of many whose names became household words.' (*Crusade in Europe* (London, 1948), p. 487.) Lord Ismay's chance to leap into the spotlight of history came in 1952.

Lord Ismay had built a career in exercising his skills in the art of planning and then in executing those plans within the limits of feasibility. He had provided the 'lubrication' necessary to enable men of strong minds and enormous responsibilities to carry out their tasks successfully. NATO had men of equally strong minds, and certainly the magnitude of Lord Ismay's task was obvious to all. The traditions of the League secretariat and the United Nations, and the British Cabinet system were valuable resources for the first Secretary-General of NATO to draw upon in accomplishing his task.

CHAPTER II

EARLY EFFORTS TO ADMINISTER NATO

ALTHOUGH the governing body of NATO—the Council of Ministers—had strong precedents in international organization and administration upon which to draw in forming this new and, in some very important respects, unique organization, for the first years of the Alliance the organization was largely *ad hoc*. Initially the Council did not have assigned to it all the politico-economic responsibilities which it later accepted, therefore the size, nature, and structure of a centralized civilian International Staff/Secretariat under the Council had to await the passage of events.

The North Atlantic Treaty—NATO's constitution—did not offer much assistance. It was vague about the administrative and political structure with which the new Organization was to be endowed. No specific mention was made of a Secretary-General or of any other officer. Article 9 provided only that 'the Parties hereby establish a Council, on which each of them shall be represented, to consider matters concerning the implementation of this Treaty. . . . The Council shall set up subsidiary bodies as may be necessary'.[1] The flexibility which the Treaty gained from not being detailed has been one of NATO's strengths, because the Organization has been able to deal pragmatically with the varied administrative needs which have arisen.

For the first year NATO's organization resembled the traditional one for accomplishing international business— employing the pre-League method described by Sir Eric Drummond. The various boards and committees, created piecemeal, were serviced by personnel seconded (on formal assignment) from their governments, and reported directly to Ministerial Committees of the Council.

[1] The complete Treaty is given in Lord Ismay, *NATO The First Five Years 1949–1954* (Paris, 1956), pp. 17–21. Hereafter called *The Five Years*.

A Defence Committee composed of the Defence Ministers of
member countries was established by the Council meeting of
September 1949; in November a Defence Financial and
Economic Committee, consisting of Finance Ministers, was
set up. Both of these committees reported directly to the
Council, which normally was made up of the Foreign Ministers
of member countries.

Under the Defence Committee was a Military Committee,
composed of the Chiefs-of-Staff of the member countries or
their representatives, and a Military Production and Supply
Board. The Military Committee, through its executive body,
the Standing Group (consisting of representatives of the
Chiefs-of-Staff of France, the United Kingdom, and the
United States) formulated the military policy of the Alliance.
After December 1950, the Standing Group, on behalf of the
Military Committee, was also empowered to determine the
requirements of the forces assigned to NATO.[2] The Military
Production and Supply Board studied programmes, drew up
plans, and co-ordinated the means by which the armed forces
were to be equipped.

The Defence Financial and Economic Committee and the
Military Production and Supply Board had permanent
working staffs located in London. The Military Committee
and its Standing Group met in Washington. To co-ordinate
matters, a Standing Group Liaison Office was set up in
London. The arrangement for meetings of the Council of
Ministers was:

The location of each session of the Council shall be determined
by the Chairman after consultation with other members of the
Council. For general convenience the ordinary annual session should
normally be held at about the same time and in the same general
geographical area as the annual session of the General Assembly.
Other ordinary sessions should whenever practicable be held at
some convenient location in Europe.[3]

[2] ibid. p. 35.
[3] ibid. p. 173. The *Daily Worker* (London) interpreted this policy in the
following way: 'Underlining the fact that the Atlantic Pact organization is
in direct opposition to the UN, it was announced yesterday that the annual
meetings of the full North Atlantic Council will be held at the same time
and the same place as the UN Assembly'. (4 May 1951.)

This was the structure of NATO until May 1950 when the Council decided that some changes were needed. Lord Ismay has analysed the reasons for these changes:

When the Council met in London on the 15th May 1950, they were brought up against the fact that there was a lack of co-ordination between NATO's military and civilian agencies. The military authorities were awaiting information from the Defence Financial and Economic Committee on what resources would be available to meet the Medium Term Defence Plan; this [Plan] required a much higher level of forces than member countries were actually planning. At the same time, the Defence Financial and Economic Committee was awaiting specific information from the military authorities about priorities and especially the costs of the plan. Long memoranda were being exchanged on the subject without much result.[4]

THE ORGANIZATION IN DECEMBER 1949[5]

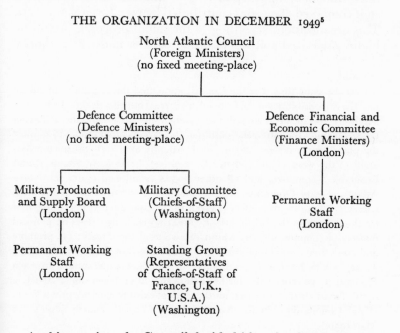

At this meeting, the Council decided 'that the time had come for the creation of a permanent civilian body which would be

---

[4] ibid. p. 28. The Medium Term Defence Plan had been prepared by the military planners to cover the four-year period beginning from 1950.

[5] ibid. p. 26.

responsible for carrying out the policies of the NATO governments in the intervals between meetings of the North Atlantic
Council'.[6] Deputies to the Council Representatives (as the
Foreign Ministers were called) were appointed, to meet in
continuous session. They were called Council Deputies, and
were headed by a chairman elected from among them. Mr.
Charles M. Spofford, the United States Deputy was elected
chairman. As chairman, Mr. Spofford was made responsible
for directing the permanent working staff of the Organization.[7]
This placed him in an ambivalent position. On the one hand,
he served as a member of the board of directors of NATO, so to
speak—and furthermore as its chairman; on the other hand, he
was the executor of the Council's decisions.[8] To help in this
latter function, the Deputies were authorized to establish a
staff composed of persons contributed by member governments.
This organization, according to the initial proposal, 'would be
highly organized and would bring together under its authority

[6] ibid.

[7] At the same time that the Council appointed the Deputies, 'to ensure
that the responsibilities of the Council are carried out effectively', the Foreign
Ministers specifically charged the Council to 'undertake the following
tasks: (a) study the inter-relationship of the various programmes to support
the plans for the defence of the North Atlantic area and ensure co-ordination of the work of the Defence Committee, the Defence Financial and
Economic Committee, and all other bodies established under the North
Atlantic Treaty Organization; (b) recommend to governments the steps
necessary to ensure that effect is given to the co-ordinated plans prepared
for the defence of the North Atlantic area; (c) exchange views on political
matters of common interest within the scope of the Treaty; (d) promote
and co-ordinate public information in furtherance of the objectives of the
Treaty while leaving responsibility for national programmes to each
country; (e) consider what further action should be taken under Article 2
of the Treaty, taking into account the work of existing agencies in this field'.
(Final Communique of the North Atlantic Council, Fourth Session, 18
May 1950.)

[8] In 1955 the member governments made the Secretary-General
Chairman of the Council; thus Lord Ismay also found himself in the
position of participating in the taking of decisions he would be charged
with implementing. His position was not directly analogous to Mr.
Spofford's in that Lord Ismay was a NATO international civil servant
whereas Mr. Spofford was not.

the secretariats of all the organizations of the Treaty, at least in the preliminary stage, those which are located in London.'[9] Thus by May 1950 a central co-ordinative body had been created, but there was still no permanent international secretariat paid from an international budget.

Eight months later, in February 1951, a Working Group on the Establishment of an International Budget for the NATO Staff was formed.[10] In its considerations this Working Group recommended the establishment of an international budget only in that area of the non-military side of the Alliance which was directly under the chairman of the Council Deputies. This included only the organization which served the Deputies, the Deputies' chairman, and the Council of Ministers when it was in session.

In line with this recommendation, the Deputies approved the establishment of an international budget in May 1951; and in July an international secretariat was set up, which included the Planning and Co-ordination Group, the Office of Administration, the Office of Statistics, the Office of Budget and Accounts, the Conferences and Committees Division, and the Information Service. This organization was placed under the direction of an Executive Secretary, Mr. Nigel E. P. Sutton of the United Kingdom, former Secretary-General of the Inter-Allied Reparations Agency. The Executive Secretary assisted the Chairman of the Council Deputies in his dealings with member governments and co-ordinated the organization and work of the Deputies, and the work of the civilian agencies. He was also responsible for the administration and supervision of the international staff of the Organization.[11]

The highest-level body which worked under the Deputies' chairman was the Planning and Co-ordination Group,

---

[9] NATO Doc. D-D/10.

[10] NATO Doc. D-D (51) 45. The question of an international budget had been considered in August 1950 by a Subcommittee on Administrative and Procedural Questions, but not affirmatively. In January 1951 Mr. Spofford recommended to the Council that an international budgetary system should be adopted in lieu of the seconded system. (NATO Doc. D-D (51) 30.)

[11] *The NATO Handbook* (London, Jan. 1952), p. 22. Mr. Sutton's official title was 'Secretary to the Council and the Deputies'.

consisting of Mr. Amory H. Bradford of the United States, Mr. Sivert A. Nielsen of Norway, M. Jean Cahen Salvador of France, and M. Rene Stinglhamber of Belgium. All of these officers had been loaned to NATO. The Group assisted the Chairman and the Executive Secretary in the day-to-day organization of the work of the Council Deputies, followed up decisions of the Deputies, and prepared reports to the Council.

General control of the Organization was strengthened at this time by redefining the North Atlantic Council to include, as appropriate, not only Foreign Ministers, but also Defence and Finance Ministers. It was to be a council of governments and not one of individual ministers. The Council's Defence Committee and Defence Financial and Economic Committee (formed in 1949) were absorbed into the Council.[12] The Military Representatives Committee, which had been established in December 1950, took over the work of the Military Committee; and the Defence Production Board, established at the same time, took over that of the Military Production and Supply Board.[13] The Military Committee continued to meet, but only periodically, at the level of Chiefs-of-Staff. The Military Production and Supply Board went out of existence. A Financial and Economic Board was created to continue many of the activities of the Defence Financial and Economic Committee. These agencies were allowed their own permanent staff, but they were all placed under the control of the Deputies. Thus the prestige, as well as the power, of the Council Deputies was enhanced.[14]

[12] The wording of this action as 'absorbed' rather than, say, 'abolished', was necessary in order to avoid having to amend the Treaty which specified that there should be a Defence Committee composed of the Defence Ministers (Article 9). The terms of reference of the Defence Committee were issued in the Final Communique of the North Atlantic Council, First Session, 17 Sept. 1949.

[13] See Ch. XI of this study for a discussion of the activities of the Defence Production Board.

[14] Sir Alfred Zimmern, a prominent figure in the League of Nations proposed at this time that a 'streamlined executive' of five men should be formed to lead NATO. One should be American, one British, and the third either British or Canadian, with the other two places for nationals of other

In sum, by the end of 1951 NATO had a permanent, continuously-sitting central organ called the Council Deputies, with its own unified secretariat, and three major operating agencies: the Defence Production Board, the Financial and

THE ORGANIZATION IN MAY 1951[15]

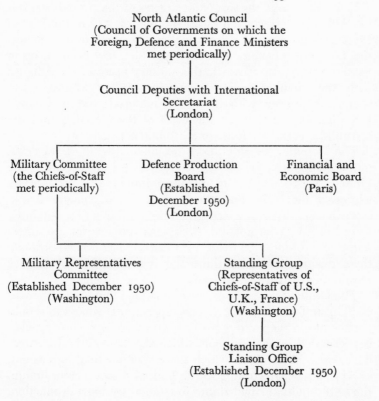

North Atlantic Council
(Council of Governments on which the
Foreign, Defence and Finance Ministers
met periodically)

Council Deputies with International
Secretariat
(London)

Military Committee
(the Chiefs-of-Staff
met periodically)

Defence Production
Board
(Established
December 1950)
(London)

Financial and
Economic Board
(Paris)

Military Representatives
Committee
(Established December 1950)
(Washington)

Standing Group
(Representatives of
Chiefs-of-Staff of U.S.,
U.K., France)
(Washington)

Standing Group
Liaison Office
(Established December 1950)
(London)

Economic Board, and the Military Representatives Committee together with the Standing Group. This structure remained essentially unchanged throughout Lord Ismay's

---

Powers. He felt this arrangement would give to the Alliance unfettered leadership, which many people felt was lacking. (*Daily Mail*, 26 July 1951.) In various ways this suggestion has been repeated over the years.

[15] *The Five Years*, p. 42.

tenure of office. Thereafter the problem in NATO was not one of general organization but of function and control. It became apparent in 1952 that, to render function more explicit and control more effective, the provisions of the Treaty for the civilian side of NATO must be developed even further in line with the growing functions of the Alliance.

Discussions as to the sort of arrangement that would best suit the Alliance were carried on in the months before the Lisbon Ministerial meeting of February 1952. They fell to two bodies: the Temporary Council Committee, which had been set up in September 1951 to reconcile the military needs of the Alliance with the member nations' capacity and/or willingness to support these needs with money and material; and the Council Deputies. It was through the work of the Deputies that the controlling considerations were brought forth.

The Deputies' considerations fell along two lines. The first line was supported by the United States and the second by the United Kingdom. In its memorandum the United States expressed the belief that the organizational changes should serve to consolidate and strengthen the machinery for obtaining co-ordinated governmental decisions, provide for an international staff under an executive to administer and co-ordinate these decisions, and continue the reconciliation of military requirements with politico-economic capabilities.

The United States Deputy recommended that the permanent civilian staff should perform more operational work and should participate in the various working groups composed of specialists seconded by governments which the Council had created. This was a point about which there was not total agreement, as will be seen. According to the United States memorandum, the staff should be divided into functional sections: Production, Finance, Economics (raw materials, manpower, transport), Infrastructure, Planning, Statistics, Reports, Records, Screening and Costing, Secretariat, Information, and Legal Capabilities Review (a small supervisory group to pull together the contributions of other staff sections).[16]

There should be a Council of Permanent Representatives, the members of which would have ministerial rank but would

[16] NATO Doc. D-D (52) 17.

not need to be members of their nations' Cabinets. A Secretary-General would act as the permanent Chairman of the North Atlantic Council with the rank of Vice-Chairman, and would preside in the absence of the Chairman. The chairmanship should rotate among the Foreign Ministers of member countries, but the chairman would usually preside only when the other Foreign Ministers were assembled. To serve the Council each country should maintain delegations, patterned on the United Nations model, at headquarters, which would be in the Paris area.

The United Kingdom memorandum proposed a slightly different organization. It agreed that there should be a Secretary-General at the head of an international staff, and with access to the Council and the power to submit recommendations to the Council. But it said that the staff should be 'strong in quality, though not in numbers'.[17] The Council, instead of being the chief body over a unified 'operating staff', should have two main committees—a Military Committee and an Economic and Production Committee. The Secretary-General should not be responsible for the staff of the Military Committee or of the Standing Group. The Economic and Production Committee should absorb the Financial and Economic Board and the Defence Production Board, and their staffs should be under the Secretary-General.

The Permanent Representatives should elect a Vice-Chairman from among themselves who would preside at all non-Ministerial meetings, and the site of the Council should be in London.[18] In addition there should be various *ad hoc* bodies set up to handle specific problems as they arose.

As can be seen, the United Kingdom did not favour as strong a central organization as did the United States. Under the British proposals the Secretary-General would be a weaker figure, who would have to share with the Council's standing committees control over the staff of the non-military agencies. In the main, he would be a co-ordinator and supervisor of civilian activities—literally a secretary-general. He would not

[17] NATO Doc. D-D (52) 19.
[18] The question of the location of the unified headquarters—London or Paris—was not easily settled. See Ch. III of this study.

have as strong a position *vis-à-vis* the Council as that envisaged by the United States. Whereas, according to the American memorandum all NATO activities would be grouped directly under the Council through the Secretary-General who would be an active participant in the Council, according to the British memorandum civilian activities would be separated from military activities and would be divided into two parts: secretariat duties (relating to the Council and Council Committees); and 'operating duties', the latter working under the rubric of the Economic and Production Committee. Lastly, under the United Kingdom's plan the Secretary-General would not be an officer of the North Atlantic Council. In this last respect he would be similar to his predecessors in the League of Nations and the United Nations.

The Deputies discussed both proposals, and finally adopted the following policies, which were accepted by the Council at its Lisbon meeting:

A Secretary General should be appointed by, and be responsible to, the Council. He should not be a member of any national delegation. He should be responsible for organizing the work of the Council and directing the work of the International Staff/Secretariat. He should initiate and prepare matters for Council action and ensure that appropriate steps are taken to follow up Council decisions. He should have direct access to all NATO agencies and to governments.

The Secretary General should serve as Vice-Chairman of the Council and preside in the absence of the Chairman.[19]

For top management the Deputies were replaced by a continuously sitting Council composed of Permanent Representatives, who were supposed to be 'sufficiently close to their governments and entrusted with adequate authority to enable the Council to discharge their collective tasks and to reach prompt decisions'.[20] The new Council was given an unequivocal mandate to 'assume responsibility for the tasks hitherto performed by the Council Deputies, the Defence Production

---

[19] *The Five Years*, p. 55.

[20] ibid. The comment in the U.K. memorandum mentioned above, that the very term 'Deputies' implied a lack of authority, was thus heeded.

Board, and the Financial and Economic Board'.[21] Thus, what were called 'operating staff' or 'operating duties' by the British were incorporated into the new structure to make the 'International Staff' component of the 'International Staff/Secretariat'. As will be seen later, Lord Ismay was not entirely in favour of this. Perhaps his attitude was a reflection of his national experience.

In any event, the Defence Production Board became the Production and Logistics Division; the Financial and Economic Board became the Economics and Finance Division; the Information Service, at first incorporated into a newly-created Political Affairs Division, later became the Information Division. To eliminate the geographic problem of co-ordination, all these agencies were gathered into a central headquarters in Paris. Except for the Military Commands, the Military Representatives Committee, and the Standing Group, the prefabricated annexe to the Palais de Chaillot, which had been constructed for the 1950 meeting of the General Assembly of the United Nations, became NATO's centre of operations.

The Standing Group Liaison Office was moved from London to Paris, and the Standing Group Liaison Officer was given the tasks of representing the views of the Standing Group to the Council and ensuring, through his staff, that Standing Group views were made known to all the appropriate committees and working groups of the Council. Similarly he kept the Standing Group informed of the views expressed by the Council.

This re-arrangement was not intended as a personal reflection on the Deputies, their organization, or their chairman. The changes were made because heretofore problems of control and allocation of function had not been sufficiently worked out to meet the complex responsibilities of the Alliance. The Deputies had been neither the harness nor the horse, to paraphrase one of Lord Ismay's sayings. As *The Times* explained:

Some concern has, it seems, been caused at the London headquarters of the North Atlantic Council by reports . . . that the Council of Deputies has not been successful in co-ordinating the work of the NATO agencies, and that it may be wound up. It is pointed out that much has been achieved under the leadership of

[21] ibid. p. 56.

Mr. Spofford, the deputies' chairman. If integration of the defence efforts of the member countries has met with difficulties, this cannot fairly be laid against the deputies themselves.[22]

Exactly how much had the Organization been changed by the reshuffling of agencies and the appointment of a Secretary-General? The North Atlantic Council itself had not changed. Periodically the Foreign, Defence, and Finance Ministers would meet on the Council, which was in continuous session, although now with Permanent Representatives rather than Deputies taking care of the day-to-day work. It still possessed the power of ultimate decision in NATO. But the influences and techniques according to which these decisions were made were altered and amplified at Lisbon.

For one thing, the Secretary-General was clearly made the chief executive officer of NATO, unhampered by any national affiliation. Whereas the Deputies' chairman had also had to represent the views and interests of the most powerful member State of the Alliance, Lord Ismay was enjoined to be an international civil servant after the example of Sir Eric Drummond.

In contrast to the Secretary-General of the United Nations, the Secretary-General of NATO was made a constituent participant in the chief organ. He sat on the North Atlantic Council, in a sense, as the fifteenth member State of NATO.[23] As Vice-Chairman of the Council he presided over it in the absence of, or at the desire of, the Chairman. Since the Council usually met in permanent session with only the Permanent Representatives present, this gave the Secretary-General an active part to play in most of the matters coming to the attention of NATO's governing body. He also provided continuity of leadership, as the chairmanship rotated annually among the Foreign Ministers alphabetically by country, and the Chairman, being a Foreign Minister, rarely had time to attend non-Ministerial meetings. Further, the Secretary-General could of course 'initiate and prepare matters for Council action',[24] and he had direct access to governments.

The Council, by authorizing the creation of a strong

---

[22] 6 Dec. 1951.

[23] In 1952 NATO had fourteen member nations.

[24] *The Five Years*, p. 55.

Secretary-General, heading a unified International Staff/Secretariat which had 'operating' as well as 'secretariat' duties, had followed the United States recommendations more closely than the British ones. The evolution of the civilian side of

INTERNATIONAL STAFF/SECRETARIAT IN FEBRUARY 1952[25]

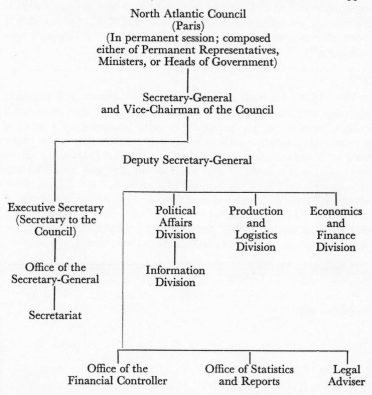

North Atlantic Council
(Paris)
(In permanent session; composed
either of Permanent Representatives,
Ministers, or Heads of Government)

Secretary-General
and Vice-Chairman of the Council

Deputy Secretary-General

Executive Secretary
(Secretary to the
Council)

Political
Affairs
Division

Production
and
Logistics
Division

Economics
and
Finance
Division

Office of the
Secretary-General

Information
Division

Secretariat

Office of the
Financial Controller

Office of Statistics
and Reports

Legal
Adviser

NATO to this stage of development, was summarized by the Chairman of the Council Deputies when he said:

The Council had no pattern to follow in creating an organization which would join together effectively twelve sovereign nations in a collective effort that cut across political, military, and economic

[25] *The North Atlantic Treaty Organization* (Paris, Dec. 1952), p. 33; 'Text of Lord Ismay's Report to the Ministerial Meeting of the North Atlantic Council at Bonn, May 1957', App. C., as contained in the *NATO Letter*, Vol. 5, Spec. Supp. to No. 6.

fields. There was a sense of urgency which was felt even more acutely
when the Korean War was launched last year. The main objective
was to get on with the job, without bothering too much about the
tidiness of the organizational structure. Committees and working
groups were established as the need for them arose to carry out
specific assignments. Inevitably it became apparent, in the light of
experience and as NATO began to evolve from a planning organization into an agency committed to the execution of plans, that a
more efficient, and neater organization of the top structure was
necessary.[26]

and

The earliest function of the Treaty Organization was purely a
planning one, initially in the military field and then in related
fields of production and supply. The work was done by a series of
committees on which each nation was represented. As it came to the
time to translate plans into action . . . an international staff or
secretariat was created to deal functionally and not through committees with the increasing number of matters that could be brought
within the area of international staff work. This area of international
action has steadily broadened over the past twelve months by a
process of accretion rather than by plan, and sometimes against
some opposition on the part of Member Governments.[27]

[26] Speech by Mr. Charles M. Spofford, former Chairman of the Council
Deputies, 10 May 1951 (NATO Speech Series No. 2).

[27] Speech by Mr. Charles M. Spofford, 5 March 1952 (NATO Speech
Series No. 12).

CHAPTER III

THE FINAL FORMATION OF A NATO
INTERNATIONAL HEADQUARTERS

ONE of the chief problems which confronted the Deputies in planning the reorganization of NATO was how to 'provide proper representation of national interests at the highest level and at the same time to allow speed in action and decision'.[1] This statement sums up one of the underlying themes of this book and also of NATO itself. The events surrounding the Lisbon conference clearly offer an excellent example of this problem. Progress toward unanimity and the decisions taken were immersed in national susceptibilities.

First, the date of the conference. At the Ministerial Meeting of the Council held in Rome in December 1951, the next meeting had been set for 2 February 1952 in Lisbon. In January the meeting was postponed to 16 February, primarily because the French government hoped to be able to conclude the Paris negotiations for establishing the European Defence Community (EDC) and to debate these agreements in the National Assembly before the Lisbon meeting. The Foreign Ministers of the six negotiating Powers—France, Italy, the German Federal Republic, and the Benelux Powers—had been working towards agreements to incorporate the German Federal Republic into EDC, and, in turn, to demarcate the relationship of EDC to NATO. If these arrangements could be concluded it was assumed that NATO could then continue its over-all planning for the defence of Western Europe.[2] Shortly after requesting the postponement of the Lisbon

[1] Final Communique of the North Atlantic Council, Eighth Session, 28 Nov. 1951.

[2] A complete description of the tortuous pre-Lisbon EDC negotiations can be found in the unpub. diss. by A. F. Meisch (Oxford, 1958), 'The European Defence Community and European Integration', Chs. I–III.

meeting France experienced a governmental crisis, making it advisable to await the formation of another government. The Belgian government also had a Cabinet crisis at this time.[3]

In early February 1952 the Council Deputies, for their part, found it necessary to recommend to the NATO governments that the meeting should be postponed four days further, until 20 February, to enable the Deputies to complete the reports they were preparing to submit to it. These reports included the final arrangements for the entry of Greece and Turkey into the Alliance, the structure and composition of the Mediterranean Command, and the final drafting of the Temporary Council Committee's recommendations.[4] The funeral of King George VI, which was to take place on 15 February in London, provided another reason for delay because many of the Ministers attending the conference had planned to attend the funeral.

The two major political—i.e. negotiable—organizational questions which had to be resolved directly by the Council were the location of NATO's permanent headquarters and the choice of the first Secretary-General. Formal consideration of both these questions was delayed until the last day of the meeting, although they had been discussed at many informal sessions. The site of headquarters was not as important as some of the other problems before the meeting—such as the size of troop commitments, the sharing of the burden of costs, the re-armament of the German Federal Republic—but it was by no means unimportant. There is soundness in the proposition that 'the importance of choosing the most suitable site for an international organization is generally underestimated and the choice actually made is liable to be determined by political and not administrative considerations'.[5]

Besides the prestige which would accrue to the host country —still of importance in international affairs—there were other

[3] To tie the EDC and German questions into an agreed 'package', the British proposed on 31 Jan. that the French, U.S. and U.K. Foreign Ministers should meet in London on 13–14 Feb.

[4] See Ch. X of this study for a detailed account of the Temporary Council Committee's work.

[5] Alexander Loveday, *Reflections on International Administration* (Oxford, 1956), p. 7.

advantages to be gained. The most obvious practical consideration was that the nation whose Foreign Office was closest to international headquarters would have the most effective liaison with headquarters. To be able to work so closely with one's Foreign Office would be a distinct advantage. Besides ease of communication, the ready availability of 'back-up', or rank, or merely depth, of representation for the myriad committees that were constantly meeting would provide influence, pressure, or flexibility not readily available to other delegations.[6]

Moreover, the presence of national delegations in the host country, especially in its capital city, would expose them to certain domestic influences. For instance, the local press would be read, and the impact of the host country's international commitments upon local issues would be observed. The delegates would be influenced, either positively or negatively, by happenings in their host country as well as by happenings at home.

These internal influences would also have a very personal effect on the delegations and on the international staff. If the cost of living in a particular city was exorbitantly high it would be demoralizing and could lead to recruitment difficulties. The locale in which the headquarters building was situated could affect the social relationships among the staff, and the relationships of the staff to the community. Lastly, the foreign exchange benefits which would accrue from an increase in the foreign population of the city, and the housekeeping costs of headquarters would be of some importance.

These are general considerations which underlie the question of the location of the headquarters of any international organization. There were also more specific, and more specifically political, considerations related to NATO. At Lisbon the British Foreign Secretary, Mr. Anthony Eden, argued that London should become the site of the permanent headquarters because of its medial location between Western Europe and North America. This atittude was consistent with

---

[6] The different methods used in transmitting documents and messages between the delegations and their Foreign Offices could delay proceedings —whether by diplomatic pouch, telephone, radiogram, or airmail.

the British desire to remain economically, politically, and militarily only semi-committed to the Continent. An Atlantic partnership concept was more acceptable than a European Community concept which would tie Britain to the Continent. In British eyes at that time their future was tied as much, if not more, with America and the Commonwealth.

From the Continental viewpoint, the British attitude implied that, if war came, Western Europe might not be vigorously defended and the so-called peripheral strategy of defence at the Pyrenees and the Channel might be applied. Therefore most of the NATO Continental Powers favoured Paris, situated in the heart of the nation upon which would hinge the ground defence of Western Europe. The Americans wanted to reassure these doubting Continental nations, so, overcoming an earlier reluctance to locate the civilian headquarters so near the main military headquarters (SHAPE was near Paris), they supported Paris.[7]

As to convenience, both cities could lay plausible claims. The existence of newly renovated housing in Belgrave Square in London which had been prepared for the Deputies' organization and the Defence Production Board staff gave weight to the British argument that it would be cheaper not to relocate. All the inconveniences of arranging housing, furnishings, currency exchange, and extra-territorial privileges would have to be re-endured. But Paris offered another argument for

[7] Discussion over the choice of London or Paris reached back to early 1951, when SHAPE was being set up. At that time the military leaders had agreed with the British against Paris for the political headquarters. One newspaper report, taking a very large view, speculated: 'If NATO goes to Paris, it will be inextricably connected with the Supreme Headquarters Allied Powers in Europe (SHAPE) and the defence of Europe. Certainly the safety of Europe is one of the prime strategic interests of NATO; but it is not the only one. Apart from SHAPE, the North Atlantic Council will also control the Middle East Command with its headquarters in the Eastern Mediterranean, and the North Atlantic Command with headquarters in Norfolk, Virginia. As a central point for all three commands, London is better than Paris. But, if eventually the strategy of the Pacific is brought under the same control, then perhaps London should yield to Ottawa as the appropriate centre of all these defence arrangements.' (*Observer*, 3 Feb. 1952.)

convenience. If headquarters were in Paris, then member nations could utilize for NATO representation their delegations to the other international organizations in Paris. Not only was the Organization for European Economic Co-operation there, but in 1952 plans were being made to establish the EDC headquarters there also. With the proliferation of international representational activity since the end of World War II many nations had experienced difficulty in providing adequate delegations to all the conferences, councils, and associations which were being formed. When the various agenda included subjects ranging from the broadly diplomatic to the narrowly technical (but nonetheless important), the problem could at times become very difficult. This was especially true for the smaller Powers, but no nation was immune from this problem.

The counter-argument that Paris's facilities for absorbing yet another international organization were over-strained, was in turn countered by assurances from the French Foreign Minister, M. Robert Schuman, that the French government would facilitate the proper arrangement of siting and housing for headquarters, the International Staff/Secretariat, and the delegations.[8] Both cities had an adequate supply of non-officer grade men and women for local recruitment, and both were cultural centres full of attractions and activities to satisfy the entertainment and aesthetic needs of members of the delegations and the International Staff/Secretariat.

All of these arguments, important as they were, gave way to other political considerations. The question of location became tied in with the question of leadership. Specifically, the question of national representation in the top posts of the new organization assumed prime importance. Here again prestige was not to be discounted. A nation naturally likes to have its nationals occupying the more important posts in the international organizations to which it belongs. It can be a reflection of a nation's influence—if not of its power. Also, apart from any question of loyalty, an international administrator is inevitably influenced in his methods of work, his sympathies, his attitudes toward himself and his associates, by his own

[8] See Ch. VIII of this study, for a discussion of the International Staff/ Secretariat's housing problem.

experience. The social, political, cultural, and economic environment in which he was educated and in which he built his career prior to becoming an international administrator is reflected in his international activity. This fact of life, by its very nature, is likely to redound favourably rather than unfavourably on the interest of the nation from which he comes. Lastly, since it was impossible to equip the Organization with truly 'non-national' civil servants, it was not unreasonable for a nation to prefer its own nationals in responsible positions over those of another.[9]

In the Deputies' organization the top posts had been occupied by the Americans and the British. The Chairman of the Council Deputies was an American and his Executive Secretary was British. This arrangement was not carried over into the new organization. Mr. Spofford wanted to return to his New York law practice, having originally expected to serve abroad for only eighteen months from 1950, and Mr. Sutton did not find it convenient to remain. Therefore the field was clear for the new Secretary-Generalship.

At Lisbon, when reorganization was being actively considered, it was only natural that there was some feeling that the position should go to a national of a smaller Power. One advantage of selecting a small-Power national was that he could mediate among the larger Powers. His appointment, implying that he was to be neutral towards all, including his own country, would be an affirmation of the principle that no single Power should dominate the Alliance. And, if he did decide on any issue to take a position which was opposed by many of the member nations, he could not easily be accused of 'throwing his country's weight around'. It was also a well-known fact that since World War II the smaller nations had produced statesmen of the first calibre.[10]

[9] The idea that an international civil servant is not faced with the question of divided loyalty because, ultimately, the interests of his nation should also be the interest of the organization is attractive but can present problems in application.

[10] See the Chatham House pamphlet, *The International Secretariat of the Future* (London, 1944), pp. 26–32, for a discussion of the opposing view that the leader should be from a large Power, and also that he should be young, which Lord Ismay was not.

The most widely-mentioned possibility was Canada's Minister for External Affairs, Mr. Lester Pearson. He had been an enthusiastic supporter of NATO, and an advocate of an 'Atlantic Community' concept embracing economic, social, and cultural ends as well as military ones. He was also the 1952 Chairman of the NATO Council. Mr. Pearson neither confirmed nor denied that he was to become the first Secretary-General; he contented himself with saying that the possibility of his assuming the post was 'hypothetical'.[11] Other names mentioned were those of Dr. Dirk U. Stikker, Foreign Minister for the Netherlands, and M. Paul-Henri Spaak, the Belgian Foreign Minister, both of whom later occupied the post.[12] But the argument about the site of headquarters spilled over into the question of who should be the first Secretary-General.

It was not until the last session of the Council meeting that the decision was made to place headquarters in Paris, and, as a complement to this, to appoint a Briton as Secretary-General.

Three primary reasons were offered for extending the invitation to a Briton: first, some of the nations preferred a civil servant to a politician for Secretary-General; second, Mr. Pearson reportedly was hesitant to relinquish his post as Canadian Foreign Secretary; and third, most of the member nations favoured Paris for headquarters.[13] It seemed a suitable arrangement to give Britain the honour of providing the first Secretary-General since headquarters would not be in London. The United States Secretary of State, Mr. Dean Acheson, proposed the British Ambassador in Washington, Sir Oliver Franks, and the Council agreed. Dr. Cunha, the Portuguese Foreign Minister, then suggested that the Council should telephone Sir Oliver to inform him of its decision and invite him to accept the post. If he accepted, the Lisbon meeting would close on the highest level of achievement. Mr. Pearson put the call through, getting Sir Oliver from his breakfast

---

[11] *Financial Times*, 19 Feb. 1952.

[12] M. Spaak's name had been mentioned in Dec. 1951 when the TCC's report was first submitted to the Council.

[13] Portugal and Iceland originally supported Britain in favouring London.

owing to the difference in time between Washington and
Lisbon.[14] Mr. Pearson, as Chairman of the Council, had already
told newsmen that the Council had 'unanimously and enthusiastically' agreed to ask Sir Oliver to take the position.[15]
The Ambassador, to everyone's surpise, did not accept immediately; instead, he requested forty-eight hours to consider
the offer.

Not waiting the forty-eight hours for Sir Oliver Franks's
reply, the Ministerial meeting was adjourned, leaving the
matter to be settled by the Deputies, who were enjoined to
continue in their duties until they were able to complete the
arrangements for reorganization. It was expected that this
would take a few weeks. When Sir Oliver subsequently declined
the invitation, a majority of the nations continued to favour the
appointment of a Briton.[16]

The uncertainty in NATO as to the identity of the Secretary-
General cast some doubt upon the wisdom of some of the
organizational decisions taken at Lisbon. In particular, the
Deputies had second thoughts about granting to a less-than-
top-level appointee the power of direct access to governments

---

[14] As early as a week before the Council's decision, Franks had been
mentioned in the Press as a strong candidate. The first call to reach Sir
Oliver that morning came from Mr. Charles Campbell, chief of the British
Information Service in New York, who was reported to have got the
Ambassador out of his bath.

[15] Although not a world figure Franks was well-known. Before entering
public life he had been a philosophy don. In 1948 he relinquished the
Provostship of the Queen's College Oxford, to organize the European
response to the Marshall Plan offer. After the formation of OEEC he went to
Washington. (*Who's Who, 1956*, p. 1049.) Later he became Chairman of
Lloyd's Bank and most recently he returned to Oxford as Provost of
Worcester College.

[16] With Sir Oliver Franks's refusal, the Deputies were placed in an
awkward position; whoever of the first rank of the free world's statesmen
subsequently accepted the post might suffer a loss of prestige. It would not
be flattering to any nation to have one of its first-line diplomats or Cabinet
ministers the second choice. The only person who could gracefully accept
the position was Mr. Pearson, because it was common knowledge that he
had been favoured for the post. But this would not have fitted into the
quid pro quo agreed to at Lisbon.

and the right to initiate proposals in the Council.[17] Without these powers the new Secretary-General would be not much more than a high-level administrator, with a narrower range of activity than the Deputies' Chairman had possessed. This would defeat one of the purposes of the reorganization—the heightening of the power and prestige of the head of the newly-integrated International Staff/Secretariat. Happily the Deputies escaped from this quandary when Mr. Churchill made available to NATO his Secretary of State for Commonwealth Affairs, General Lord Ismay.[18] *The Times* exulted:

> The appointment of Lord Ismay as secretary-general of the NATO more than retrieves the initial setback caused by the premature announcement that the post had been offered to Sir Oliver Franks. Indeed, of all the candidates whose names have been mentioned Lord Ismay would seem to have the strongest qualifications for the post. There could be no better proof of its importance in the eyes of the British Government than that the Prime Minister should be willing to spare the man who has long been his closest adviser on matters of defence. . . . In Lord Ismay administrative ability is backed by good sense, personal modesty, and tact of the kind which makes men forget that they represent different nations.[19]

The *Daily Worker* groused:

> The post of Secretary-General of NATO was created on American insistence because they wanted to give the impression that the

---

[17] *New York Times*, 6 Mar. 1952. The purpose of these alterations was not to reduce the Secretary-General's effectiveness as administrative head of the International Staff/Secretariat, but to adjust his relationship with the Council in his role as an international diplomatist. A denial of the right of direct access to governments did not mean that the Secretary-General and his staff could not write letters to governments or deal with government representatives; it meant that he would not have that free and ready attention given to him by the limited circle of top governmental decision-makers which was essential if he was to carry on any kind of personal diplomacy.

[18] Other Britons who had been mentioned for the post were Sir Edwin Plowden, then Chief Planning Officer of the Treasury and Chairman of the Economic Planning Board, and a member of the Executive Bureau of NATO's TCC, and Sir Gladwyn Jebb, then U.K. Representative to the UN.

[19] 13 Mar. 1952.

Atlantic War Pact Organization was not under their control. They insisted on a British representative for this job, which was first offered to the British Ambassador in Washington, Sir Oliver Franks, and refused by him. Lord Ismay was Mr. Churchill's personal Chief-of-Staff in the recent war and in his new job will retain his connections with the Tory Premier.[20]

The most reflective comment was the caution offered that 'the post will be one, by all accounts, in which it might be easier to lose an established reputation than to make a new one'.[21]

[20] 13 Mar. 1952.
[21] *Daily Telegraph*, 7 Mar. 1952.

PART II

THE MACHINERY FOR POLICY-MAKING
IN NATO HEADQUARTERS

'On the one hand, he is a diplomat dealing with the most delicate and confidential issues of international politics. On the other hand, he is an administrator, responsible for the conduct of an office containing six or seven hundred employees.'

Sir Alfred Zimmern

'. . . it should regard as its first duty to collate the relevant documents and to prepare the ground for these decisions without suggesting what these decisions should be; . . . once these decisions had been taken by the bodies solely responsible for them, it should confine itself to executing them in the letter and in the spirit.'

League of Nations Report

CHAPTER IV

THE NORTH ATLANTIC COUNCIL:
COMPOSITION AND ROLE

IT is of special significance that Lord Ismay, in contrast to his predecessors in other international organizations, served in a dual capacity as head of the International Staff/Secretariat and as Vice-Chairman (later Chairman) of the Council. The confluence of these two functions made the Secretary-General the point at which the purely political crossed with the administrative. Lord Ismay was fully aware of this situation, and saw it as an opportunity for effective service.

Although no formal conditions were placed upon his acceptance of the post of Secretary-General, Lord Ismay wanted it to be understood that he was to preside over the Council in the absence of the Chairman.[1] He also made it clear that he wanted freedom of action in his dealings with the Council, including the right to initiate business and to have direct access to member governments.

In retrospect his insistence upon clarification of these matters may appear to have been unnecessary, but at the time of his

---

[1] Lord Ismay's right to chair the meetings of the Permanent Representatives was never seriously questioned. However, the first time that the Chairman could not attend a meeting of the Council in Ministerial session, there was some talk of having another Minister take the chair. Lord Ismay objected to this, pointing out that the Council already had a qualified and logical Chairman—meaning the Secretary-General—and should use him in this capacity. Thereafter the precedent was set for the Secretary-General to chair both Ministerial meetings and the Council of Permanent Representatives in the absence of, or at the request of, the Chairman. In 1956 this procedure was officially confirmed when Lord Ismay was made the Chairman of the Council and a Minister was elected on an annually rotating basis for the largely honorary and ceremonial post of President of the North Atlantic Council. (Interview with Lord Ismay, 28 May 1959; *The North Atlantic Treaty Organization* (Paris, 1957), pp. 38–39.)

appointment there was justification for it. As noted in Chapter III, after Sir Oliver Franks declined the invitation to become Secretary-General, the Ministerial Council at Lisbon delegated to the Council Deputies the task of obtaining a Secretary-General and the Deputies had seriously considered narrowing the powers of the office if a person of sufficiently high rank could not be found to occupy it. Lord Ismay felt that, if he did not have unfettered authority, he would be less of a figure than the Deputies' chairman had been, and consequently the aim of reorganizing the civilian structure of NATO would be defeated in some measure from the outset. He was of course assured that he would have the powers he asked for.

As the *de facto* executive and presiding head of the Council, especially when it met at the Permanent Representatives' level, the Secretary-General could have used his position to propose his own programme or to adopt a critical (albeit constructive) attitude toward some of the workings of the Council. In view of the weaknesses displayed in the Deputies' structure and the increasing magnitude of the work to be performed (in 1952 it was full steam ahead for re-armament), an aggressive leader would have been strongly tempted to follow this course.

Such a development would not have been entirely unexpected, for at the time the position was created the functions of the Secretary-General were characterized variously as those of 'a civilian Eisenhower',[2] a 'super-expeditor',[3] and a director-general.[4] He was to possess 'drive, imagination and persuasiveness',[5] and should be a person 'of the highest caliber, a personage with an international reputation for efficiency and intellectual integrity, skilled in dealing with the kinds of problems certain to arise within a group comprising the representatives of many nations'.[6]

The magnitude of the Secretary-General's task was measured in such statements as: 'The Secretary-General's chief function

[2] *New York Times*, 27 Feb. 1952.   [3] *Daily Mail*, 22 Feb. 1952.

[4] According to some political scientists, this term implies stronger executive leadership than the term 'secretary-general', although perhaps more in the administrative than in the political sense.

[5] *New York Times*, 27 Feb. 1952.

[6] *New York Herald-Tribune*, 28 Feb. 1952.

. . . will be to speak directly to the member Governments
with all the authority he can build up around his office as the
voice of the NATO community as a whole';[7] 'this new permanent authority [the International Staff/Secretariat] would
be placed under the chairmanship of a permanent secretary-
general or chairman who would not be a member of any
national delegation but would have an international status
within NATO somewhat similar to that of Trygve Lie in the
United Nations';[8] '[the] permanent chairman . . . would thus
clearly wield considerable authority and bear wide responsibilities'.[9]

From the American viewpoint these descriptions were
apposite for, throughout the preliminary experience of NATO,
as indicated earlier, the United States had advocated strong
leadership for the Council and the civilian staff; most often it
had been the British who had favoured more decentralized
executive leadership.[10] Lord Ismay, as the first incumbent,
could set the pattern for the Secretary-Generalship. As one
observer put it: 'Working without direct precedents to guide
him, the secretary-general has had to impose upon the new
administrative machinery with which he was provided the
cohesive stamp of an individual personality'.[11]

Lord Ismay decided not to adopt an aggressive and independent role as Secretary-General. Though he had thought it
necessary to claim unfettered authority at the time of his
appointment, he did not assume the attitude of a full member
of the Council, though in a sense he was one (especially after
the Council Resolution of December 1956); he preferred to
regard himself as 'an international servant of NATO', whose
function was 'stewardship'.[12] Unlike his immediate successor,

---

[7] *New York Times*, 13 Feb. 1952.   [8] ibid. 18 Feb. 1952.

[9] *Manchester Guardian*, 27 Feb. 1952.

[10] See pp. 27–29 above.   [11] *The Times*, 19 Dec. 1953.

[12] Speech delivered by Lord Ismay, 12 Mar. 1953 (NATO Speech
Series No. 33). When Lord Ismay talked of himself as the 'servant' of the
Council he was thinking as much in terms of the military tradition as in the
British civil servant tradition. He was fond of representing himself as an
'old soldier'. For instance, in a speech to the diplomatic correspondents in
1952, he said: 'It is an ordeal for a soldier—and a cavalry soldier at that—
to address an audience who are not only masters in the realm of diplomacy,

M. Paul-Henri Spaak, he considered it appropriate to wait
for the Council to initiate or authorize a course of action
before he promoted it publicly. He was also very careful
not to appear to 'lecture' his Council colleagues. But it must be
realized that M. Spaak's more forthright diplomatic initiatives
were only partly due to the difference in style and personality
of the two men. They were also due to the difference in their
situations. By the time M. Spaak assumed the leadership of
NATO, he had the precedent, the organizational structure,
the confidence, and the goodwill which Lord Ismay had
established to build upon. When Lord Ismay began his term
of office he was relatively unknown internationally, although
well-known in American and British military circles. He had
been called to a position which, initially, had been the centre
of lengthy discussions and speculation. And, most important
of all, he had to deal with fourteen (later fifteen) member
nations, each of which jealously guarded its own interests.
For instance, in 1953 M. René Mayer, the French Prime
Minister, complained that Lord Ismay was not being tough
enough with member countries. Lord Ismay replied: 'What
would you expect? The first thing I would do would be to
demand that France should increase its conscription term to
twenty-four months. The next thing I would do would be to
tell the British they must cut the expensive burden of their
social services. Neither country would do this. I cannot get
tough.'[13] The roles of arbiter, mediator, conciliator, and co-
ordinator seemed to fit more appropriately his situation, his
experience, and his personality. The ultimate in tributes to
his effectiveness in these roles was paid by Mr. William
Batt, former chief of the United States Mutual Security

---

but who are also experts at giving expression to their views. My father
would never let me forget the hackneyed story of the cavalry officer who
was so stupid that his brother officers noticed it.' (NATO Press Release,
12 June, 1952.) One observer saw him thus: 'Ismay, whose gentle, slightly
protuberant blue eyes, turned-up nose and stubborn jaw have earned him
the nickname of "pug", likes to amuse strangers with a breezy imperson-
ation of the simple old soldier. In fact, however, he has one of the sharpest
minds in international public life.' (Edmund Taylor, *Washington Post*,
15 Apr. 1956.)

[13] As related by C. L. Sulzberger, *New York Times*, 22 May 1957.

Administration Mission and Chairman of NATO's Defence Production Board. He said, in a speech made at a banquet given by the English-Speaking Union:

Looking back I am convinced that Lord Ismay was divinely chosen (although Sir Winston had something to do with it, too) for those difficult formative years of NATO. With no real constitutional authority, with little more than a hot office in the Palais de Chaillot, a limited budget and 14 prima donna nations, he produced all the harmony there was in the enterprise.[14]

Producing harmony was something Lord Ismay was good at. In his new position he could use both formal and informal arrangements to achieve it, and informality was not uncongenial to him. He himself observed: 'I always find it easier to do business face to face with people.'[15]

An account of an interview with Lord Ismay, in which his methods of doing business were discussed, was subsequently published:

When a particularly sticky problem comes up before the Permanent Council . . . he invites them all to luncheon in his Paris residence. In this 'NATO' house, furnished and decorated by Lady Ismay with objects and materials from all the member nations, he gives them a magnificent meal—at which no shop is talked. Then they get down to their discussions. By the time the party breaks up possibly ten of the 15 members will have accepted the decision, and the other five, whose ideas may be all different, will have agreed to take it up with their governments. 'You tell them the situation, say X, Y and Z have agreed, and I am sure you will win them over.' The next week, of the five dissidents, three possibly will have obtained their government's approval. Lord Ismay then turns to the intelligent persuasion of the two intransigents. And eventually they come back and tell him: 'Our governments don't like it; their ideas on this matter are quite different. But for the sake of NATO's solidarity they will accept the decision.' Had he ever had a decision turned down for lack of unanimity? 'No, not yet. But there are certain matters which, knowing I would never get agreement, I have just shelved for the time being. One eventually develops a sixth sense which tells you just how far you can go.'[16]

---

[14] *The Times*, 5 June 1957.   [15] *Daily Telegraph*, 20 Feb. 1953.
[16] Interview with Mr. Geoffrey Hoare, as printed in the *News Chronicle*, 21 Feb. 1956.

On a more official level the Council had at its disposal three types of meetings. The first type was the normal session, to which each Permanent Representative could bring four or more advisers, depending upon the business under discussion. The second type was the restricted session for the consideration of more confidential matters. Each Representative could bring one or possibly two advisers to these meetings. The third type was the informal session, at which only the Representatives were present: there was 'no agenda, no record, no commitments—and therefore no formal decisions [were made]' at an informal session.[17]

The chief advantage of the informal session was that it enabled 'Permanent Representatives to inform their governments of the climate of opinion in the Council, and in particular to report the preliminary views of their colleagues on important questions which are destined to come up later for Council decisions'.[18] By dealing with more sensitive matters in this way, a possible disagreement or potential dispute could be resolved before it reached a more formal stage of discussion, where a government would have greater difficulty in adjusting its position. A government could assimilate the impressions and information gained through these informal contacts before deciding on its formal position.[19]

Thus, a government's formal instructions to its Permanent Representative did not always signal the opening of negotiations, but sometimes signified that the subject had been sufficiently brought along through preliminary discussions to warrant

[17] *The Five Years*, p. 58.

[18] ibid. The number of informal—or private—meetings progressively increased. Lord Ismay reported: 'In 1952, there were 17 such meetings; in 1953, 23; in 1954, 35; in 1955, 43; and in 1956, 66.' He went on to observe: 'Nevertheless, it must be recognized that the practice of consultation in the Council has not as yet developed sufficiently to meet the demands of political changes and world trends.' (Text of Lord Ismay's Report to the Ministerial meeting of the North Atlantic Council at Bonn, May 1957, as contained in *NATO Letter*, Vol. 5, Spec. Supp. to No. 6.)

[19] Lord Ismay said: 'One naturally hopes that some of the ideas brought out in these informal discussions will ultimately be the subject of formal papers which will be considered in open Council.' (*The Times*, 16 May 1952.)

the opportunity of transferring it to a more formal plane. For, by formalizing negotiations, all the interplay of traditional diplomacy among sovereign States would begin: an interplay which, without adequate preliminary exchanges of views, could prove to be divisive as well as conciliatory in effect.

The policy of holding at least one meeting a week of the Council of Permanent Representatives had already been established. Lord Ismay wished for at least three Ministerial meetings a year as well.[20] This wish was never fulfilled: it became the pattern to hold two Ministerial meetings a year—one in December at which military and economic matters were emphasized, and one in April at which there was an exchange of views on political matters.[21]

A recurring difficulty was the integration of the Ministerial meetings into the schedule of domestic political activities of member countries. The delay in the assembling of the Lisbon Conference has been described in Chapter III. Another example of difficulty in timing was the necessity to start the Ministerial meeting of April 1953 in the middle of the week because the Danish elections were being held the previous weekend, the original time for the meeting. Danish politics interfered again later in 1953 when Mr. Kraft, the Danish Foreign Minister and that year's Chairman of the Council, cabled to Lord Ismay:

On the 18th of September, 1952, I succeeded my brilliant colleague Mr. Lester Pearson as Chairman of the North Atlantic Council. Denmark's tenure of the chair is now coming to an end. I should have liked to have been able to come to Paris to hand over to my successor. I fear, however, that this is now impossible. The 22nd of September is election day which makes it imperative for me to be in Denmark during the preceding week. I should be most

[20] In this Lord Ismay was confirming a Lisbon decision.

[21] The report of the Committee of Three on Non-military Co-operation in NATO, which was approved at the Ministerial meeting in December 1956, made the following recommendation: '. . . (a) that in order to strengthen the process of political consultation Foreign Ministers should each year make an appraisal of the political progress of the Alliance: the basis of this annual political appraisal is to be a report submitted by the Secretary-General; . . .' This annual appraisal has been submitted.

grateful, therefore, if you would notify the Council accordingly. Would you tell the Council of my deep disappointment that affairs in Denmark make it impossible for me to come to Paris at this time?[22]

Lord Ismay's concern to preserve his position as an impartial international civil servant continued throughout his period of office. In this connexion he was fond of quoting a comment made to him by Sir Winston Churchill after he had agreed to go to NATO. Churchill had said: 'Now that you are going to serve fourteen different countries, I hope that you will not consider it absolutely essential to put Great Britain absolutely last on every possible occasion.'[23]

One of the most interesting examples of this concern was his decision to pay an official visit to the United Kindgom (as distinct from his frequent private visits to make speeches at various gatherings or to stay at his farm in Gloucestershire). An official visit from the Secretary-General meant that the British government had to receive him as its guest and with the same degree of protocol as it would accord a top-ranking representative of a foreign government. His visit was all the more interesting because his former chief, Mr. Churchill, was among his hosts. He accepted the 'full-dress' treatment, which included lunching with the Queen at Buckingham Palace and with the Lord Mayor of London at the Mansion House. It was suggested at the time that 'this is probably the first time that a British subject has officially visited his own country'.[24]

However, Lord Ismay's internationalism did not mean that he ceased to think and act like an Englishman. Quite the contrary. He observed traditional English manners and dress. On the days of Council meetings he wore the appropriately diplomatic black coat and striped trousers, and on his official visits to member nations he appeared with bowler, black suit, and umbrella.[25] The following anecdote illustrates his 'Englishness' even more aptly:

[22] NATO Press Release, 18 Sept. 1953.
[23] *The Times*, 16 May 1952.   [24] *Daily Telegraph*, 30 June 1954.
[25] On hot summer afternoons in his office he would occasionally change into a sports shirt, but if a visitor appeared he would put on his coat and tie.

Being an impartial arbiter did not inhibit Ismay's own feeling of being personally English. Sometimes, in NATO debates, he would admit this with a grin. When the EDC was still a possibility, French Foreign Minister Bidault asked him to suggest that Britain join the proposed European Army. Ismay . . . argued that England could not sacrifice the traditions of its army built up over centuries; it could not permit these to be absorbed in a supranational force. 'Of course', Bidault observed wryly, 'you are perfectly willing to sacrifice the traditions of Napoleon and Blücher—only not those of Wellington.' Ismay conceded he was right.[26]

But it seemed that in some respects Lord Ismay got the worst of both worlds. For instance, in February 1953 he had planned to travel aboard the liner *Queen Elizabeth* on an official visit to Canada and the United States. When he found that the British Foreign Secretary, Mr. Anthony Eden, and Mr. R. A. Butler would be travelling in the same ship, he switched over to the liner *United States*. Thus, in order to preserve his reputation for impartiality, he had to forgo what would probably have been a pleasant and fruitful voyage with former close associates who were also influential in NATO affairs.[27]

Thus, as the servant of the Council and at the same time its Vice-Chairman (later Chairman), clothed with the rights of direct access to governments and initiative in Council matters, and as an 'internationalized' civil servant, Lord Ismay set to work to do what he could within the limits of the Organization. Despite his initial claiming of these rights, he habitually acted through the Council, and said: 'I cannot speak or issue instructions on my own authority. I can only speak in the name of the Council and on the authority of the Council.'[28]

As explained earlier, this situation was partly due to his interpretation of his job, to his personality, and to his style, but it was also in large measure due to the definition of the

---

[26] As related by C. L. Sulzberger, *New York Times*, 22 May 1957.
[27] *Daily Telegraph*, 28 Feb. 1953.
[28] NATO Press Release, 13 Nov. 1952. The Ministerial meeting in Dec. 1956 strengthened his powers. After the report of the Committee of Three on Non-military Co-operation in NATO had been adopted, Lord Ismay felt in a stronger position to promote his viewpoint. He would quote relevant recommendations from the report as his authority for taking an initiative.

Council. The Council was officially defined as a 'Council of governments, represented by Ministers for Foreign Affairs and/or Ministers of Defence and/or other competent Ministers, especially those responsible for financial and economic affairs, as required by the agenda of each meeting. When appropriate, member countries could be represented by heads of governments . . .'.[29]

It was, then, first and foremost a Council of governments. NATO, during Lord Ismay's tenure, never laid claim to being a supra-national entity. Quite the contrary. Repeatedly in public pronouncements NATO officials said that the Alliance was an alliance of sovereign States, possessing no supra-national powers. An accurate assessment of the direction that NATO gave to the concept of national sovereignty was made by Mr. Lester Pearson when he said: '. . . the formal surrender of sovereignty, in its old form, is not now so decisive an issue as the provision of a new assurance through adequate international measures that power, traditionally the main attribute of sovereignty, will not be used for wrong purposes and against the general interest.'[30] Put in more positive terms it was felt that: 'Although sovereignty remains in reserve, as a political and psychological safeguard, a growing degree of renunciation is and must be accepted in practice for NATO to work at all.'[31]

In other words, methods of accommodation, compromise, and round-the-table bargaining, within the fundamental assumption that the State would remain the sovereign party to this process, applied to NATO. Any paramount consideration, directed in fulfilment of whatever purposes were agreed to be of the general interest, would still be under the rubric of an international—as opposed to a supra-national—system. It was the purpose of NATO not to supplant national action but to supplement and reinforce it through co-operative enterprise. The Committee of Three on Non-Military Co-operation in NATO recognized this condition of interdependence, when it declared:

[29] *The Five Years*, p. 55.
[30] Speech delivered 30 Apr. 1956. (NATO Speech Series, No. 77.)
[31] From an editorial, *New York Times*, 12 Dec. 1952.

The fundamental historical fact . . . is that the nation-state, by itself and relying exclusively on national policy and national power, is inadequate for progress or even for survival in the nuclear age. As the founders of the North Atlantic Treaty foresaw, the growing interdependence of states, politically and economically as well as militarily, calls for an ever-increasing measure of international cohesion and co-operation. Some states may be able to enjoy a degree of political and economic independence when things are going well. No state, however powerful, can guarantee its security and its welfare by national action alone.[32]

The key words used by the committee were 'interdependence', 'cohesion', and 'co-operation'. This was as far as NATO could go.

Lord Ismay, as pointed out earlier, pictured the Council as the controlling body of the Alliance. He accepted the fact that his mandate came from the member governments through the Council. He also knew that, under the unanimity rule, each member country had a veto. Therefore, in order to ensure consistency and direction in policy, one of the Secretary-General's prime duties became the achievement of harmony and mutual understanding, among member governments in the first instance and among the Permanent Representatives in the second.

To achieve unified leadership certain assumptions had to underlie the Council's operations. First and foremost of course was the assumption that all member nations were agreed that they should meet together to take decisions. There must be no walking out of meetings. A second assumption was that there must be a willingness to seek a solution, which in some cases would mean submerging a particular national interest in favour of the interest of all. Thirdly, there must be a willingness to pursue a particular national interest through the medium of the Council rather than through other means.[33]

During the first few months of Lord Ismay's tenure of office it seemed doubtful whether the Council in fact would possess

[32] See 'Report of the Committee of Three on Non-military Co-operation in NATO' as reproduced in *NATO Letter*, Vol. 5, Spec. Supp. to No. 1.

[33] A close examination of the evolution of political co-operation and consultation as regards the Council and the Secretary-General under Lord Ismay's leadership is made in Ch. V.

enough authority to enable it to come to effective agreements. Although it had been established 'in permanent session with effective powers of decision'[34] the demonstration of these powers appeared to be slow in coming. As early as August 1952 (five months after Lord Ismay's appointment) there was public speculation that the Council machinery was breaking down. The principal causes of this alleged breakdown were said to be the increasing use of bilateral negotiations among the member nations and the tendency to make unilateral decisions.

As one observer put it: 'Instead of using the Paris staff they [i.e. member nations] are now either dealing with their problems unilaterally or bringing them direct to Washington. The result is a deepening fear that the whole machinery for NATO is being gravely undermined'.[35] Two examples were offered in support of this observation. The first was Mr. Churchill's statement in reply to criticism of Britain's unilateral announcement of a 'stretch-out' of its rearmament programme. Churchill declared:

To suggest that we have no right to make necessary, or even beneficial, changes in our own military organization and expenditure without a general meeting of all NATO powers would be an abrogation of our rights and an alteration of our ordinary practice such as I have not hitherto seen in peace or war.[36]

Thus he rejected the publicly-hailed uniqueness of NATO as an 'alteration of . . . ordinary practice'.

The second example was the French government's tendency, when M. Antoine Pinay was Prime Minister, to deal directly with Washington about French financial problems arising from rearmament. One of the causes of this disregard of the NATO machinery was the American Congressional policy of appropriating Mutual Defence Assistance, i.e. rearmament funds, on an annual basis, whereas the Western European nations felt that they must have an assurance of specific financial assistance covering more than one year in order to place

[34] *The Five Years*, p. 55.
[35] *New York Herald-Tribune*, 18 Aug. 1952.
[36] As quoted in the *New York Herald-Tribune*, 18 Aug. 1952.

production orders and to plan their own fiscal programmes. Their pressure on Washington for greater aid commitments was thus not ill-founded. The result of this bilateral activity was, however:

> . . . that national representatives to the Atlantic Council do not have enough authority. Changes in the timing of the United States and British defense build-ups have been decided and announced, so far as they have been announced, in Washington and London. There is no evidence that the Atlantic Council in Paris has had any influence on the action of either of the two largest member nations. There is no evidence that there has been any 'co-ordination' at the organizational level.[37]

One possible reason why this problem arose was that in the early days—from January 1951 to May 1952—during General Dwight D. Eisenhower's tenure as Supreme Allied Commander Europe, the Supreme Commander, more than any other person or body had been the public embodiment of NATO. It was inevitable that after General Eisenhower's departure in 1952, at the time of the Lisbon reorganization, there would be discussion of whether—and how—to redefine the relationship of the military with the civilian and political sides of the Alliance. In any event, military affairs tended to continue to be handled in Washington rather than in Paris.

Closely related to this problem was the question, never resolved, and probably not completely resolvable, as to who or what agency should decide when and where to use atomic weapons. The separation of the strategic bomber forces of the United Kingdom and the United States from the regular command structure of NATO and the foreshadowed emergence of a multilateral NATO nuclear capability gave rise to the problem of command and control of these deterrent and retaliatory weapons. More specifically, could a NATO commander or a single member nation issue an order to use nuclear weapons without full consultation with member governments, presumably through the Council? Lord Ismay said: 'Everyone realizes that the use of the A-bomb is a political decision. No commander could take it without consulting his

[37] *New York Times*, 14 Aug. 1952.

government.'[38] He affirmed that the 'enormous decision' must remain a political and not a military responsibility.[39]

But even he could not escape from giving a somewhat vague description of the Council's relationship with the military:

> . . . the Council have considerable responsibility toward the military authorities. In each country there is a government whose military advisers are the Chiefs-of-Staff, and these in turn direct the commands. On that analogy the Council are an international cabinet. Their military advisers are the Military Committee, which in turn gives directions to the Supreme Commanders. Thus the Council are responsible for giving political guidance to the military authorities and for providing them, so far as economic capabilities permit, with the men, equipment and the infrastructure which they require for the discharge of their responsibilities to defend the NATO area.[40]

Lord Ismay unquestionably felt that the military authorities should be subordinate to the political authorities. He believed that one of his major achievements at NATO was his establishment of the precedent that the military authorities, from the Standing Group down, should co-ordinate their plans and programmes through him to the Council and should co-operate in every way with the work of the International Staff/Secretariat. This procedure was very important, for the economic and financial and the production and logistic functions were all dependent upon information which had to be supplied by the military planners. It took several years, however, and much shifting and hauling, to work out the procedures for ensuring the smooth flow of information between the Palais de Chaillot and the Standing Group and Military Commands. The process, as described in later chapters, had not been perfected by the time Lord Ismay retired, but he had at least tried to make procedures as effective as he could.

[38] *New York Herald-Tribune*, 31 Oct. 1956.

[39] In this statement Lord Ismay was responding to a press furore caused by a speech Lord Montgomery gave in October 1956 at the Royal United Service Institution in London in which he conveyed the impression that NATO would 'use the bomb and ask afterwards'. (NATO Speech Series No. 84.)

[40] *The Five Years*, p. 61. For the original terms of reference of the Council, see *The Five Years*, pp. 172–3.

Lord Ismay believed firmly that it was through a strong
Council that NATO could be made more effective. Whenever
a vacancy occurred on the Council he suggested to the appointing government the importance of selecting a man who
held its highest confidence and who could effectively influence
both the attitude of his own Foreign Office and also those of
his colleagues on the Council.

There are arguments both for and against the appointment
of a Council of Permanent Representatives consisting of
extremely high-ranking men. The intention of the decisions
taken at Lisbon was to affirm the primacy of the NATO
Council as 'the apex of the Atlantic alliance'.[41] But, as the
apex, the Council might be subject to the suspicion that it
threatened national interests rather than favoured them. Both
the large and the small Powers on the Council had reason to
fear any development in that direction. The large Powers
wanted to minimize the restrictions on their freedom of action
and the small Powers wanted to minimize domination by the
large Powers.

Lord Ismay wanted the Council to be a body capable of
making explicit enough decisions for him, as its servant, to
execute them effectively.[42] In a speech in which he discussed the
powers of the Council, he made these three points: 'First, the
North Atlantic Council is in effect an International Cabinet
so far as concerns NATO affairs. Secondly, the authority of
the Council is in no way altered by the presence or absence of
Ministers. Thirdly, the Council has in fact been in permanent
session in Paris. . . .'[43] In his eyes, as mentioned earlier, the
Council, acting as an international cabinet, should receive all

[41] The phrase comes from an editorial, *The Times*, 2 Mar. 1953.

[42] For example, when Lord Ismay visited Washington in Mar. 1953 he
urged that 'a strong man be deputised at NATO by the Administration so
that it could continue to move ahead and take increasingly important joint
decisions'. (*New York Herald-Tribune*, 11 May 1953.) At that time the post
was vacant owing to the resignation of Mr. William Draper. It was rumoured
also that Lord Ismay prevailed upon the British government to maintain
'a top-calibre British diplomat' at NATO after Sir Frederick Hoyer Millar
left. An old friend of Lord Ismay's, Sir Christopher Steel, got the position.

[43] Speech by Lord Ismay, 8 Sept. 1952. (NATO Speech Series, No. 22);
Speech by Lord Ismay, 5 Nov. 1954. (NATO Speech Series, No. 62.)

papers and policy proposals and issue decisions and policy statements—in other words, its procedure should resemble that of the British Cabinet system.

In this same speech Lord Ismay emphasized the authority of the Council. He said: 'It was recently suggested that important matters requiring urgent decisions were being held up because there had been no Ministerial meeting for a long time. This criticism overlooks the fact that the Council, as now constituted, has precisely the same powers of decision, irrespective of whether Governments are represented by Ministers or by their Permanent Representatives.[44] In saying this, Lord Ismay was implying that the Permanent Representatives and/or the Ministers constituted the *same* Council—that the Council itself was always in session, possessing the same powers, regardless of its composition.

Technically speaking this was true. But an analysis of the composition of the Permanent Representatives to the Council showed that perhaps, after all, they were not so very different from the former Council Deputies. Of the twelve men who had served as Deputies, eight had subsequently been appointed to serve as Permanent Representatives.[45] Thus, if the Permanent Representatives were to exercise greater powers of negotiation, decision, and supervision, this more energetic and forceful behaviour would have to emanate from the same men who had found their actions restricted as Deputies. Moreover, the diplomatic rank—or governmental status—of the Permanent Representatives was no higher than that of the Deputies.[46]

[44] ibid.

[45] Cf. *The NATO Handbook* (London, Jan. 1952), p. 30, with *The North Atlantic Treaty Organization* (Paris, Dec. 1952), p. 25. The Deputies carried over were: M. André de Staercke of Belgium, herr de Steensen-Leth of Denmark, M. Herve Alphand of France, Hr. Gunnlangur Petursson of Iceland, Sr. Alberto Rossi Longhi of Italy, Jonkheer A. W. L. Tjarda van Starkenborgh Stachouwer of The Netherlands, and Sir Frederick Hoyer Millar of the U.K. Mr. L. Dana Wilgress, the Canadian Deputy, was appointed Permanent Representative in Aug. 1953, the interval between Apr. 1952 and Aug. 1953 having been filled by Mr. A. D. P. Heeney.

[46] The careers of the men who served as Permanent Representatives during Lord Ismay's tenure of office were as follows. The Belgian representative had never been a Minister and had not entered diplomatic life

It therefore became apparent that, if the Permanent Representatives were to become something greater than the Deputies, the initiative would have to flow from the ultimate source of control, the member governments.

Lord Ismay pointed out the need for stronger governmental support for the Permanent Representatives when he declared in 1957 at the last Ministerial meeting he attended as Secretary-General:

---

until 1950. Canada was represented throughout most of the period by a professional diplomat who had for a brief time served as Deputy Minister of Trade and Commerce in Mr. Mackenzie King's government. Denmark was represented successively by three men, all career Foreign Service officers. France had two diplomats, then a former Minister of Labour and Social Security turned diplomat. The German Federal Republic appointed as its first and only representative a professional diplomat. Greece sent as its first representative a man who had been a long-time Deputy, a some-time Cabinet member, and for lengthy intervals in between, a high-level diplomat. This man was succeeded by a career diplomat. Iceland sent first a professional Foreign Service officer, then a man who had combined an academic career in international law with international diplomatic experience. Italy had, successively, two career diplomats. From Luxembourg came first a career diplomat, and then an attorney who after World War II had entered the diplomatic service. Norway was represented first by an economist turned diplomat, and then by a high-level professional diplomat. The Netherlands sent first a career diplomat who had served as Governor-General of the Netherlands East Indies, and after him another career diplomat. Portugal and the U.K. were both represented by career diplomats. The representative from Turkey deserves special treatment, for he was Mr. Fatin R. Zorlu, later Minister of Foreign Affairs. 'In May, 1952, M. Zorlu was appointed Permanent Representative of Turkey to the North Atlantic Council. He was elected to the Turkish Parliament on 2nd April 1954, and appointed Minister of State. He became Vice-President of the [Turkish] Council of Ministers while retaining his post as Permanent Representative to the North Atlantic Council, until December 1955.' Mr. Zorlu was succeeded by a professional diplomat. Lastly, the U.S. was represented first by a New York banker, then by a textile representative, and then by a former Assistant Secretary of State for European Affairs who had been an executive of a pharmaceutical company. This situation should be construed more as a characteristic of American political life than as an adverse reflection on either the ability of the men appointed or on the importance which the U.S. attached to NATO. (Taken from the official NATO biographies.)

. . . there is still a tendency in some quarters to regard the Council of Permanent Representatives as a sort of Second Eleven, which is empowered to decide matters of relatively small importance, but, in the case of more important problems, to do no more than make preliminary studies with a view to their consideration and decision at Ministerial Sessions. In the interests of efficiency, it is important that the plenary authority of the Permanent Council should be generally recognised.[47]

Apparently this plenary authority had not been generally recognized during his term of office, and it is difficult to avoid the conclusion that there was some qualitative difference between the Council when the Permanent Representatives were meeting and the Council when the Ministers were attending. For instance, it was contestable whether the Permanent Representatives could decide the same kinds of questions that the Council could in Ministerial session. It was true that even Ministers inevitably had to refer back to their governments on major issues. However, this did not alter the fact that Ministers travelled to NATO Headquarters twice a year to transact business of a nature different from that associated with the Permanent Representatives. The Ministers received reports which the International Staff/Secretariat, the delegations, and their respective Ministries had specifically prepared for them; they decided upon matters which had been purposely, and at times laboriously, brought to the decision stage by the Permanent Representatives; they performed the symbolic function of demonstrating to the world the unity of the Alliance; they underlined the important place which NATO occupied in their respective foreign policies; and lastly they negotiated and co-ordinated the great issues of the Cold War.

The Permanent Representatives, by contrast, were responsible for the day-to-day supervision of the workings of the Alliance; they hammered out its major policies step by step. It was the Permanent Representatives who supervised the various Council Committees and working groups through which the bulk of the International Staff/Secretariat's business was carried on. The importance of the contribution which the

[47] 'Text of Lord Ismay's Report to the Ministerial Meeting of the North Atlantic Council at Bonn, May 1957', as contained in the *NATO Letter*, Vol. 5, Spec. Supp. to No. 6.

Permanent Representatives made in solving NATO's problems is illustrated by the following analysis of a Council meeting:

> The full-dress Council will . . . sit down around the green-baize table with neatly sharpened pencils, the advisers and specialists clustered behind the delegates in whispering knots, to study two kinds of questions. For convenience, let us call them Category A and Category B questions. Category A questions are the routine questions of administration of effort—chiefly money, figures, divisions, who pays for what and how. Category B questions are questions of strategic and military policy—upon these hangs the destiny of the West. Most of the bitterness, haggling and irritation will fester over the less important Category A questions.[48]

Category A questions were those which more often than not were left to the Permanent Representatives to resolve.

In summary, the Permanent Representatives and the Ministers dealt with different aspects of a greater function—that of providing centralized, multi-national leadership for the Alliance. The two sets of representatives, both constituting, in a legal rather than a functional sense, the same Council, complemented each other's work. Together they fulfilled the 'job description' given them by M. Bidault, former French Minister of Foreign Affairs and a former Council Chairman:

> The Atlantic Council has indeed the highest responsibility for all such matters as the peaceful settlement of international disputes involving Member States, as the development of relations designed to strengthen their free institutions, as their economic co-operation, as the mutual assistance they are liable to give each other in the event of armed aggression, as the compulsory consultation whenever any one of them sees a menace to its territorial integrity, political independence and security.

He went on to say: 'One may wonder at times where fundamental directives and political decisions which, for all of us, are wider than the national framework, are worked out. Well, we should once again declare that it is in no other place but here.'[49]

---

[48] Theodore H. White, *Daily Mail*, 3 Dec. 1952.

[49] Speech delivered 14 Dec. 1953 (NATO Press Release No. 66.) A 'decision' by the Council was often really the legal act of confirming—or ratifying—agreements already worked out at other levels in the International Staff/Secretariat or through other channels, as mentioned earlier.

CHAPTER V

THE NORTH ATLANTIC COUNCIL:
NEGOTIATION AND CONSULTATION

ONE of the most significant evolutionary developments in the role of the Secretary-General during Lord Ismay's tenure of office was his emergence as an agent able to participate in the negotiations and consultations which accompanied the multilateral formulation and execution of foreign policies. This development was the result of the NATO nations' gradual recognition of the fact that they could not separate their military and economic policies from their foreign policies on either a regional or a world-wide basis. But this recognition did not come easily, nor did it necessarily produce satisfactory results.

The Assistant Secretary-General for Political Affairs, speaking rhetorically, discussed the pre-Lisbon history of this question shortly after taking up his post in 1952:

What would then be the scope and nature of the political questions which could appropriately be discussed and even settled within NATO? We get little indication of the answer to this qustion by looking back on the previous activities of the Council. Only a few questions of a fairly limited nature have so far been brought up for general discussion. These included, of course, the discussion which led to action taken on the question of associating Germany in Western defence and the accession of Greece and Turkey to the NATO. In addition, the Council Deputies had carried out an interesting exchange of views and information on various subjects. The emphasis was, however, on an informal exchange of information without comment by governments. I think it is correct to say that so far the subjects discussed have been chosen somewhat at random.[1]

Thus Lord Ismay had no firm tradition or habit of consultation on political subjects among the Alliance members to build upon. The general rule was that questions concerning

[1] Speech by Sr. S. Fenoaltea, 13 June 1952. (NATO Speech Series, No. 20.)

geographical areas not included within the confines of the Treaty could be discussed only in so far as they referred to one of the member countries.[2] But, speaking of the creation of NATO, Lord Ismay had said: 'I am convinced that the present solution is only a partial one, aimed at guarding the heart. It must grow until the whole free world gets under one umbrella'[3] —'We cannot do our business except on a global basis.'[4]

Two possible methods of establishing this 'global basis' were postulated by Lord Ismay. The first was to expand the mandate of the Standing Group; the second to create a similar agency which would perform a function wider in scope than planning purely NATO military policy. In both proposals Lord Ismay undoubtedly had in mind some sort of extension of the Anglo-American Combined Chiefs-of-Staff operation during World War II, which, with the addition of France, had been reborn

---

[2] Article 6 of the Treaty had provided: 'For the purpose of Article 5 an armed attack on one or more of the Parties is deemed to include an armed attack on the territory of any of the Parties in Europe or North America, or the Algerian Departments of France, on the occupation forces of any Party in Europe, on the islands under the jurisdiction of any Party in the North Atlantic area north of the Tropic of Cancer or on the vessels or aircraft in this area of any of the Parties.' This Article was modified by the Greece-Turkey Protocol, signed 22 Oct. 1951, upon the accession of these two countries to NATO. The revised text read: 'For the purpose of Article 5, an armed attack on one or more of the Parties is deemed to include an armed attack: (i) on the territory of any of the Parties in Europe or North America, on the Algerian Departments of France, on the territory of Turkey or on the islands under the jurisdiction of any of the Parties in the North Atlantic area north of the Tropic of Cancer; (ii) on the forces, vessels, or aircraft of any of the Parties, when in or over these territories or any other area in Europe in which occupation forces of any of the Parties were stationed on the date when the Treaty entered into force or the Mediterranean Sea or the North Atlantic area north of the Tropic of Cancer.' (*The Five Years*, pp. 18–21.) The accession of the German Federal Republic in 1955 did not alter the geographical responsibilities of the Alliance.

[3] *Manchester Guardian*, 9 Oct. 1952. In Nov. 1951 there had been a suggestion that a NATO Consultative Assembly should be instituted which would sit alongside the Council similarly to the Strasbourg Assembly and the Council of Europe. This suggestion would have broadened the range of political topics taken up in NATO. But it was never adopted.

[4] *The Times*, 20 Feb. 1953.

in the Standing Group. But whichever agency was used, according to Lord Ismay, its activities should be qualified in two ways: first, it should operate only in wartime; second, it should be subordinate to the Council, especially as regards political guidance. He had definite reasons for making these qualifications. In regard to the first of them he said:

> Anyone can see that war, beastly though it is, is much easier to run than peace. In wartime you are in the presence of the concrete and not the abstract. The number of problems is limited, and if you adopt the wrong solution, you soon get a stern corrective. But in peace the number of problems is larger and they can be solved only by the assumption of hypotheses which are really little more than guesswork.[5]

As to the second qualification, Lord Ismay knew that within the confines of the Alliance the smaller Powers already had reservations about any proposal to create a 'political Standing Group' which would have removed them from the realms of decision-making and the formulation of policy. These Powers had from the inception of NATO been worried lest they would be dominated by their larger allies. As far back as 1950 they had insisted on the creation of the Committee of Military Representatives of their Chiefs-of-Staff 'in order to ensure, on the one hand, that all member nations not represented on the Standing Group are kept in touch with its work and, on the other hand, that the Standing Group is kept informed of the points of view of those other nations'.[6]

For them the question was: since the political and economic representation of their interests in NATO had come through the Council, why should they allow another body to be created which would restrict the range of their influence and possibly remove from their purview certain vital questions of both a military and political nature? In fact the Big Three continually had to reassure their smaller allies that they were not being neglected when the Big Three met without them. The United States, the United Kingdom, and France frequently announced that they would keep their partners advised about the subjects of their discussions, and that they would seek the smaller Powers' advice and consent—preferably through NATO's

⁵ *New York Times*, 26 Feb. 1953.   ⁶ *The Five Years*, p. 68.

consultative machinery—before adopting policies directly involving their interests. For instance, when the Big Three Foreign Ministers met in Washington in June 1953—the first such meeting after Lord Ismay had assumed office—they gave formal assurances to their NATO colleagues that they would be kept fully informed about any discussions which impinged on Alliance matters. This would include such topics as Germany, the Soviet peace offensive going on at that time, the proposed European Defence Community (EDC), and Indo-China.[7]

In 1954 the Council approved a 'Resolution on Political Consultation' which committed the Ministers to make a sustained effort to inform one another of their 'views on political questions of common concern'. Because the Resolution also underlined the limits beyond which the Council was unwilling to go, it is quoted in its entirety:

THE NORTH ATLANTIC COUNCIL

HAVING REGARD to the obligations assumed by the Parties to the North Atlantic Treaty

RECOGNIZING

(A) That the security and unity of the Atlantic Community depend not only on collective defence measures but also on co-ordinated diplomatic policies: and

(b) that developments in the international situation affect each of the Parties;

---

[7] The many conferences held at all levels about arrangements for incorporating EDC into the NATO framework, and, after the demise of EDC, the arrangements for bringing the German Federal Republic into NATO, occupied a substantial amount of the Council's attention. But, in terms of the methods used by the Council to gain for itself greater direct participation in negotiations, these discussions did not change matters much. This observation is borne out by the manner in which the Council acknowledged the conclusion of the negotiations: 'The Council noted that all the agreements reached at the London Conference and at the subsequent meetings of the Four and Nine-Power Conferences form part of one general settlement which is directly or indirectly of concern to all the North Atlantic Treaty Powers and which was accordingly submitted to the Council. The Council welcomed this settlement.' (NATO Press Release M2(54)2.)

REAFFIRMS the views of the Committee on the North Atlantic Community endorsed by the Eighth Session of the Council at Rome;[8]

AGREES that the Council should be used when appropriate for exchanges of views on political questions of common concern;

RECOMMENDS

(A) that all member governments should bear constantly in mind the desirability of bringing to the attention of the Council information on international political developments whenever they are of concern to other members of the Council or to the Organization as a whole; and

(b) that the Council in permanent session should from time to time consider what specific subject might be suitable for political consultation at one of its subsequent meetings when its members should be in a position to express the views of their governments on this subject.[9]

At the Ministerial meeting held in July 1955, immediately preceding the Geneva Four Power Summit Conference, the Council arranged that one of the Big Three's Permanent Representatives should report to it on their discussions. The Italian Foreign Minister, Signor Gaetino Martino, voiced the feeling of smaller Powers about this arrangement when he said:

At the meetings of the Atlantic Council in Paris, complete agreement has been achieved on the way in which the representatives of the Western powers should conduct the negotiations which are now beginning at Geneva. The United States, Great Britain, and France will speak with one voice at this conference on behalf of the whole Atlantic Community. They will endeavour to arrive at an understanding with the U.S.S.R. as to a feasible solution of the main difficulties which lie at the root of the present tension in Europe. The principle which we have preached for many months, that all members of the Community should take an active part in framing a common European policy, has been fully realized. What we need is not a directorate of Great Powers, but a group of powers acting on a mandate from the Community as a whole. . . . We have, above all, insisted on the necessity of a more and more intimate and active collaboration between all the Atlantic countries, in order that each may make its contribution to the solution of common problems.[10]

[8] See fn. 14, this chapter.   [9] NATO Press Release 15-54M.
[10] ANSA, 18 July 1955.

One way that the Big Three facilitated NATO planning for the Geneva Conference was to give to the Council's Permanent Representatives an advance outline of the 'chapter headings' of the proposed topics for discussion. The Representatives could report this information to their Foreign Ministers who would then have time to prepare their responses before they met together in the Council to give expression to NATO policy.

Lord Ismay expanded upon this procedure:

Prior to this Conference [the Summit] the French, British and U.S. Governments exchanged views among themselves on all the problems that were likely to be discussed, and tentatively agreed on the line they should take. Their collective views, as they took shape, were periodically reported to the North Atlantic Council, so that the twelve partners who were not going to be represented at Geneva could express their opinions on the proposals, and put forward any suggestions they thought fit. In this way all the partners, and not only the three who were to be represented at the Conference took part in the preparatory work. Finally, the three Foreign Ministers who were going to Geneva, came to Paris the day before the meeting, and had a full dress conference with their colleagues from the other twelve countries. Thus they could take their places round the Council table in Geneva, fortified by the knowledge that they would be acting in accordance with the wishes of their fellow members of NATO.[11]

The year 1955 also witnessed several other moves within NATO which appeared to lead toward increased political consultation and co-ordination of foreign policies. The first move occurred at the May Ministerial meeting, at which the Council devoted part of its time to an examination of the situation in the Middle East, and particularly to Soviet aims therein. The Middle East threat had been discussed along with what Lord Ismay called 'a whole host of difficulties' which confronted the Alliance. Other problems along NATO's geographic margins at that time were the friction between Greece, Turkey, and Britain over Cyprus, and the French difficulties in North Africa, particularly in Algeria.[12] None of

[11] Speech delivered 30 Sept. 1955. (NATO Speech Series, No. 69.)
[12] In Cyprus the British insisted on retaining control until satisfactory arrangements could be made to preserve British control over their military installations, and to bring peace between the hostile Greek and Turkish

these difficulties erupted into the Council with any compelling force however. More encouraging to the development of political co-operation was the spate of meetings held in the second half of 1955 and flanking the 'Little Summit Conferences' which were an aftermath of Geneva. Some of the leaders of the smaller Powers, such as M. Spaak of Belgium, urged that the Council should become a 'political Council of the free world', and it seemed that such was becoming the case.[13]

To cap all this activity the Council, at its Ministerial meeting in December 1955, took up the question of improving economic and social co-operation in NATO. The Italian Foreign Minister suggested that there should be more emphasis in NATO on Article 2 of the Treaty, which provided for the strengthening of social and economic ties. He wanted collaboration first in establishing European common markets, and second in giving aid to developing countries. The Canadian Foreign Secretary, Mr. Lester Pearson, who had supported the idea of greater NATO activity in the social and economic sphere ever since the Organization's earliest days, supported this proposal. The Ministers thereupon instructed their Permanent Representatives to investigate and report upon the matter.[14]

---

communities. The French were faced with a rebellion in Algeria which had turned into a war of independence.

[13] A variation on the earlier proposals regarding the Standing Group was also offered at this time. It was proposed that the Standing Group should be enlarged by the addition of a fourth member who would be chairman, and who would not be a national of any of the three countries composing the Standing Group. Thus the Standing Group would represent more truly the entire Alliance, and not so exclusively the three leading Powers. (*New York Times*, 16 Dec. 1955.)

[14] The earlier Ministerial Committee had been set up at the Ottawa Conference of Sept. 1951, which included representatives from Belgium, Canada, Italy, The Netherlands and Norway. (*The Five Years*, p. 44.) This was known as the Pearson Committee. It reported to the Lisbon meeting. Nothing concrete came from this earlier effort. (ibid., pp. 151–2.) The Council's later action was officially reported in the Final Communique of the Ministerial meeting of Dec. 1955: 'The Council recognised that recent developments in the international situation made it more necessary than ever to have closer co-operation between the members of the Alliance as envisaged in Article 2 of the Treaty. They decided to instruct the Permanent

At the Ministerial meeting in May 1956 the Council gave added impetus to this matter by appointing a special Committee of Three on Non-military Co-operation in NATO, composed of Mr. Lester Pearson, herr Halvard Lange of Norway, and Signor Gaetino Martino of Italy. The Committee was instructed 'to advise the Council on ways and means to improve and extend NATO co-operation in non-military fields and to develop greater unity within the Atlantic Community'.[15]

Shortly after the Ministerial meeting of May 1956 the greatest strain of NATO's political life up to then began to develop, and the issue was directly related to the question of consultation over events involving the embroilment of NATO nations in non-NATO areas. The foundations of the crisis were laid when the United States, on short notice, withdrew its offer to help finance the Aswan Dam planned for Egypt. Shortly after the British followed suit, thus provoking a storm of resentment in Egypt which culminated in the nationalization of the Suez Canal by the Egyptian government on 26 July 1956.[16] This led in October–November to the sending of a combined Anglo-French Expeditionary Force to the Canal Zone in the face of violent Egyptian objections. The Force's mission was, ostensibly, to halt Israeli–Egyptian fighting in the area, which had threatened the flow of traffic through the Canal.

Council to examine and implement all measures conducive to this end.' (NATO Press Release M4 (55) 2.)

[15] Final Communique of the North Atlantic Council Ministerial meeting, 5 May 1956. The Committee's terms of reference were contained in the 'Report of the Committee of Three on Non-military Co-operation in NATO', as reproduced in the *NATO Letter*, Vol. 5, Spec. Supp. to No. 1. Further references to the report will be as it appeared in the *Letter*. The only portions of the report which were not made public were those pertaining to certain economic matters. The entire report was submitted to the Council as NATO Doc. C-M (56) 26.

[16] See *Documents on International Affairs, 1956*, ed. Noble Frankland (London, 1959), pp. 73–239, for a survey of the situation as it had unfolded. The withdrawal of British military forces from the huge Suez base had been the subject of prolonged and tortuous negotiations between Britain and Egypt for several years, and had not contributed to Anglo-Egyptian amity.

Lord Ismay pointed out that this event did not directly affect NATO, because the Treaty called for action only if one of its members was menaced, and, he noted, no member of NATO had been attacked. Nonetheless, immediately after the military action the Permanent Representatives of the Council met in closed session every day for a week. The key point at issue was the fact that neither the United Kingdom nor France had consulted their Allies before taking action. Thus the two primary items on the agenda of the Ministerial meeting held in December 1956—the Report of the Committee of Three and the Suez Crisis—were closely related.

The entire situation gave rise to definitive discussions in the Council about the limitations which should accompany any extensive practice of consultation among Alliance members. These discussions brought out the various viewpoints—and the attendant complications—which had previously been tacitly understood to exist but which had been glossed over. No longer could the Council overlook the divorce from reality which events so amply demonstrated had existed between its public statements and its practice.

Undoubtedly, on balance, the importance of the December Ministerial meeting rested on the need to restore a badly shattered unity to the Alliance. The American Secretary of State, Mr. John Foster Dulles, on arriving in Paris for the meeting declared: 'It is our firm resolve to find a means of burying past discords and opening the way to a fruitful and peaceful co-operation.'[17] He believed that the best way to accomplish this aim was to have, in addition to the regular Council sessions, individual talks by the Secretary of State with the Foreign Ministers of France and Britain, rather than the more traditional Three Power joint talks which had taken place at past Ministerial meetings. To give time for these separate talks the Council agreed to meet in formal session for only two hours each morning and each afternoon, thereby allowing time during the two days of the meeting for private sessions between Ministers and among groups of Ministers.

These deliberations revealed that any general principle for

---

[17] *The Times*, 10 Dec. 1956.

complete consultation about and alignment of foreign policies simply did not square with the international facts of life. For instance, while it might appear sensible for the NATO countries involved in Africa to attempt to align their foreign policies in that region, it would have been asking too much to require all the other NATO Powers to associate themselves actively with such a policy. A good example of the difficulty of alignment was the increasing American reluctance to support British and French—to say nothing of Dutch, Belgian, or Portuguese —policies toward their colonial or ex-colonial areas.

Mr. Dulles believed that consultations should not be allowed to hinder effective national action. He pointed out that the United States had concluded defence pacts with (at that time) forty-four countries, all of which called for consultation. Would it be practicable, he asked, for the United States to submit for prior consultation at NATO matters which, under other treaties, were of more direct concern to the thirty other countries with which she had pacts? The most important consideration, according to him, was that consultations should take place *before* a crisis arose, in order that member nations might be apprised of one another's opinions in advance of national action. The fact that Mr. Dulles had made this point very strongly at the Ministerial meeting of the previous May probably contributed to the vigour of his restatement of it in December. At the time of the earlier meeting, he had said:

. . . at Paris last week we had to ask ourselves whether what has been done is good enough. There has been a marked development of the consultative process. But it still remains the fact that matters of vital importance to the Atlantic Community are not being given timely consideration on a community basis.

I have already referred to the problem of the Middle East which had never been seriously discussed by the North Atlantic Treaty Council even though the future of Western Europe is deeply engaged by developments there.

We have seen in North Africa where serious disturbances within a part of the North Atlantic Treaty area have brought about a shifting of forces from continental Europe which alters the capability of defense as against a possible aggression from Eastern Europe.

There is the problem of Cyprus which deeply concerns three parties to the North Atlantic Treaty, the United Kingdom, Greece and Turkey.

I do not suggest that any of these problems should today be made a matter of common consideration around the NATO Council table. At the point to which these particular problems have now developed, there can reasonably be questions as to whether consultation is or is not desirable. Neither do I imply any criticism of the past, for there has never been agreement or understanding that problems of this type should be discussed. But surely the Atlantic Community is not adequately organized if matters of this nature, which could shake the Community to its foundations, develop over the years without any effort at broad consultation between the members.[18]

In other words, Mr. Dulles implied that political consultations could take place more effectively in times of relative tranquility or when a chain of events was still controllable than after a crisis had become acute.

Other Ministers at this time also voiced some of their major international political concerns. Herr von Brentano, Foreign Minister of the German Federal Republic, at the Ministerial Council meeting of the Western European Union (WEU), which immediately preceded the NATO Council meeting, asked what could and would be done by the West in the event of a rising in Eastern Germany comparable to the one which had taken place in Hungary. Turkey raised a similar question at the NATO Council meeting when its delegate wanted to know what NATO would do to meet a situation in which Turkey became involved in hostilities with a Soviet-assisted Syria.[19]

A proposal by Turkey that NATO should grant stronger support to the Baghdad Pact was received without enthusiasm. The Scandinavian countries, in particular, which had hesitated about agreeing to the inclusion of Greece and Turkey in NATO in the first place, were opposed to any further formal geographical extension of the Alliance. The Norwegian Foreign Minister, herr Halvard Lange, agreed that the minimum requirement was co-ordination, but he also made the qualification that NATO members could not be expected to bear

---

[18] Speech delivered 8 May 1956. (NATO Speech Series, No. 78.)
[19] *Manchester Guardian*, 11 Dec. 1956.

responsibility in areas where they had no possibility of exerting their influence.[20]

A more hopeful note was struck by Herr von Brentano when he suggested that a special NATO cabinet of under-secretaries of state should be formed which would meet every two months to co-ordinate policies. Worthy as this suggestion may have been, however, it was never acted upon. One consequence of it would have been an inevitable down-grading of the Permanent Representatives.

The most all-inclusive proposal was made by the British Foreign Secretary, Mr. Selwyn Lloyd. He suggested that there should be a single Atlantic Assembly patterned on parliamentary lines and recruited from national parliaments. He thought that political and military direction for the Assembly should be provided by NATO (within which would be WEU), and that economic co-operation should be under, and in association with OEEC.[21] However, as Mr. Lloyd made clear, the idea of consultation did not mean merely giving the right to other nations to criticize or obstruct. To have an effect on a nation's foreign policy, consultation would also have to mean sharing in the responsibility for decisions. In Mr. Lloyd's eyes, any nation would be justified in hesitating to accept this responsibility.

The outcome of the meeting, in the face of all these perplexities and varied suggestions, was the unanimous adoption of the entire Report of the Committee of Three on Non-military Co-operation. This report is a milestone in NATO's 'legislative' history and therefore merits detailed consideration.

The Committee was forthright in its condemnation of the narrow use which had been made of the Council in the realm of political consultation. It declared:

[20] *New York Herald-Tribune*, 13 Dec. 1956; *Christian Science Monitor*, 12 Dec. 1956. Turkey was in a uniquely strategic position to raise such a question, as she was a member not only of NATO and the Baghdad Pact, but also of the Balkan Pact, with Yugoslavia and Greece. All Turkey had to do, in case of a threat to its soil, was to let the aggressor violate its frontiers, and all three Pacts might come into operation.

[21] A similar proposal had been made to the Council of WEU by the Italian Foreign Minister, Signor G. Martino. He had called for a 'political association' within WEU with, however, a directly elected Assembly.

NATO has not been destroyed, or even weakened by the threats or attacks of its enemies. It has faltered at times through the lethargy or complacency of its members; through dissension or division between them; by putting narrow national considerations above the collective interest. It could be destroyed by these forces, if they were allowed to subsist. To combat these tendencies, NATO must be used by its members far more than it has been used, for sincere and genuine consultation and co-operation on questions of common concern. For this purpose, resolution is more important than resolutions; will than words.[22] It is easy to profess devotion to the principle of political—or economic—consultation in NATO. It is difficult and has in fact been shown to be impossible, if the proper conviction is lacking, to convert the profession into practice. Consultation within an alliance means more than exchange of information, though that is necessary. It means more than letting the NATO Council know about national decisions that have already been taken; or trying to enlist support for those decisions. It means the discussion of problems collectively, in the early stages of policy formation, and before national positions become fixed. At best, this will result in collective decisions on matters of common interest affecting the Alliance. At the least, it will ensure that no action is taken by one member without a knowledge of the views of the others.[23]

The Committee went on from this general statement of faulty practice, to recommend certain principles and practices which would help to create a climate in which full and frank consultation could take place:

(a) members should inform the Council of any development which significantly affects the Alliance. They should do this, not merely as a formality but as a preliminary to effective political consultation;

(b) both individual member governments and the Secretary-General should have the right to raise for discussion in the Council any subject which is of common NATO interest and not of a purely domestic character;

(c) a member government should not, without adequate advance consultation, adopt firm policies or make major political pronouncements on matters which significantly affect the Alliance or any of its members, unless circumstances make such prior consultation obviously and demonstrably impossible;

[22] Report of the Committee of Three, p. 5.
[23] ibid. p. 6.

(*d*) in developing their national policies, members should take into consideration the interests and views of other governments, particularly those most directly concerned, as expressed in NATO consultation, even where no community of view or consensus has been reached in the Council;

(*e*) where a consensus has been reached, it should be reflected in the formation of national policies. When for national reasons the consensus is not followed, the government concerned should offer an explanation to the Council. It is even more important that where an agreed and formal recommendation has emerged from the Council's discussions, governments should give it full weight in any national actions or policies related to the subject of the recommendation.[24]

The Secretary-General was authorized to prepare an annual report upon which Ministers at the spring meetings of the Council could 'make an appraisal of the political progress of the Alliance and consider the lines along which it should advance'.[25] The report should include an analysis of the major political problems of the Alliance; a review of the extent to which member governments had consulted and co-operated on such problems; and an indication of the problems and possible developments which might require future consultation, so that difficulties might be resolved and positive and constructive initiative taken.[26] In addition the Committee recommended that:

To assist the Permanent Representatives and the Secretary-General in discharging their responsibilities for political consultation, there should be constituted under the Council a Committee of Political Advisers from each delegation, aided when necessary by specialists from the capitals.[27]

The Assistant Secretary-General for Political Affairs was made Chairman of the Committee of Political Advisers, and the Political Affairs Division was strengthened in order to be able to prepare the requisite background papers for this Committee.[28]

[24] ibid. p. 7.   [25] ibid. p. 7.
[26] ibid. p. 7. This is a paraphrase of the relevant paragraphs.
[27] ibid. p. 7.
[28] See *The North Atlantic Treaty Organization* (Paris, 1959), p. 42, for a description of the enlarged duties of the Political Affairs Division.

The Secretary-General, as noted earlier, was made Chairman of the Council, and given the 'right and duty' of bringing to its attention matters which he believed might threaten the solidarity or effectiveness of the Alliance.[29] In the important realm of the settlement of inter-member disputes, the position of the Secretary-General was now considerably enhanced. He was empowered 'to offer his good offices informally at any time to the parties in dispute, and with their consent to initiate or facilitate procedures of enquiry, mediation, conciliation, or arbitration; and . . . where he deems it appropriate for [this] purpose . . . to use the assistance of not more than three Permanent Representatives chosen by him in each instance'.[30]

These grants assigned a considerable degree of discretion to the Secretary-General. They gave him not only the right to judge when he should take an active part in the disputes of member States, but also the right to select which members he desired to assist him in resolving those disputes amicably. The member States had become his colleagues in a joint endeavour, whereas before they had been his 'masters'. If the Secretary-General of the United Nations had not become the 'World's Moderator' as President Roosevelt had expected that he would, the Secretary-General of NATO was offered the possibility of becoming the 'Atlantic Community's Moderator'.[31]

Clearly, through these words and actions of the Council and through the discussions which had surrounded the entire subject of political consultation, both the Council and the

[29] Report of the Committee of Three, p. 8.

[30] ibid. p. 8. The Council's 'Resolution on the Peaceful Settlement of Disputes and Differences between Members of the North Atlantic Treaty Organization' is contained in *The North Atlantic Treaty Organization* (Paris, 1957), p. 64.

[31] Schwebel, p. 14. Lord Hankey, who served as Secretary to the British Committee of Imperial Defence and the Cabinet, made this comment: 'I begin to doubt whether the United Nations, or the Conferences of Foreign Ministers or for the matter of that the over-rated Summit Talks or, even NATO, with the much smaller task of preserving good relations between nations already committed to concerted action in the event of a possible war against a common enemy, will be able to provide a deterrent to another major war, without more adequate machinery than they possess.' (Private memorandum to Robert Jordan, 31 Aug. 1959.)

Secretary-General had assumed new stature. Lord Ismay in this respect gained the satisfaction of being able to retire from office leaving NATO stronger in arrangements for political consultation than he had found it. The Council affirmed that 'the foundation of NATO was the political obligation which member governments had taken for collective defence'.[32]

Lord Ismay ranked the need for member governments to consult together frequently and fully on their foreign policies wherever these policies might range, in the forefront of his 'last will and testament' made when he retired. He drew up a set of 'Rules for NATO Conduct' which set forth his feelings on this subject:

It is the privilege of the old retainer to speak his mind to his masters. So, greatly daring, I am going to address this parting message to them. It is called 'Rules for the Conduct of NATO'.

Rule Number One: Do not forget that, although the Alliance was born of fear, and security had to be given first priority, it is not merely a military alliance of the old-fashioned sort. If it is to survive it must be strong, not only militarily, but politically and morally. It is therefore imperative that the partners should keep in the closest touch with each other on all matters great and small which affect the Alliance. This means that none of you should take action or reach firm decisions on such matters without consulting your allies or, at the very least, without keeping them fully informed. As I have explained, effective machinery for the purpose exists; there is therefore no excuse.

Rule Number Two: It is a cardinal sin for one of the members to do anything which might disturb or even seriously weaken the Alliance. At the same time, there are bound to be quarrels in the best regulated families. If, therefore, you find yourselves at logger-heads with one of your partners, pause for a moment and reflect that you and he are fundamentally like-minded people, dedicated to the principles of democracy, individual liberty and the rule of law. This being so, you can even question his judgement, but you ought not to question his motives. That is the thought that should govern your conduct towards the quarrel. The main thing is to settle it as quickly as possible. Let not the sun go down upon your wrath. If

[32] *The North Atlantic Treaty Organization* (Paris, 1957), p. 62.

you can settle it between yourselves without involving your other friends, so much the better.

. . . . . .

Above all, if there is any dirty NATO linen to be washed, do not wash it in public.

. . . . . .

Rule Number Five: The North Atlantic Treaty has definite limitations. It is only defensive and it applies only to NATO territory. But do not forget that the world in which we live is now a small place and that there may be developments outside the NATO area which may exercise a permanent influence on the security of that area. NATO must therefore always have an agreed policy for dealing with such developments as they occur, and must pursue that policy resolutely.

All that I have tried to say can be summed up very simply. NATO must behave like a family, all of whose members are engaged in the same business—the business of preserving the peace and of making the world a safer and a happier and a kinder place for all peoples. We have only to be vigilant, resolute and, above all, united: we have only to be true to ourselves and to each other. And all will be well.[33]

It was a sad time at NATO—especially in the International Staff/Secretariat—when Lord Ismay retired. In the realm of the settlement of political disputes, regardless of the difficulties in achieving effective political consultation, the measure of Lord Ismay's success in inspiring the confidence of member governments in the Secretary-General can be estimated from the fact that all the possible nominees for his successor were men pre-eminent in the field of international diplomacy.

Rumours of Lord Ismay's retirement had cropped up periodically almost from the first year of his leadership. As early as September 1953 it had been hinted that he wanted to retire and might be succeeded by Mr. Lester Pearson. In December 1953 he felt compelled to declare that reports that he would submit his resignation early in 1954 were 'quite untrue and without foundation.'[34] The basis of the reports was

---

[33] Speech delivered 4 June 1957. (NATO Speech Series, No. 89.)

[34] *Manchester Guardian*, 19 Dec. 1953. The question of his retirement caused so much attention at this time that even the Foreign Office had been questioned. (*Manchester Guardian*, 18 Dec. 1953.)

the notion that in 1952 he had been given a two-year term which was expiring. This was not accurate; Lord Ismay had not agreed to a specific term of service when he accepted the post.[35] In April 1954, it was rumoured that Lieutenant-General Sir Ian Jacob, Director-General of the British Broadcasting Association (BBC) and one of Lord Ismay's principal assistants during World War II would be offered the position. Perhaps Lord Ismay's age and health—he was 65 when he was appointed and at the time was suffering from fibrositis—led to these rumours.

Finally, in May 1955 Lord Ismay told the Council that he was thinking of retiring, but he received so heartfelt an expression of its desire that he should remain for at least another year, that he consented to do so.[36] The Council nevertheless knew that it had to find a successor not later than the Ministerial meeting of December 1956. The four most widely-rumoured candidates for the post were Mr. Lester Pearson, M. Paul-Henri Spaak, M. Paul van Zeeland, and herr Halvard Lange.[37] Mr. Pearson eliminated himself by supporting M. Spaak.[38]

M. Spaak was the most favoured candidate. He had been an important leader in the movement for European integration, and had played a very positive role in NATO as Belgium's Foreign Minister. Throughout the discussions of December 1956 he had forthrightly advocated a closer correlation between NATO's military and political policies, and greater use of the Council as means of achieving this objective.[39] His appointment to succeed Lord Ismay in May 1957 was welcomed as an

[35] Interview with Lord Ismay, 28 May 1959.

[36] Interview with Miss Mary Green, former personal secretary to Lord Ismay, 2 Jan. 1959.

[37] *Manchester Guardian*, 8 Dec. 1956. It is interesting to note that these same men had been prominent among the possible candidates in 1952.

[38] As far back as 1948 M. Spaak had been suggested for the post of Secretary-General of OEEC because the U.S. had wanted an outstanding European political figure in the position, whose prestige would facilitate reconciliation of national views and interests. But the British, true to their policy of weak ties in European international organizations, opposed this. The same pattern occurred in NATO. (See Ch. II.)

[39] *New York Times*, 3 Dec. 1956.

indication that the Council had come to a fuller recognition of the important place political issues occupied in preserving the harmony of the Alliance and the unity of the Western Powers. As one distinguished observer put it:

> During [Lord Ismay's] stewardship NATO's main problem was to develop a workable military arrangement to police the free world's borders. But now, despite imperfections in the defensive picture, the alliance's difficulties have shifted in emphasis to politics. It is therefore fitting that Spaak, one of Europe's outstanding statesmen, should take over. . . . By the time Spaak succeeds Ismay there may be alleviating circumstances. Surely several among the Foreign Ministers . . . will no longer hold their same positions.
>
> As a group, unfortunately [the NATO Foreign Ministers] have failed. This is not their personal fault. But methods their Governments chose to follow—polite agreement to disagree or to ignore disagreement—led to an accord to forget all disaccord. Such methods produced a never-never land of unreality. This is certainly NATO's last meeting of the old team. Already permanent ambassadors to its Council are being changed. By the time Spaak sits down next spring with different Foreign Ministers, there will be new personality relationships.[40]

[40] C. L. Sulzberger, *New York Times*, 10 Dec. 1956.

CHAPTER VI

THE OFFICE OF THE SECRETARY-GENERAL, INCLUDING THE EXECUTIVE SECRETARY AND THE SECRETARIAT

To understand how policy was made, it is necessary to examine the organization and methods of the secretariat part of the International Staff/Secretariat. Outside the broader designation of the 'Office of the Secretary-General', which had been placed under the responsibility of the Executive Secretary, there existed the Secretary-General's office proper. This office consisted of the private offices of the Secretary-General and the Deputy Secretary-General and their personal staffs, and the Emergency Planning Office. Before Mr. van Vredenburch, the first Deputy Secretary-General, arrived Lord Ismay had only two assistants. His private secretary was Mr. Peter Scott from the British Foreign Office, whom he had known previously in India. His deputy private secretary was M. G. de Boisgelin, from the Quai d'Orsay.[1]

Whereas Mr. Scott performed most of the traditional duties of a private secretary—handling appointments, official correspondence, reports, memoranda, etc.—M. de Boisgelin's duties were not as clear-cut. Initially his major task had been to maintain contact with the French delegation to NATO, which served as the agent for the host country in matters relating to the International Staff/Secretariat's move to Paris. One of his first 'extra-curricular' assignments was to procure an official residence for the Secretary-General. The difficulty of this assignment is illustrated by a press comment made in August 1952, nearly five months after Lord Ismay had arrived:

[1] Before M. de Boisgelin was appointed he was privately interviewed by Lord Ismay—an indication of the care the French government took to ensure that no nominee for the post appeared to have been 'forced' on Lord Ismay.

Like many other foreigners working in Paris, Lord Ismay is having accommodation trouble. In June I heard him say he was Stateless, because he was serving 14 different governments; and Homeless, because he hadn't been able to find a flat. He is still without a flat . . . and continues to stay at the Hotel Bristol.[2]

More significant administratively, the presence of a French-speaking official in the Secretary-General's office ensured that the temptation for Lord Ismay's English-speaking staff to work exclusively in English would be resisted. The official NATO languages were English and French, and papers in either language could thus readily be accepted.

After Mr. van Vredenburch's arrival, M. de Boisgelin became private secretary to the Deputy Secretary-General. He and Mr. Scott continued to process the papers of both the Secretary-General and Deputy Secretary-General as one office; Mr. Scott was careful to keep M. de Boisgelin informed about the Secretary-General's out-going papers, thereby keeping intra-office co-ordination strong.[3]

[2] *Daily Mail*, 26 Aug. 1952. Several months later NATO bought him a house in the Villa Said, a private street located in one of Paris's best districts. Other noteworthy residents of the Villa Said have been Anatole France and M. de Boisgelin. According to M. de Boisgelin, Lord Ismay never abused the availability of his private secretary. Another, more informal service performed by M. de Boisgelin was to introduce Lord Ismay into French horse-racing circles.

[3] The co-ordination of papers for the Secretary-General's attention has been hypothetically described as follows: '. . . it will normally be found that a matter requiring the attention of the Secretary General gives rise to the following action: (*a*) Letter from Mr. X to the Secretary General. (*b*) Note from the Secretary General to the appropriate senior officer—Assistant Secretary Y, for instance—asking for his comments and a draft reply. (*c*) Assistant Secretary General Y calls in one of his associates—Z—and asks him to prepare comments and a draft reply. (*d*) Z sends to the registry for the appropriate file, and prepares comments and draft reply; he then signs the comments and forwards them to: "The Secretary General for the attention of the Deputy Secretary General" and the whole file arranged in the following order is sent to the Secretary General's office: (1) Comments of Assistant Secretary General Y. (2) Draft reply, in double spacing. (3) Note from the Secretary General. (4) Letter from Mr. X. (5) File of the question completed to date. If, as is nearly always necessary, reference to previous papers would facilitate comprehension of the question under

When Mr. Scott was posted as Counsellor to the British Embassy in Vienna, M. de Boisgelin assumed responsibility for the entire office, becoming Lord Ismay's private secretary. Later in Lord Ismay's tenure of office he was occasionally referred to as the *chef de cabinet*, but in fact he never held the powers traditionally associated with this title.[4]

Lord Ismay had as his personal secretary Miss Mary Green, who was seconded from the British Cabinet Office and who had been with him throughout World War II and in India. She handled his official, semi-official, and personal correspondence, kept the files of his speeches and assisted in their preparation, and was responsible for his personal interests.

In the more broadly conceived 'Office of the Secretary-General', the Executive Secretary, Lord Coleridge of the United Kingdom (in 1952 he was Captain The Hon. R. D. Coleridge, C.B.E.) directed the work of the office and co-ordinated the general activity of the International Staff/Secretariat. The Executive Secretary had a threefold mandate. First, he was the Secretary to the Council and in that capacity his duties were defined as follows:

[He] is responsible to the Secretary-General for programming its work and for seeing that action is initiated on decisions of the Council. He is also responsible for supervising secretaries of the committees of the Council, and for directing the work of the Conference Service of the Organization.[5]

In the early years of Lord Ismay's tenure of office, the Council had twelve committees and working groups, divided into six

consideration, these are suitably tabbed. (*f*) The Deputy Secretary General examines the file and either returns it to Assistant Secretary General Y, if he does not agree with the position adopted, or else sends it on to the Secretary General. (*g*) If the Secretary General accepts the draft, it is re-typed, signed and dispatched. The file is then returned to Assistant Secretary General Y with a copy of the final letter, which has previously been shown to the Deputy Secretary General. (*h*) After it has been seen by Assistant Secretary General Y and his direct associates, including Z, the dossier is returned to the registry.' (NATO, Doc. ON (56) 68.)

[4] M. Spaak's *chef de cabinet*, M. Saint-Mleux had more responsibility than did M. de Boisgelin, and he used his authority in the traditional way.

[5] NATO Staff Manual, 2 Feb. 1953, item 1021.

categories, and also various *ad hoc* working groups. The categories, with their committees and working groups were: Annual Review—Annual Review Committee; Infrastructure —Infrastructure Committee and Infrastructure Payments and Progress Committee; Civil Co-operation—Information and Cultural Relations Committee and the Working Group on Labour Mobility; Budget—Civilian Budget Committee and Military Budget Committee; Production—the Working Group on Correlated Production Programmes in Europe; Emergency Planning—Planning Board for Ocean Shipping, Planning Board for European Inland Surface Transport, Committee on War-Time Commodity Problems, and the Committee on Civil Organization in Wartime.[6]

By 1957 the number of committees had grown to twenty-five: Committee of Political Advisers, Committee of Economic Advisers, Working Group on Labour Mobility, Annual Review Committee, Committee on Information and Cultural Relations, Infrastructure Committee, Infrastructure Payments and Progress Committee, NATO Pipeline Committee, Committee on European Airspace Co-ordination, Defence Production Committee, Security Committee, Civilian Budget Committee, Military Budget Committee, Senior Civil Emergency Planning Committee, Planning Board for Ocean Shipping, Planning Board for European Inland Surface Transport, Civil Aviation Planning Committee, Petroleum Planning Committee, Industrial Raw Materials Planning Committee, Food and Agriculture Planning Committee, Coal and Steel Planning Committee, Civil Defence Committee, Medical Committee, Manpower Planning Committee, Civil Communications Planning Committee.[7]

As will be described below, some of the secretaries to these committees had not been placed under the Executive Secretary at the outset; but by and large the Executive Secretary was the focal point for the secretariat activities of the International Staff/Secretariat, and assigned the secretaries to their committees.

Lord Coleridge inherited his secretariat function from the Deputies' Executive Secretary and from the Planning and

[6] *The North Atlantic Treaty Organization* (Paris, 1953), p. 51.
[7] *The North Atlantic Treaty Organization* (Paris, 1957), p. 72.

NORTH ATLANTIC COUNCIL COMMITTEE STRUCTURE[8]
(1953)

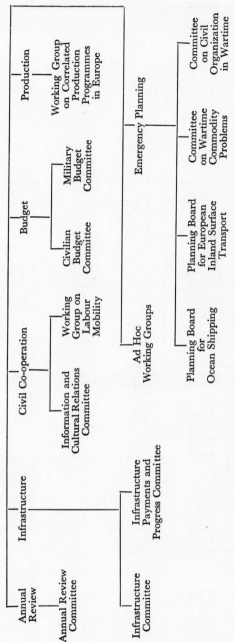

[8] *The North Atlantic Treaty Organization* (Paris, 1953), p. 57.

NORTH ATLANTIC COUNCIL COMMITTEE STRUCTURE[9]
(1957)

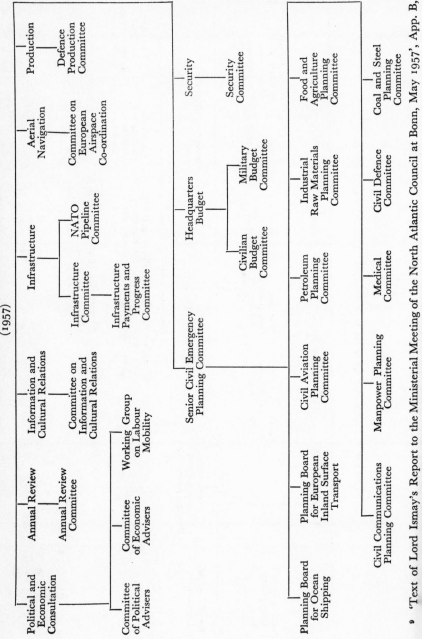

[9] 'Text of Lord Ismay's Report to the Ministerial Meeting of the North Atlantic Council at Bonn, May 1957', App. B,

Co-ordination Group of the Deputies' organization. This group had assisted the Deputies' Chairman and his Executive Secretary in the day-to-day organization of the work of the Council Deputies, had followed up decisions of the Deputies, and had prepared reports for the Council. Lord Coleridge also inherited the work which had formerly been done by the secretaries attached directly to the various Boards, Committees, and working groups of the Deputies' Organization and which had not been made responsible to the Deputies' Executive Secretary.[10]

The second area of Lord Coleridge's mandate consisted of a non-secretariat duty, internal administration. Lord Ismay had stipulated:

[Lord Coleridge is] responsible for the internal administrative arrangements of the international staff, and in this capacity supervises the work of the General Services. He assists the appropriate Assistant Secretaries General in coordinating establishment tables for the staff.

He is responsible for personnel matters in general, for supervising the work of the Personnel Office and for the equitable interpretation of staff regulations.[11]

In other words, the Deputy Secretary-General, the three Assistant Secretaries-General, the Head of the Information Service (later the Information Division), the Financial Controller, and the Statistician reported to the Secretary-General. Everything else, including the Conference Section, Personnel Section, General Services Section, Registry Section, and Security Section, came under the Executive Secretary.[12] This administrative responsibility imposed an onerous burden on the Executive Secretary, and exposed him to pressures and problems relating to the various Divisions and Independent Offices of the International Staff/Secretariat with which he would not otherwise have had to cope.

The third area of Lord Coleridge's mandate came from Lord Ismay's habit (as a man trained in the military tradition)

[10] *The NATO Handbook* (London, Jan. 1952), p. 22. See also Ch. II of this study.

[11] Staff Manual, item 1021.

[12] *The North Atlantic Treaty Organization* (Paris, Dec. 1952), p. 33.

OFFICE OF THE SECRETARY-GENERAL[13]
(1952)

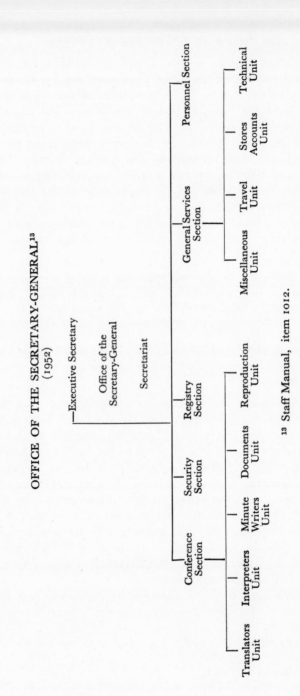

[13] Staff Manual, item 1012.

of viewing his chief administrative officer as a chief-of-staff. He therefore gave Lord Coleridge this general mission:

On those aspects of the work of the Organization which are not the direct responsibility of one particular Assistant Secretary-General, he maintains, at the appropriate level liaison with delegations and with the Office of the Standing Group Liaison Officer, and prepares or co-ordinates reports for the Secretary-General.

. . . . .

The Executive Secretary performs such other special functions as may from time to time be assigned by the Secretary-General.[14]

The strictly secretariat work of the Executive Secretary *vis-à-vis* the Council followed the traditional pattern. At Council meetings—the Permanent Representatives met at least once a week, usually on a Wednesday—the Executive Secretary sat next to the Secretary-General. Immediately behind the Executive Secretary sat his deputy. After the meeting a paper was prepared from the notes of the Deputy Executive Secretary and the minute writer and submitted to the Executive Secretary. If he approved it, the draft was co-ordinated with the Deputy Secretary-General, then drawn up as a Council minute, translated, and reproduced. This minute was distributed to the delegations and to those members of the International Staff/Secretariat who were entitled to it. If the delegations had any corrections which they wished incorporated in the minute, their requests for amendment were made to the Executive Secretary. In addition, Lord Coleridge followed through any action which the Council had approved, by co-ordinating the matter with the appropriate Assistant Secretary-General, delegation, or other agency and by keeping Lord Ismay informed of whatever action had been taken.

To prepare for a Council meeting, the Executive Secretary assembled a draft agenda based on matters submitted to him by Lord Ismay, by the Assistant Secretaries-General, and by the delegations, and on matters carried over from the previous agenda. After the draft had been co-ordinated with all the parties concerned the final agenda was assembled and a folder prepared for the Chairman of the Council (or the Vice-Chairman, as appropriate), introducing the subjects to be raised.

[14] Staff Manual, item 1021.

This folder included briefs whose purpose was to suggest what the position of the Chairman might be on the various topics. The suggested position would have been ascertained, of course, from the background and history of the matter and from the interests and parties involved. Usually the suggestion was prefaced by the statement, 'you may like to say'. The folder also contained a notation if a delegation had disapproved of an item on the agenda, had proposed or would propose a reservation or amendment, or had reacted unfavourably to the item in a committee.

To achieve final co-ordination of the business to be presented to the Council, the Secretary-General convoked a staff meeting, attended by the Deputy Secretary-General, the Assistant Secretaries-General, the Standing Group Liaison Officer, the Financial Controller, and the Executive Secretary. In practice the Deputy Secretary-General conducted these meetings, with M. de Boisgelin acting as secretary, unless there was a matter so important that the Secretary-General's presence was required, and then Lord Ismay would occasionally call a special meeting. He preferred to remain out of routine matters and this meeting was usually a tidying-up session before the Council met.

The secretaries to the various Council committees worked with their committees, with the delegations, with the technical experts in the Divisions where appropriate, and with other relevant Sections of the International Staff/Secretariat. It was part of their duties to co-ordinate the work of their committees with all these parties, and to draw up all the papers and documents pertaining to the work of their committees in a manner acceptable to Lord Ismay and to the Council.[15]

[15] The general policy was: 'All Council documents (agenda, reports, memoranda, summary records, etc.) will be submitted to the Office of the Secretary General [i.e. the Executive Secretary] for approval before being sent to the Conference Service for duplication and distribution. 2. Committee and Working Group documents will not be submitted to the Office of the Secretary General for prior approval, but will be circulated under the authority of the Secretary of the Committee after consultation, as necessary, with the Chairman. 3. The records of the Council and of Committees should be as short as possible. Observations of particular speakers

The strength of the Secretariat's position—and hence that of the Executive Secretary—was enhanced by the fact that Lord Ismay preferred papers drawn up for him to be in the British administrative style. A British-type memorandum included first, the presentation of the problem, then a listing, with discussion, of the alternatives which might be possible in its solution, and lastly the recommendations which could be made in the light of the foregoing considerations.

The so-called Continental administrative style, in contrast, allowed for the resolution of the problem in a different manner. The Continental memorandum was not written with the aim of presenting a clear-cut recommendation: this was left for the reader himself to draw from the discussion of the various alternatives. In other words, by the British method the decision-making process tended to be initiated from the bottom, but by the Continental method the decision-making process was concentrated at the top of the administrative structure. Because the implications of this difference in approach permeated the work of the International Staff/Secretariat, a closer look at the two systems is appropriate.

The Cabinet of a Continental Minister consisted of various specialists in the work of the Ministry, who worked out the policies of that Ministry, drawing if necessary on information from the operating units. The various Cabinet committees which might be established to handle a problem were serviced by *rapporteurs*—committee members who were experts in the subject. The two facets of administration—the formulation of policy and supervision of its execution—remained tied to the Cabinet or the Minister's office. The *directeur de cabinet* handled the former and the *chef de cabinet* the latter.

In the British system the problem was formulated, expanded, and co-ordinated by each level of the administrative hierarchy before it reached the Minister. As to execution, if the decision

should normally be attributed only when a representative is making a formal statement or reservation in the name of his government. 4. Reports by Committees or Working Groups to the Council should be as concise as possible, summarizing the main aspects of the problem under review, and terminating with the conclusions or recommendations agreed on by the Committee or Working Group.' (NATO Doc. ON (52) 41.)

was taken at Ministerial level, each echelon of the Department made sure that it carried out the responsibilities imposed upon it by the decision. If the decision was made at Cabinet (or inter-Departmental) level, the Cabinet secretariat made sure that the Departments concerned were properly informed.

Thus it can be seen that each system required its own manner of thinking, its own approach. The Joint Sub-Committee on a European Civil Service set up by the Council of Europe's Consultative Assembly, recognized this problem when it observed:

. . . it will become no less necessary or urgent to instil some form of *intellectual discipline* [their underlining] which if not uniform is at least sufficiently coherent in its variety, into the staff of the organizations. The number of different national backgrounds, languages and forms of education are at present often the cause of difficulties. . . . While this is undoubtedly an enriching factor as far as individual contacts go, it must be supplemented by training all staff in similar working habits and methods and a way of thinking which is sufficiently uniform and well fitted to the needs of international work.[16]

In the realm of the Council's business the Executive Secretary's work was clearly defined. But, when lateral inter-Divisional memoranda and non-Council papers which had originated in the Divisions were sent to the Secretary-General or the Deputy Secretary-General, the role of the Executive Secretary became less clear. Many of the officers in the Divisions and their subordinates had had little experience in the British 'brief-writing' system. Their methods of doing business at times resulted in work which, although it would have been acceptable in their indigenous administrative context, did not conform to what Lord Ismay expected. Consequently it often fell to Lord Coleridge and his secretariat to introduce uniformity in style and presentation, and consistency in substance, into the work of the Divisions. This involved redrafting some of the Divisional papers. Thus no clearly-delineated line could be drawn between those matters which should and those which should not involve the Executive Secretary. To avoid the danger of unintentional

[16] Council of Europe Doc. AS/Jur-Bud (11)2.

reinterpretation in the course of redrafting, papers were often fully co-ordinated after having been redrafted.[17]

From this brief survey it can readily be concluded that the Executive Secretary, in his position as Secretary to the Council, as well as in his work as unofficial chief-of-staff to Lord Ismay, exercised a direct influence on the work of the entire International Staff/Secretariat, and on all the Council's functions.[18] In the broadest sense the operations of the International Staff/Secretariat, from Lord Ismay through the Council, its various committees and working groups, and the delegations, revolved around the Office of the Secretary-General, and hence the Executive Secretary. This did not mean that the Executive Secretary was involved in all aspects of the business of these agencies, but it did mean that at some stage the Executive Secretary would become a participant if the business was to come to the point of Council decision. He was the link between those who made the decisions, i.e. the Secretary-General, the Council, and the Council Committees, and those who prepared and executed them.

In addition, in his area of responsibility as head of internal administration, the Executive Secretary not only engaged in activities which affected the secretariat function but also in those which affected everyone in the International Staff/Secretariat who was below the grade of Deputy Assistant Secretary-General, or Head of an Independent Office. The scope of these activities increased steadily until in 1956 the NATO Management Survey Team made the following recommendations:

The internal administration of the International Staff/Secretariat has been the responsibility of the Executive Secretary. His role as Secretary of the Council and principal staff officer of the Secretary-General and Vice-Chairman of the Council imposes a very heavy burden and the conference and administrative tasks of the Organization have proved to be more difficult and comprehensive than

---

[17] See Ranshofen-Wertheimer, Ch. I, for a discussion of this problem based on the League of Nations' experience.

[18] Although the military side of the Alliance—the Standing Group, Military Representatives Committee, Supreme Commands, etc.—does not figure in this study, nevertheless it should be noted that where the work of these bodies bore on the Council's domain, the Executive Secretary would also deal with them.

originally envisaged. Accordingly, a separation of these functions is considered desirable.[19]

As an alternative to the system originally set up by Lord Ismay, the Team recommended that the position of Director of Administration should be created. Its holder would be responsible for:

. . . the internal administration of the International Secretariat. Generally speaking he would be the co-ordinator of the nine services (Personnel, Security, General Services, Budget and Finance, Language, Reproduction, Graphic Presentation, Registry and New Building) under his control and direction. With the help of a Management Assistant, he would be responsible for the functioning of the entire organization of the Secretariat, for the preparation of the Annual Budget, for the provision of conference facilities and for the administration of the Staff. He should maintain close relationship with the Assistant Secretaries-General and the Executive Secretary so that the services will adequately respond to the needs of the substantive activities of the Organization.[20]

The Secretary-General and the Council approved this recommendation. In August 1956 the Financial Controller, M. A. Bastin of Belgium, was appointed Director of the Administration Division and was made accountable directly to the Secretary-General through the Deputy Secretary-General. He assumed this position without relinquishing his Controllership duties.[21]

---

[19] NATO Management Survey Team, General Report, 1 May 1956, par. 19. The Team was constituted under the provisions of NATO Doc. C-R (55)53.

[20] General Report, par. 27 (f). See Ch. VIII for a further discussion of the duties which the Director of Administration assumed from the Executive Secretary.

[21] The Staff Committee, on behalf of the Staff Association, resolved on 20 Aug. 1956 that it 'unanimously welcomes the announcement of the creation of the post of Director of Administration'. (NATO Doc. CP/56/57-N/37, Annex 1). In Sept. 1958 the Secretary-General, M. Spaak, made a further administrative change: 'The service of the Financial Controller to revert to its independent position and the Financial Controller to be given increased responsibilities in the control of budget operations. M. Bastin to retain the functions of Financial Controller. The other services hitherto comprised in the Administrative Division to remain grouped together

The Team also recommended that the three secretaries serving the Infrastructure, Armament Production, and Budget Committees, and which were assigned to their respective Divisions, should be transferred to the Executive Secretary's office. This recommendation was made on the principle that the secretariats of policy-making committees should not reside in the Divisions. The Council approved the principle, and the secretariats serving the Infrastructure Committee (except the financial accounting services), the Committee on Armament

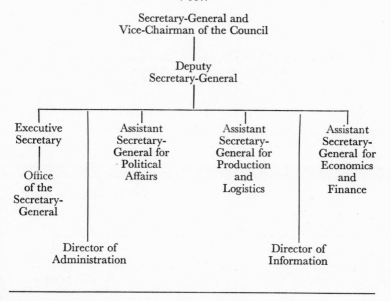

INTERNATIONAL STAFF/SECRETARIAT[22]
(1957)

within a "Personnel and Administrative Service" directly under the Secretary General, the Head of this Service to be Cdr. de Vries [the Personnel Officer]. The preparation and presentation of the budget will be within his purview.' (NATO Doc. ON (58)39.) This action placed internal administration under M. Spaak's *chef de cabinet*, reflecting a general shift under M. Spaak's leadership toward Continental administration.

[22] NATO Doc. ISM (57) 4; 'Text of Lord Ismay's Report to the Ministerial Meeting of the North Atlantic Council at Bonn, May 1957.' App. D., as contained in the *NATO Letter*, Vol. 5, Spec. Supp. to No. 6.

Production (formerly the Defence Production Committee), and the Budget Committee, were placed under Lord Coleridge. Each of these Council Committes had under it a network of subcommittees and working groups.[23]

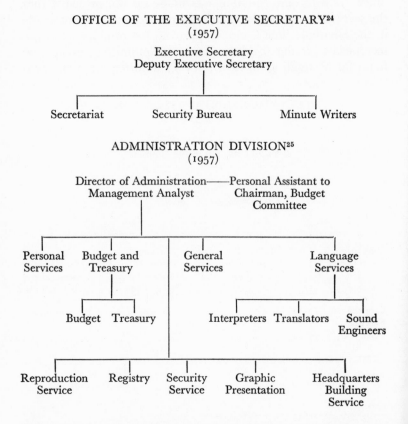

OFFICE OF THE EXECUTIVE SECRETARY[24]
(1957)

Executive Secretary
Deputy Executive Secretary

Secretariat   Security Bureau   Minute Writers

ADMINISTRATION DIVISION[25]
(1957)

Director of Administration——Personal Assistant to
Management Analyst   Chairman, Budget
Committee

Personal   Budget and   General   Language
Services   Treasury   Services   Services

Budget   Treasury   Interpreters Translators Sound
Engineers

Reproduction   Registry   Security   Graphic   Headquarters
Service   Service   Presentation   Building
Service

To assist the Council and the Committees in their work, each member nation maintained a delegation in Paris. This delegation consisted of two types of staff: diplomatists for representational purposes on NATO's various committees and working groups, and technical experts brought in for specific

[23] The Executive Secretary also retained the responsibility for coordinating security matters with member countries.
[24] NATO Doc. ISM (57) 4.   [25] ibid.

purposes. The delegation also served as the go-between for the International Staff/Secretariat and the governments. It was organized on lines similar to those of an embassy. A Permanent Representative usually held the rank of Ambassador; an Assistant Permanent Representative, if he was from a larger power, was a Minister, otherwise he was a Counsellor. The delegation was divided functionally, paralleling the structure of the International Staff/Secretariat. For instance, the French delegation had an Economic and Financial, a Production, and a Military Section.[26] Smaller delegations designated individuals, usually of Counsellor rank, to perform similar duties on the committees and working groups, rather than having a Section. A technical expert usually did not hold a diplomatic rank but would most probably work with the delegation Counsellor or special attaché in his field. Occasionally an expert was seconded directly to the International Staff/Secretariat, especially if his work was more than temporary.

The International Staff/Secretariat often found that, if it needed to inform the Council of a certain programme, it was helpful to work with the delegations and the Permanent Representatives. Thus the International Staff/Secretariat could inform the Council, or more often the Council Committee supervising the relevant activity, from two directions: through the Permanent Representative of a delegation, and through the International Staff/Secretariat's own administrative channels. Sometimes the crucial elements in communication were the Committee's chairman and secretary; between them they provided the most important connecting link between the Committee or the Council and the International Staff/Secretariat. They worked together on the agenda and on ensuring compliance with the Committee's decisions. Often, if one or other of them did not take the initiative, the committee or working group did not meet for long periods.

Lord Ismay most often communicated with governments

---

[26] NATO, *Liste des délégués au conseil de l'Atlantique Nord*, 1 July 1958. Rank had played an important part in the Council's acceptance of Lord Ismay's leadership. The fact that he had been a Cabinet Minister made him in the eyes of the Permanent Representatives and the Council Ministers, 'one of them'. (Interview with Lord Ismay, 28 May 1959.)

through the delegation. He avoided writing directly to government leaders because he felt that it would help to raise the prestige of the Permanent Representatives if he worked through them. In fact he would have preferred the delegations to play a greater part than they did in conducting the business of NATO. He believed that the 'staff' aspect of the International Staff/Secretariat should have been undertaken almost entirely by the delegations not by the Divisions. According to him, the delegations should have retained the expertise needed to work out production and logistics problems and economic and financial arrangements. He would have liked to limit the functions of the International Staff/Secretariat to those of a service agency which would provide the secretariat for the Council and its committees and working groups, which in turn would bring together technical experts to deal with specific issues. In other words he wanted to reproduce the Cabinet secretariat method in NATO

Indeed the Division he thought most appropriate to the new organization was the newly-created Political Affairs Division because he considered himself administratively weak in background research staff. This was the least 'operative' of the operating Divisions. He also felt that, as he had not engaged in this sort of international diplomacy before, the creation of such a staff of political experts would be personally useful. It should be noted that, under the Deputies, preparatory memoranda or documents had not been drawn up by a purely international staff. The work had been done for Mr. Spofford by either the American delegation or the Planning and Co-ordination Group. The other Deputies had relied on their own delegations, and, for the Council generally, *ad hoc* committees and working groups had been appointed, made up usually of representatives of those member countries that wanted to take part in the business on hand.

As it turned out the political affairs specialists on the delegations, rather than the Political Division, continued to perform the greater part of this function. This was another reflection of the twofold fact that the Secretary-General's international political position had not developed far enough to warrant his using a large staff of political experts, and that important political decisions were worked out according to

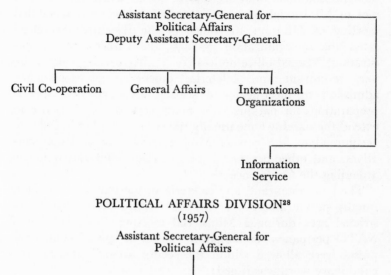

POLITICAL AFFAIRS DIVISION[27]
(1952)

Assistant Secretary-General for
Political Affairs
Deputy Assistant Secretary-General

Civil Co-operation   General Affairs   International
Organizations

Information
Service

POLITICAL AFFAIRS DIVISION[28]
(1957)

Assistant Secretary-General for
Political Affairs

General Affairs Section   Research Section

national interests, and were made in the Council.[29] The two
major 'operative' functions requiring technical expertise during
Lord Ismay's tenure of office, Annual Review and Infrastructure, came to be lodged with the International Staff/Sec-
retariat. The over-all result was that the division of work
between the International Staff/Secretariat and the delegations
became rather the opposite of what Lord Ismay had originally
envisaged.

[27] *The North Atlantic Treaty Organization* (Paris, Dec. 1952), p. 33.
[28] NATO Doc. ISM (57) 4.
[29] The Political Division was built up after M. Spaak became Secretary-
General. This was a reflection partly of M. Spaak's tendency to engage in
'personal diplomacy' and partly of the member countries' gradual willingness to use the Council for fuller co-ordination of their foreign policies. This
tendency began to develop during Lord Ismay's tenure of office, especially
from the period of the Geneva Conferences and later the Suez Crisis. Lord
Ismay welcomed it. He has characterized himself as the wet nurse of NATO,
and M. Spaak as the governess.

8

Turning to more mundane matters, what arrangements did the International Staff/Secretariat make when the Council met in Ministerial session? Several days before a scheduled meeting of Ministers the office of the Executive Secretary (after the re-organization in 1956, the Director of Administration)[30] issued office notices concerning parking, use of the bar, restaurant and cafeteria, processing of documents, admission to meetings, and seating arrangements. Special preparations for parking were made with the Paris police to extend the parking zone usually reserved to NATO in order to accommodate 'the cars of Ministers, Permanent Representatives, and other designated personalities, civil and military, attending the Conference'.[31]

The bar, restaurant, and cafeteria in the Palais de Chaillot, usually public areas, were brought within the secure or restricted area during a Ministerial meeting. Only holders of NATO permanent or temporary passes or special conference passes were allowed within the secure area. A special precautionary word was issued:

. . . all visitors should be advised to enter the building by the Seine entrance. Staff members are particularly requested to receive only visitors with official business to transact, and to ensure that in each case the visitor's pass is correctly timed and signed at the conclusion of the interview, and that the visitor is escorted at all times while within the secure area.[32]

Dining facilities were kept open late into the night for the convenience of those persons who had to remain on duty beyond normal working hours. Bar hours were extended from 10.30 a.m. to dawn.[33]

The expansion of the volume of documents for translation, reproduction, and distribution during a Ministerial meeting necessitated the special channelling of requests. A specific

---

[30] Even after the 1956 administrative alterations the Executive Secretary was still responsible for all arrangements for Ministerial meetings held away from Paris.

[31] NATO Doc. ON (54) 57.   [32] ibid.

[33] ibid. Special restrictions were placed on the use of dining facilities when the Secretary-General was giving a reception or cocktail party.

person was designated in the Executive Secretary's office (after 1956, in the Conference Services of the Administration Division) to receive and act upon requests for these services. All persons sending documents were enjoined to refrain from directly contacting the Documents Office, the typing pools, or the Registry, and to use the delegated intermediary.[34] A list of telephone and office numbers of the members of the International Staff/Secretariat, the Standing Group, and the delegations was issued; thus people could contact whom they desired without having to make extensive enquiries.

A policy for admission and seating at the Ministerial sessions was laid down and rigidly enforced. It was:

The Secretary General has ruled that the number of members of the International Staff attending the Ministerial Meeting shall be kept to the minimum necessary to the efficient conduct of future business resulting from this meeting. . . .[35]

The Secretary General wishes to restrict to the minimum the number of the Secretariat who are present at any one time. Assistant Secretaries General, heads of independent offices and the Standing Group Liaison Officer are asked to issue the necessary instructions to ensure that only those members of the staff whose presence is necessary for the agenda item under discussion are in the Council Chamber or use these seats during the Ministerial Meeting. . . .[36]

If groups of Ministers meet individually, or if a restricted plenary meeting takes place, only such members of the staff as are designated by the Secretary General will attend.[37]

Before each session a seating plan for the head of the table and for the row behind was approved and published by the Secretary-General. This plan left no one in doubt as to who should sit where; in gatherings where not only international protocol had to be considered, but also the susceptibilities of the International Staff/Secretariat and the delegations, this action was both efficient and politic. Generally, twelve seats on the dais were provided for 'essential advisers of the International Staff' and twelve more for Naval, Military, and Air Force advisers. The twelve seats reserved for the International Staff/Secretariat were usually allocated in the following

[34] NATO Doc. ON (53) 85.   [35] NATO Doc. ON (56) 75.
[36] NATO Doc. ON (53) 79.   [37] ibid.

manner: 'Each Assistant Secretary General and Head of an independent office may nominate no more than two members of his staff to occupy these seats'.[38] By restricting the number of seats, and permitting the presence of only those persons concerned either with the agenda item under discussion or with the conduct of future business arising from the discussion, the Secretary-General made it necessary for the International Staff/Secretariat to shift personnel in and out of each session. The entrance guards had to be told who should be allowed to enter.

The arrangements for public sessions of the Council were somewhat different. A larger room was used and persons not requested to attend were strictly prohibited. 'Heads of divisions and offices have been asked to decide which members of their staff should attend the meeting, and to distribute the necessary *special* [NATO underlining] passes giving access to the Council room. Ordinary NATO passes will not be accepted by the guards.'[39] At public sessions all staff members were required to 'be in their seats by 10.15 a.m. so as not to interfere with the photographing of Ministers which will be taking place from 10.15 onwards'.[40]

The language problem was one of the reasons why Lord Ismay conducted Ministerial meetings even when he was still only Vice-Chairman of the Council. The Chairmanship (after 1956, the Presidency) rotated annually by country. If the Foreign Minister of a particular country was ill-equipped to do business either in French or English, he found it not only convenient but almost a necessity to rely heavily on the Secretary-General. He had the option of speaking in his native language, but if he did so he was required to provide his own interpreters to render his speech into one of the two official

[38] NATO Doc. ON (54) 63. A variation on this procedure was to allow that: 'each Assistant Secretary General and the Executive Secretary may nominate no more than three members of his staff to occupy these seats'. (NATO Doc. ON (56) 75.)

[39] NATO Doc. ON (55) 23. The Executive Secretary usually decided how many persons from each Division or Independent Office would be allowed to attend the public sessions, and then the Division or Office made the selection. (NATO Doc. ON (54) 28.)

[40] NATO Doc. ON (55) 23.

languages. The only exception to the two-language rule during Lord Ismay's tenure of office occurred in 1955 at the ceremonies welcoming the entrance of the German Federal Republic into NATO: the remarks of the Chancellor, Dr. Konrad Adenauer, who could speak only German, were translated by NATO. The Germans did not press for the inclusion of their language as a third official language while Lord Ismay was Secretary-General.[41]

When Mr. Ole Björn Kraft, the Danish Foreign Minister, became Chairman of the Council he candidly recognized the language problem. He said:

It is with humility that I take over the Chairmanship in succession to such distinguished men as Mr. Acheson, M. van Zeeland and Mr. Pearson. I wish to remind the Council that my task is rendered even more difficult than that of my predecessors by the fact that the discussions of the Council are conducted in languages neither of which is my mother tongue, and I ask you to grant me the favour of indulgence.[42]

One way around this situation was for the Chairman to leave the bulk of the work to the Vice-Chairman, who in any event usually presided over meetings of the Permanent Representatives. Considering the demands which pressed upon a Foreign Minister apart from his duties as Chairman of the NATO Council, this development was natural. The Chairman visited the Palais de Chaillot only occasionally during the intervals between Ministerial meetings, and on those occasions he often came to perform a ceremonial function such as addressing a special group or welcoming certain dignitaries; and in September of each year he came to hand over to his successor.

The Chairman's knowledge of the intricacies of the problems which might arise at a Ministerial meeting was therefore somewhat limited. It fell to the Executive Secretary to ensure that he was fully briefed before each meeting. Sometimes this could be done at the Palais de Chaillot, if the Chairman arrived four or five days prior to the meeting. Otherwise, Lord

---

[41] Interview with Lord Coleridge, 2 Aug. 1958.

[42] NATO Press Release, 18 Sept. 1952. Over the years, however, NATO gave increasing financial assistance for the publication of indigenous language versions of official publications.

Coleridge travelled to the Chairman. Other Ministers were briefed by their delegations.

The public briefings which preceded, accompanied, and followed a Ministerial meeting, in the opinion of many press and special media people, left much to be desired. The problems and activities of the Information Division (originally the Information Service) are discussed in Chapter IX but it is nevertheless appropriate here to point out some of the characteristics of this vital function as they related to the Council.

Generally the formal public information treatment consisted of a terse announcement that a meeting was to be held; then, during the meeting the formal speeches of the Ministers were released, and at the conclusion of the meeting a carefully agreed final communique, summarizing what the Council wished the world to know about what had happened, was issued. At the April Ministerial meeting there were always some special press releases and speeches commemorating the anniversary of NATO. An ardent note on the significance of the anniversary was struck by Lord Ismay in an address given at the 1953 annual Thanksgiving Day Dinner of the American Society in London. He concluded his remarks by saying: 'We have only to do our duty, all the 14 nations that are bound together in bonds of faith and friendship in this great experiment in international relations; and then it may well be that the date of the signature of the North Atlantic Treaty, the 4th April, will be celebrated as another Thanksgiving Day by generations still unborn.'[43]

In the later years of Lord Ismay's tenure of office, particularly in view of the public interchange of correspondence between the U.S.S.R. and the Western Powers, Council meetings were subjected to increasing newspaper surveillance over the content of discussions. In earlier years so much of the business of the Alliance had been either so technical, i.e. financial or logistic, or so militarily restricted, that the opportunities for newsworthy treatment of these meetings were limited. It was not rare to find a newspaper summary of a Ministerial meeting confined to such a terse statement as this:

A Ministerial session of the North Atlantic Council, attended by fourteen Foreign Ministers and the Deputy Prime Minister of

[43] 26 Nov. 1953. (NATO Speech Series, No. 52.)

Turkey, was held in Paris today under the chairmanship of Mr. Stephanos Stephanopoulos, the Foreign Minister of Greece. The Foreign Ministers of France, the United Kingdom and the United States consulted with their colleagues in preparation for the Geneva [Summit] Conference. This continued the consultations already held in the Council by the Permanent Representatives. The Council were in full agreement in their reaffirmation of the unity of purpose of the Atlantic Alliance. Mutual consultations will continue.[44]

Although the following statement doubtless expressed an essential ingredient in the life of NATO, it did not arouse public interest: 'Ministers emphasized the value and significance of the political consultation which has increasingly developed in the North Atlantic Council.'[45] At times the phraseology became somewhat stilted and even platitudinous:

It is above all the fact that our joint intentions are clearcut and definite which binds us together: without this our efforts would fail to be understood by the public opinion of our countries as well as by that of other free countries who look to us with hope . . . we must draw even closer the links which unite us and show ourselves capable of boldness and elasticity in our concepts, and of firmness in our determination.[46]

These pronouncements of course had a ring of truth, but at the same time they left the impression that the Ministers were talking around the issues which in fact determined whether the Alliance was alive or not. This situation is a common characteristic of international gatherings: its advantage is that no person using this kind of language can be accused of committing an indiscretion; its disadvantage, from the viewpoint of the interested observer, is that it leaves unreported the volumes of words done up in reports, surveys, and memoranda which are the substance of any Ministerial meeting. It also leaves unreported much of the real intercourse of any gathering of such high-level persons, for besides the intra-NATO roles played by the Council, the Secretary-General, and the International Staff/Secretariat, there were also the extra-NATO implications and impressions of their actions. Lord Ismay recognized that the kind of understanding the public had of the International Staff/Secretariat and its Secretary-General was vitally important to the success

---

[44] NATO Press Release No. M2 (55) 1. [45] ibid. No. M3 (55) 1.
[46] ibid. 15 Dec. 1952.

of the Alliance. This recognition led to the development of NATO's press, public relations, and information programme.

Closely connected with the general public's understanding of NATO was Civil Emergency Planning. As early as 1952 attention had been given to the need for civilian planning, for soon after the creation of the International Staff/Secretariat, the Council set up a Committee on Civil Organization in Time of War.[47] The following year the Council authorized the creation under this committee of two more specialized committees: the Civil Defence Committee and the Committee on Refugees and Evacuees. These committees brought together experts in these fields from member countries so that they could examine the problems which might arise in a national emergency and suggest methods of resolving them.[48]

The work of the Civil Defence Committee had become so extensive by 1954 that in April of that year Lord Ismay appointed Sir John Hodsoll of the United Kingdom as Chief Technical Adviser to the committee and M. Raymond Rudler of France as Assistant Chief Technical Adviser. The Chief Technical Adviser reported directly to Lord Ismay who took a strong personal interest in this work. He told how, early in his tenure of office, he took up the cause of civil defence:

The day after my first arrival in Paris, I went to see President Eisenhower who was then commanding at SHAPE, and we had a talk about my new job. He suggested that among other things I should do my best to get Civil Defence going in all the countries of the coalition. I determined to follow his advice, but it was not too easy to get started. Civil Defence is of course a national responsibility, and a country can do as little or as much as it likes. A tendency—perhaps a natural one on the part of most of them—is to give priority to the Fighting Services and to make Civil Defence the Cinderella.[49]

One of the first tasks of the Chief Technical Adviser was to supervise the conduct of special studies in order to incorporate

[47] *The Five Years*, p. 143.

[48] Pending the entry of the German Federal Republic into NATO a special civil defence committee was established to enable experts from that country to meet with experts from the NATO countries.

[49] Speech delivered 13 Jan. 1955, as contained in *NATO Civil Defence Bulletin*, Vol. 2, No. 2, pp. 1–2.

the results of them into memoranda to be distributed to member countries. These memoranda dealt with such subjects as: air-raid warning systems; protection against the effects of blast, especially with regard to shelters; blackout and camouflage; protection against the effects of incendiary bombs; precautions to be taken to reduce personnel casualties and damage in industrial areas; protection against poison gas; the rescue of trapped persons and the treatment and removal of the injured; special problems created by the possible use of atomic and radio-active weapons, including the special effects of heat radiation, radio-activity and atomic blast.[50]

It soon became apparent that problems of civil defence, economic mobilization, and defence production were closely related. The needs of civil defence had taken on such proportions that in 1955 the Committee on Civil Organization in Time of War was abolished, and a Senior Civil Emergency Planning Committee was created, under which were placed the following hitherto semi-independent boards and committees: the Planning Board for Ocean Shipping, the Planning Board for European Inland Surface Transport, the Civil Defence Committee, the Coal and Steel Planning Committee, the Industrial Raw Materials Planning Committee, the Food and Agriculture Planning Committee, the Manpower Planning Committee, and the Medical Committee.[51] The various working parties in the field of Civil Defence, such as those on fire services, warning, water, gas, electricity and sewers, protection of ports, co-operation in peacetime disasters, continued their work.

Lord Ismay became chairman of the Senior Committee, and the Executive Secretary became secretary. Sir John Hodsoll's office, called the Emergency Planning Office, was attached to the Office of the Secretary-General and was granted a small separate budget.[52] The Chief Technical Adviser became the Senior Civil Defence Adviser.

The main function of the Emergency Planning Office was

[50] *The Five Years*, p. 144.

[51] *The North Atlantic Treaty Organization* (Paris, 1957), p. 72; See also chart, p. 88 above.

[52] NATO Doc. ISM (57)4. Interview with Wing Commander Sir John Hodsoll, C.B., Senior Civil Defence Adviser, 13 Aug. 1958.

to co-ordinate the work of the various boards and committees. It was purely advisory and consultative. It gathered information and wrote proposed programmes to be presented to the committees. It continued to publish memoranda and booklets and to assemble a library of films, film strips, and books on civil defence and emergency planning topics.[53] In 1954 a *NATO Civil Defence Bulletin* was started, in which news and notes were exchanged about the activities and programmes in member countries. The *Bulletin* was distributed both through the delegations and directly to interested persons in these countries.

One of the difficulties which faced the Emergency Planning Office was the lack of uniformity in NATO member countries as to the government agency through which the Office should work. Like NATO's public relations programme, recommendations about emergency planning had to be carried out through the appropriate governmental channels. Some countries combined civil defence and civil emergency planning in one agency; others separated them. For instance, in Norway the Minister of Justice was responsible for civil defence and the Prime Minister for civil emergency planning. In Portugal the Minister of Defence was responsible for both, as was the Minister of the Interior in the German Federal Republic and in Italy. In Denmark, The Netherlands, Belgium, Greece, and Turkey there was no agency for civil emergency planning and the Minister of the Interior was responsible for civil defence.[54]

A very useful function of the Office, which tended to compensate for the decentralized nature of national emergency planning and civil defence, was the preparation and submission of an annual report to the Council. The report's significance was described thus: 'This parallels to some extent the Annual Review of the defence effort and thus enables NATO to assess the whole defence position of the Alliance on both the civil and the military sides.'[55] By 1956 the work of the Emergency Planning Office had become so diversified that the Management Survey Team of NATO made the following comment and recommendation:

[53] ibid.   [54] ibid.

[55] *The North Atlantic Treaty Organization* (Paris, 1959), p. 59.

At the present time, work in the Emergency Planning field is being performed directly by the Secretary General and the Executive Secretary. With the heavy responsibilities and duties of his office, the Secretary General might not be able to continue to perform this function. Arrangements should therefore be made to enable one of the Assistant Secretaries General to deputise for the Secretary General as Chairman of the Senior Emergency Planning Committee. The team felt that emergency planning work, which is now being reviewed in the light of new assumptions, might be developed and that it warranted the establishment of a division concerned with these activities. It is proposed that this division be placed under the Assistant Secretary General for Infrastructure as he would thus assume duties which would balance more evenly the load placed on the Assistant Secretaries General.[56]

This recommendation was not adopted, but after Lord Ismay's retirement the Executive Secretary was given full responsibility for civil emergency planning and the Office of Emergency Planning was placed in his Office instead of in the Secretary-General's.[57]

Probably the greatest weakness in NATO's emergency planning work was the uncertainty of military assumptions as to the sort of disaster that might occur. To try to overcome this weakness the Emergency Planning Office worked with the Air Defence Division of SHAPE. But the military agencies would not assume responsibility for the military organization of the home front. This was left to governments. The result was that only piecemeal progress in relatively limited areas of civil defence could be made. In the opinion of some qualified observers only an actual outbreak of hostilities could justify the governments and the military authorities in taking large-scale civil defence action. More encouraging was the possibility that, if there was an outbreak of war, the various emergency planning committees and boards conceivably could fill a role analogous to that performed by the Anglo-American Combined Boards in World War II. In that event the preliminary experience of having worked together and thought about the various forms of arrangements which could be put into effect would prove beneficial.

[56] General Report, par. 27(e).
[57] *The North Atlantic Treaty Organization* (Paris, 1959), p. 88.

Underlying all efforts in this field was the inability of either the military commands, the Council, or governments to define precisely what the role of NATO would be if an outbreak of hostilities occurred.[58] After 1954, when the concept of atomic or nuclear reprisal had been adopted officially, talk of massive retaliation by air made more vital the need for renewed emphasis upon the idea that civil defence was not a fruitless undertaking. As in defence production, the concept of a thirty-day war, consisting essentially of a nuclear exchange, left national planners unenthusiastic about taking stringent and unpopular measures which probably would not have an opportunity to be applied before the war ended. To arrange national planning to meet all the possible contingencies which might arise would result in a greater expenditure of national funds and a greater degree of civilian self-discipline in peacetime than had yet proved attainable. Speeches by prominent figures such as Field-Marshal Viscount Montgomery of Alamein, Deputy Supreme Allied Commander Europe, emphasizing the need for extensive planning so that some order could be brought in to the chaos which would follow the devastation, called attention to this problem.[59]

All in all, civil emergency planning was a prime example of a situation where the frustrations which arose from uncertainty as to the conditions to be met and the means available to meet them could easily have led to discouragement. The fact that the work was taken up by Lord Ismay and personally encouraged by him and by the International Staff/Secretariat, in the face of such frustrations, reflected the Secretary-General's determination not to neglect any aspect of NATO's civilian activity.

[58] To help clarify this situation, a Working Group on Application of New Assumptions to Emergency Planning Work of the Defence Production Committee was set up in Apr. 1956. The Working Group submitted a report to the Senior Committee which said: first, that the governments should get the necessary legislation adopted in order to build a framework for further co-ordinated planning; second that the Working Group was not certain that the Defence Production Committee should be working in the emergency planning field in view of the existence of committees on industrial raw materials, manpower, etc.

[59] See, for example, Lord Montgomery's speech 'The Panorama of Warfare in a Nuclear Age', delivered to the Royal United Service Institution in London, 10 Oct. 1956. (NATO Speech Series, No. 84.)

PART III

ADMINISTRATIVE PROBLEMS OF AN INTERNATIONAL CIVIL SERVICE IN NATO

'Personally, I feel profoundly convinced that a high morale in an international staff can only be created and maintained by a policy of administrative liberalism consciously and deliberately pursued by persons with a faculty for leadership.'

A. Loveday

'The Secretariat is tending more and more to become a station where people serve for a period but where they do not make their careers. . . . The salaries are not sufficiently high to compensate for the loss of all chances of promotion and the prospect of being without a post after a few years. It also prevents the formation of a personnel of able technicians and still more the creation of that spirit of complete devotion to the international institutions of the League without which they cannot live.'

William Martin

CHAPTER VII

RECRUITMENT, RETENTION, AND REMUNERATION

THE early history of the civilian administration of NATO, as noted in Part I, was marked by the Organization's transformation from a body which had been set up for planning purposes to one which could execute programmes and policies by means of a permanent International Staff/Secretariat.[1] When the Council first met in September 1949 no continuous international administrative structure of any kind was contemplated.[2] By May 1950, however, it had become apparent that a permanent directing body should be established. (This body became the Council Deputies.) And in July 1951 an international budget was instituted (*above* Chapter II).

Before the introduction of the international budget, all the officers of the civilian organization of NATO had been seconded by their governments for limited periods of service. A seconded government official was one who had been placed on special duty with NATO. During his period of duty he was not paid by NATO, nor were his conditions of employment with his government altered by his assignment to NATO.

After the adoption of the international budget system the officer ranks were filled from three sources: secondment by governments (some seconded officers were paid by NATO, some were not); permanent transfer from government service to the International Staff/Secretariat; free-lance hirings made from personal applications. All persons recruited had to have

[1] This discussion relates only to the personnel policies and problems of the officer grades—that is, Grades 10 to 15, and the highest unclassified posts. These were the positions in the International Staff/Secretariat through which policy was developed and executed.

[2] Speech by Sr. S. Fenoaltea, 13 June 1952. (NATO Speech Series, No. 20.)

the approval of and be security cleared by their governments. About 40 per cent of the officers were seconded.[3]

The secondment system had several practical advantages: a turnover of some members of the International Staff/Secretariat every two or three years helped to bring fresh thinking into it and to keep it in touch with national points of view; it also gave national civil servants a valuable insight into the problems and workings of NATO; and lastly it assisted in the liaison between the International Staff/Secretariat and member governments since seconded persons were familiar with national policies and procedures and therefore could interpret NATO business more easily to their delegations.

The major disadvantage of the secondment system was that it permitted governments to nominate persons who might not be fully qualified for their new positions. For instance, they might not have been trained in secretariat work, or they might have had only limited experience in a multi-language work situation. Some member governments had difficulty in finding enough top-level persons to send to NATO because they did not have sufficient persons available both to run the government and to send abroad to serve in the proliferating international agencies and organizations which had sprung up after World War II.[4]

Non-seconded career personnel helped to maintain continuity of policy and to make up a cadre of persons experienced in the operations of international administration upon whom the seconded persons could rely. Many of these persons were

[3] NATO Management Survey Team, General Report, 1 May 1956, Par. 34. Many specialists in production were carried over from the Defence Production Board into the Production and Logistics Division, moving from a seconded to a contractual basis. There was some criticism of this because of the fact that, since these persons had been brought to NATO to perform largely self-liquidating tasks, they should not have been offered permanent contracts.

[4] Belgium, Canada, and the German Federal Republic have been cited as the three hardest-pressed countries in this respect at that time. All three experienced increased economic expansion and prosperity after World War II, which tended to make government posts generally less attractive to promising young men than opportunities in business.

employed in the linguistic, internal administrative, or secretariat work of the International Staff/Secretariat.

Shortly after his appointment Lord Ismay formulated some general principles to guide him in his staff relationships. First, he wanted to keep his staff small: he resisted acquiring any new members until all those brought over from the Deputies' organization had been utilized. Second, he wanted the Council, the International Staff/Secretariat, and the delegations to work as a single team and not to be at cross purposes. As Head of the International Staff/Secretariat and Vice-Chairman of the Council he hoped to bring the three agencies together into an effective working relationship. Lastly, he wanted to maintain a close liaison with other international organizations, especially OEEC. He felt that by doing so he could ensure that there was no duplication of international effort, that operating expenses were kept to a minimum, and that the statistics and information collected by other organizations could be used by NATO.

Lord Ismay also wanted to possess freedom of appointment to his higher staff positions and he obtained the formal recognition of this right at the time of his appointment.[5]

Special arrangements were made to ensure a fair selection of the pre-Lisbon staff in forming the unified International Staff/Secretariat. The selection procedure consisted of a combination of the wishes of the Organization and of the individual. Every new office chief was asked to submit to the Deputies' Personnel Officer (who also became Lord Ismay's Personnel Officer) the names of those persons who he felt would be needed in Paris. Then the Personnel Officer and the office chief reviewed the list in the light of the new Establishment Tables. The persons nominated were then offered contracts which would integrate them into the International Staff/Secretariat at approximately the same grade that they had held previously. To minimize the financial inconvenience of relocation, in specific cases, individuals were classified in a grade higher than their former position (and thus received higher pay). It was expected that this situation would automatically right itself through normal attrition and other factors. Subsequent experience

---

[5] Interview with Lord Ismay, 28 May 1959.

proved however that this expectation was only partially fulfilled. Once a position had been filled at a certain level, it was difficult to 'de-grade' it subsequently. If an offer was declined, recruitment for the position took place in Paris. By and large those persons who wanted to go to Paris were able to do so. In fact some French employees who had joined NATO in London in order to work abroad found themselves returning home sooner than they had expected.

These arrangements applied to the non-officer and lower officer grades. For the top posts, i.e. those that carried political overtones, Lord Ismay tried, as far as he could, to follow his own maxim: 'After all, there is a good deal to be said for allowing a man who is entrusted with a job to work with the tools which he himself considers as the best for the purpose, so long as this is possible.'

Although at Lisbon it had been prophesied that 'there will be no deputy secretary-general in the sense of a high-level personage of a nationality different from the secretary-general's', as noted in Chapter VI, Lord Ismay decided to create the post.[6] The prime virtue of this decision was that it enabled a smaller Power to have one of its nationals in the top echelon of the International Staff/Secretariat. The first Deputy Secretary-General was Jonkheer Henry van Vredenburch of The Netherlands. Mr. van Vredenburch was a career diplomat who shortly before the reorganization had been Chairman of The Netherlands delegation to the EDC Conference held in Paris. In his new position he was made Chairman of the Council's Annual Review Committee, and was responsible in general for the economic and logistic activities of the International Staff/Secretariat. The Assistant Secretaries-General for Economics and Finance, and Production and Logistics thus came within his purview.[7]

[6] *New York Times*, 13 Feb. 1952. Lord Ismay felt that the post was not essential, but that it responded to smaller Power needs. (Interview with Lord Ismay, 28 May 1959.) He also appointed a British Executive Secretary who had control over the day-to-day activities of the International Staff/Secretariat, and who was familiar with British administrative methods and had his confidence.

[7] See Ch. X for a discussion of the Annual Review Committee.

In May 1952 Lord Ismay appointed the Heads of the Economics and Finance, and Political Affairs Divisions. M. René Sergent, formerly Financial Attaché to the French Embassy in London, became Assistant Secretary-General for Economics and Finance. His Deputy was Mr. J. K. Horsfield, a high-ranking career civil servant from the United Kingdom. The Assistant Secretary-General for Political Affairs was Signor Sergio Fenoaltea of Italy. He had been active in Italian politics for many years and, after retiring in 1947 had served as Italian Ambassador to China until 1949. He was assisted by Mr. Hugh S. Cumming of the United States, a career diplomat.

In June 1952 it was announced that Mr. David Luke Hopkins of the United States would become Assistant Secretary-General for Production and Logistics. Mr. Hopkins was a banker who had been prominent in philanthropic work in Baltimore.[8] He in effect replaced two men, neither of whom had been his exact counterpart in the Deputies' organization: Mr. William L. Batt of the United States, who had been Chairman of the Defence Production Board, and, under Lord Ismay, temporary head of the Production and Logistics Division; and Mr. William Herod of the United States, who, as Co-ordinator for Defence Production, had been the chief executive officer for the Defence Production Board. Mr. Hopkins was assisted for a short time after his appointment by Mr. Herod's former Chief-of-Staff, Lieutenant-General Sir Ernest Wood of the United Kingdom. General Wood was succeeded by Mr. Charles Brown, an American attorney.

The Information Service, at that time working within the Political Affairs Division in a semi-autonomous capacity, continued to be headed by its Director under the Deputies, Mr. Theodore F. M. Newton, a Canadian diplomat. He had two deputies, Mr. William Newton of the United Kingdom, formerly with the BBC and Mr. Geoffrey Parsons Jr., of the United States, former editor of the Paris edition of the *New York Herald-Tribune*. The Director of Statistics, Mr. Glen S. Taylor of the United States, and the Financial Controller,

[8] Others speculated about for the job were then Lt.-Gen. Curtis LeMay and General Carl A. Spaatz, both American airmen who had achieved fame in World War II. (*New York Times*, 5 May 1952.) See Ch. XI for a discussion of the defence production activities of NATO.

Mr. H. D. Pierson of The Netherlands, had also served with the Deputies.

To head the secretariat and internal housekeeping activities Lord Ismay, as mentioned earlier, appointed as his Executive Secretary, Lord Coleridge, of the United Kingdom. Lord Coleridge had had extensive experience in politico-military affairs before coming to NATO. After retiring from the Royal Navy in 1939 he had served in a special section of the Committee of Imperial Defence which was charged with linking up Anglo-French military plans after the outbreak of World War II.[9] From the fall of France until 1945 he had been Deputy Secretary of the British Joint Staff Mission and Combined Chiefs-of-Staff, located in Washington. The Mission, which assisted in the co-ordination of Anglo-American military planning, was 'an Inter-Service secretariat modelled on the lines of the Chiefs-of-Staff Secretariat in London'.[10] Both the Mission and the secretariat had been under Lord Ismay's direction.

After World War II Lord Coleridge became United Kingdom Secretary to the Military Staff Committee of the United Nations, serving from 1946 to 1948. Immediately before his appointment to NATO he had represented the British Chiefs-of-Staff on the NATO Temporary Council Committee. He now took as his Deputy Mr. Robert G. Barnes of the American State Department.

This then was the disposition of the top posts in the International Staff/Secretariat. It was international in the sense that the occupants of these posts were nationals of the various member countries—mostly the large Powers—of the Alliance, and that the creation of these posts themselves reflected the interplay of interests and methods which went into the making and execution of policy. The posts, like all other officer posts,

[9] Sir Edward Spears, *Assignment to Catastrophe* (London, 1954), I, 48. Sir Edward Spears said of the trio of officers who made up this section: 'Colonel Redman . . . was the very best type of soldier, active and incisive. . . . He was flanked by an air and a naval officer. Presently I got used to seeing this inseparable trio, who were a projection of the Chiefs of Staff Committee. The airman was a colleague of mine in the House, Sir Alfred Beit, the other, Commander Coleridge, a most charming young man, destined, I am sure, for a brilliant career.' (p. 199.)

[10] John Ehrman, *Grand Strategy* (London, 1956), VI, 346.

were filled either by secondment or contractual appointment to the International Staff/Secretariat.

Whether an officer had been seconded from his government or was a career employee, he was considered to be an international civil servant who subscribed to the following pledge:

I solemnly undertake to exercise in all loyalty, discretion and conscience the functions entrusted to me as a member of the staff of NATO, and to discharge these functions with the interests of NATO only in view. I undertake not to seek or accept instructions in regard to the performance of my duties from any government or from any authority other than the Organization.[11]

Contractual employees fell into two categories. For consultants and temporary employees, the contract was normally not offered 'for a period in excess of 90 days'.[12] For persons recruited to permanent positions there were two kinds of contract: an initial one-year contract (the first three months of which were considered to be a probationary period), followed by a more permanent contract offered to those who had successfully completed the first year of employment. The long-term contract was usually offered for an indefinite period but in special circumstances it could be written for an agreed period of time.

Termination of the initial one-year contract could be effected either by the employee or by the Organization, without notice, during the three months' probationary period. After the probationary period, termination could be effected either by the employee's giving three months' notice in writing, or by the Organization's granting separation compensation amounting to three months' continuing employment. This compensation was given only if the separation was not requested for disciplinary reasons. Thus the confirmation of the initial one-year contract at the end of the three months' probationary period implied certain obligations between the two parties.

[11] NATO Staff Rules, 1 July 1955, Art. 2.
[12] Staff Rules, Arts. 3 and 4. Consultants were not, by definition, members of the International Staff/Secretariat and therefore were not entitled to perquisites appertaining to the International Staff/Secretariat under the Agreement on the Status of the North Atlantic Treaty Organization, National Representatives and International Staff.

Three months' continuing emoluments were also granted if a person's initial one-year contract was not renewed at the end of the year. If an employee resigned after the first year he was entitled to one month's salary. If an indefinite contract was offered and accepted at the end of the initial one-year contractual period, termination would be according to the terms laid down in the contract.[13]

This whole system was simplified in January 1957 when the Council made the following announcement:

> As a result of the recent discussions of the Budget Committee with regards to contracts (Article 10 of the Staff Manual) for staff members appointed after the 17th December 1956, or staff members due to receive indefinite contracts after that date, the terms in the Staff Manual are not applicable any more, but the terms of their contract will be laid down in their individual contract.[14]

Seconded persons who were offered letters of engagement specifying their terms of employment were obviously not concerned with either probationary or indefinite periods, since they were posted by their governments for stipulated two or three year terms.

In the case primarily of United States nationals seconded to NATO at the time of the establishment of the international budget, a special arrangement for remuneration was agreed to. Under this arrangement, the United States government (or any other member government) could pay the salaries and most of the allowances of its nationals seconded to NATO at a rate determined by itself.[15] NATO would then credit the government concerned with the amounts it would otherwise have paid

---

[13] Staff Rules, Art. 10. Efficiency reports were rendered by the Heads of Divisions or Independent Offices to the Personnel Officer: '(i) before the completion of their probationary period; (ii) one month before the expiration of their initial, one-year contract, and thereafter annually'. (Staff Rules, Art. 38.) For seconded officers, especially those from the U.S., the report was made according to the policy which obtained in the national administration.

[14] NATO Doc. ON (57) 2.

[15] 'Agreement on the Status of the North Atlantic Treaty Organization, National Representatives and International Staff', Art. 19. This arrangement was adumbrated in the 'Report of the Working Group on the Establishment of an International Budget', submitted in 1951.

the employee according to the NATO salary scale, and would deduct such credits from that government's annual budget assessment.[16]

The justification for this special arrangement was: first, it protected the allowances, retirement, seniority, and other benefits accruable to a civil servant by virtue of his government service; second, it enabled the civil servant to draw a salary commensurate with that drawn by his colleagues in similar grades who had not been seconded to an international organization. This was especially important to the North American governments because their wage scales were higher than those offered by NATO, which meant that if this arrangement had not been made their seconded Foreign Service staff would have had to take a reduction in pay on coming to NATO. There was no question of creating a problem of divided loyalty for these persons. The Staff Rules stipulated:

> Members of the staff who are nationals of a country which has elected to avail itself of the special provisions of Article 19 of the Agreement on the Status of NATO International Staff (whereby a member state may at its discretion pay to its nationals their salaries and emoluments and deduct taxes therefrom) will be bound to their individual governments as regards matters of salary, emoluments and taxation only. Such arrangements shall not free them from the obligations and responsibilities to the Secretary General and the Organization laid down in these Rules.[17]

For the United States, special advantages could be gained from paying its seconded nationals. First, there is a taxation tradition in the United States which frowns upon granting tax exemptions of any kind. All United States government employees are taxed on their incomes. To have made an exception for persons employed in international organizations would have exposed the Administration to criticism from both Congress and the general public. As one noted American diplomat wrote:

> The Treasury Department still takes the provincial view that American citizens serving on an international secretariat should not

---

[16] Memorandum of the U.S. Delegation to NATO, 'Arrangements Concerning Provision of U.S. Nationals for Service as Employees of the NATO International Staff/Secretariat', 22 July 1958.
[17] Staff Rules, Art. 2.

enjoy the immunities from income taxes on their salaries which alien members of the Secretariat enjoy. They insist on asserting that the granting of immunity would constitute a special favour to one group of American citizens.[18]

Secondly, the government would be better able to recruit qualified personnel—especially technical experts—for NATO if it could pay these persons more attractive salaries than they would have received under NATO's budget. This advantage was very important during the early years of the unified budget system, because it was during this period that the United States provided most of the money and technical personnel to get the military commands properly equipped and installed. The United States government often had to compete with private industry in the domestic labour market for highly trained experts in fields which were in demand. This arrangement, in sum, illustrated the disparity in economic prosperity and capacity between the largest member of the Alliance and its allies.

Taking the European member countries as distinct from the North American ones, there was a disparity between NATO salary scales and the cost of living in Paris. With Article 19, the United States and Canada were able to reduce—in fact, to eliminate—the disparity between NATO salary scales and the actual cost of maintaining an employee in Paris in a standard approximating to that which he could enjoy at home. Apart from this special arrangement the general tendency in NATO was to avoid upward adjustments in salary scales to meet rises in the cost of living and so to keep to a minimum increases in the international budget.

Since the International Staff/Secretariat's officer classification system was based upon a rough equivalent to national practice, when governments raised their salaries and NATO did not, a progressive 'cheapening' of NATO posts resulted. In the opinion of some members of the International Staff/Secretariat the effect of this was that a government would tend to

[18] Philip C. Jessup, *The International Problem of Governing Mankind* (Claremont, 1947), p. 18. He went on to comment: 'We are years behind other governments in international sophistication because during the inter-war period we cut ourselves off from membership in the League of Nations and thus deprived ourselves of the experience in international organizations which the other states obtained.'

replace its transferred seconded nationals with persons from a lower governmental grade. Thus the principle of parity of classification of position according to function would be compromised.

To the seconded person, regardless of his rank, this situation did not seem too important, because his period with NATO was limited and he knew that he would return to his normal career pattern, although some of the Americans on the International Staff/Secretariat felt that being assigned to NATO placed them at a competitive disadvantage to their contemporaries who remained within their normal duty progression.[19] But this was due more to the fact of being of a seconded status than to the salary or classification scale.

For the permanent officer, however, this condition could lead to demoralization and in some cases to resignation, as he increasingly felt that his relative position was being devalued. There was, therefore, continuous pressure from members of the International Staff/Secretariat for salary and emolument increases to keep pace with rising cost of living and governmental scales.

The general criteria for wage considerations were laid down in 1951; they were followed throughout Lord Ismay's tenure:

(a) salaries and allowances should be adequate to attract qualified personnel from various member countries in the light of the prevailing national scales and the scales of such international organizations as OEEC and Council of Europe; (b) salaries should not be so out of line with the level of salaries generally payable to officials of the host governments as seriously to embarrass those governments in relation to the level of domestic salaries; (c) salaries should not be so low as to require disproportionately large allowances to staff coming from abroad, which would create serious disparities in total income for the same grade within the Organization; (d) the allowances payable to personnel from abroad are to be regarded as compensation for expatriation and arise primarily from the fact that the costs of living bear disproportionately on members of the staff who are not normally domiciled in the place

[19] For instance, from a purely career viewpoint, it was considered more advantageous for a Foreign Service officer to be assigned with the American delegation to NATO (USRO) than to be seconded to the International Staff/Secretariat.

where they are stationed; (*e*) officers of the Organization would not necessarily be paid expatriation allowances based on duties of a representational character as would be the case if they were serving their own government in a diplomatic capacity; (*f*) governments who find that the general level of salaries and allowances is insufficient to attract their nationals to the Organization may, if they wish, arrange for payment of supplementary allowances to the latter outside the budget of the Organization.[20]

During the years 1952 to 1957, according to the issue and the interests at hand at a particular time, these criteria were emphasized or de-emphasized in varying combinations.

When the various civilian bodies of NATO were brought together in Paris and formed into the International Staff/Secretariat, the salary scales set up under the Deputies were replaced by the scales which had been adopted by OEEC. Therefore, when OEEC increased its emoluments in 1952 to keep pace with the rising living costs in Paris, the Council of NATO decided to follow suit and in May 1952 approved a first cost-of-living allowance. It was awarded on a percentage basis, according to grade, of the combined basic salary and head-of-family allowance. In addition increases of 10 per cent and 25 per cent respectively were made in expatriation and children's allowances. These increases were made retroactive to 1 January 1952 for former NATO Financial and Economic Board (FEB) staff members who had resided in Paris prior to consolidation. For the staff formerly based in London the changes were made effective from 16 April 1952, the official date at which the unified International Staff/Secretariat took over.[21]

Even as these increases were being applied, however, living costs continued to climb, and in November 1952 the Secretary-General requested a second cost-of-living allowance, which was granted by the Council in January 1953.[22] At its meeting

[20] NATO Doc. D-D (51) 89, as quoted in NATO Doc. C-M (55) 56, Annex B.

[21] For former London-based staff the increases were allotted on a percentage rate geared to the salary agreed to in the employee's new letter of appointment. (NATO Staff Manual, 2 Feb. 1953, item 2350.)

[22] In order to document the second request thoroughly the entire International Staff/Secretariat was surveyed for the following information:

of 14 January 1953 the Council agreed to grant an increase for Grades 13, 14, and 15 retroactive to 1 July 1952. This action was taken pending a final decision on an increase for Grades 4 to 15. Like the first cost-of-living allowance, it was based on a percentage of the combined basic salary and head-of-family allowance. Both allowances were recognized as not affecting the basic salary scale. Thus the Council had not approved an across-the-board increase in basic salaries to meet the rising living costs to which the International Staff/Secretariat was exposed; instead it had granted these special, more restricted allowances, in order to avoid a large-scale reconsideration of the basic salary structure.

The Staff Association, which had been formed by the employees of the International Staff/Secretariat to represent their interests to the Administration,[23] periodically pointed out that it would have been better to have reconsidered the entire salaries and allowances structure if employees were to gain equitable remuneration in relation to the cost of living.[24] Nevertheless it was not until February 1955 that formal action was taken in this direction. It began when the French delegate to a working group of the Civilian Budget Committee which was examining the Staff Rules tabled a memorandum dealing with expatriation allowances (Article 12 of the Rules). The delegate proposed that personnel not receiving the expatriation allowance should be granted a 'residence allowance' equal to 15 per cent of the expatriation allowance.[25] His argument was that an undue discrepancy existed between the recompense of

---

nationality, grade, married/single, children, location of family, type of accommodation, suitability of accommodation, total emoluments, monthly net rent, and average amount paid per month for gas, light, and heat. (Staff Manual, item 2351.)

[23] The term 'Administration' refers to Lord Ismay and the officers responsible for the internal administration of the International Staff/Secretariat.

[24] See the Annual Reports of the Staff Committee for the years 1953–5.

[25] The expatriation allowance was one of the so-called 'continuing allowances', which included the first and second cost-of-living allowances, the head-of-family allowance, the children's allowance, and the interpreters' and translators' allowance. (Staff Rules, Art. 11.)

those employees who received the expatriation allowance and those who did not (the latter being, of course, French nationals).

This proposal was forwarded to the Civilian Budget Committee, in which the Canadian delegate submitted a memorandum which, although not objecting directly to the French proposal, suggested that this problem should not be treated in isolation. He was referring to a tendency which had developed of treating NATO staff problems piecemeal. He recommended that a study should be made of the entire salaries and allowances system, with an eye directed toward the long-range implications of both the system then in effect and any other system which might be devised. It was not unlikely that he had in mind the desire of other member nations besides France to examine the situation of their nationals.

The French delegate, in turn, submitted a commentary on his original proposal in which he pointed out that the conditions surrounding the establishment of the salary and expatriation allowance scales no longer existed, and therefore it would not be inappropriate to reconsider these scales. He noted that, whereas OEEC in 1952 had granted a substantial increase in basic salaries, NATO had instead granted a more generous expatriation allowance in order to avoid the embarrassment to the French government which would have resulted if French employees in NATO had begun drawing higher salaries than French civil servants, which would have been the case at that time. The two cost-of-living allowances, being allowances, had not altered the basic salary, and in any event they were considered insufficient. The burden of the French memorandum was that the salaries of civil servants in France, and also of employees of private firms in the Paris area, had increased, but that there had been no reconsideration of the condition of French nationals in NATO in relation to the state of both the domestic labour market and their counterparts from abroad, who had been drawing expatriation allowance. The French delegate stressed that in making his suggestion he did not wish to convey the impression that his government considered excessive the total emoluments of personnel entitled to expatriation allowance.

During these discussions it was noted that the Council of Europe had been planning a survey on the status of international civil servants in Europe and that its results might affect any conclusions arrived at separately by NATO. This survey was considered a forward step in the process of pulling together the common threads of administration existing in European international organizations. But it was also generally agreed that the Council of Europe's study would not be completed for some time, and that it would be better to proceed with an independent study.

The NATO Civilian Budget Committee recommended to the Council that a study of the entire salaries and emoluments situation should be made by a group of independent experts, and the Council agreed. It authorized the Budget Committee to appoint a Group of Experts who would work within the criteria laid down in 1951, which have been quoted above. The Group consisted of five experts nominated by member governments. They were Mr. C. J. MacKenzie of Canada, M. J. Foessel of France, Dr. S. Terranoval of Italy, Mijnh J. H. van Herwaarden of The Netherlands, and Sir William Matthews of the United Kingdom.[26]

The inaugural meeting of the Group of Experts was held in the Palais de Chaillot with the Executive Secretary of NATO in the chair. It was a ceremonial occasion as well as a business meeting. At this meeting Lord Ismay conveyed to the Group his desire that the survey should be fruitful and his willingness to help make it so. In accordance with the Secretary-General's wishes, the Executive Secretary, the Financial Controller, and the Personnel Officer of the International Staff/Secretariat became the three official representatives of the Administration in providing the Group with whatever information it requested.[27]

The Executive Secretary, Lord Coleridge, who had been appointed to explain the views of the Secretary-General to the

[26] NATO 'Report of Group of Experts on Emoluments of Members of the International Staff', Oct. 1955, par. 2; hereafter called 1955 Emoluments Report.

[27] NATO, 'Working Draft on Methods of Procedure for Five Experts Designated to Study Independently NATO Salaries and Allowances', 16 June 1955. The Draft cautioned: '. . . it is important to avoid giving any impression to the National delegations of any attempt on the part of the International Staff to influence their final decisions.'

Group, kept himself informed of its progress by receiving copies of the minutes of meetings. This procedure was adopted because the Secretary-General felt that, since the delegations, through the Council, had divorced themselves directly from the survey, by their act in setting up this group of independent and disinterested experts, he should also not be directly involved in the Group's activities.[28] Thus the experts would be free to proceed as they wished and to conclude whatever they desired.

The third major party to this project, the Staff Association, decided that it should offer its views and suggestions to the experts. It did this through its executive board, the Staff Committee. Thus the experts had available to them the assistance of both the Administration and the Staff Association.

The method adopted by the experts in gathering together their report was as follows. Before proceeding to the task itself, each expert wrote down his ideas as to what the study should entail and how it should be carried out. These ideas were examined one at a time by the Group, with each member defending his own. From this the Group was able to reach consensus on the fundamental question of method. The experts decided to utilize interviews, reports, and statistics obtainable from the International Staff/Secretariat, together with comparative information from the experience and practices of other international organizations. They extended a general invitation to all employees to appear before them and interviewed members from all grades. They also interviewed the chairman of the Rental Compensation Fund.

They studied the Staff Rules, wage scales by grade, rates of overtime pay, separation benefits, medical benefits, and certain diplomatic privileges granted by the French government. They examined in detail the impact of the two cost-of-living allowances on the financial position of the International Staff/Secretariat relative to living conditions in Paris. The general posture of the experts toward their project was stated in their report:

In addition to a careful study of proposals made by the French Delegation, two main concerns have occupied the attention of the

[28] ibid.

Group of Experts. These related to the real difficulties facing incoming personnel in securing accommodation in Paris and to questions of personal security, there being at present nothing in the form either of a pension scheme or a provident fund.[29]

During the course of the survey, the representatives of the Administration made these comments: they conveyed the Secretary-General's favourable response to the French proposal to increase the allowances; they described the difficulties of recruiting and retaining the various categories of personnel required for the International Staff/Secretariat; they suggested that perhaps a revision of the rental allowance scheme would be appropriate to compensate more adequately for Paris's high rents; and they advocated the establishment of either a provident fund or a pension scheme to provide for the employees' long-term security. The latter suggestion about long-term security was in contrast to the earlier, pre-Lisbon position that, owing to the nature of the Alliance as an international politico-military body subject to the vicissitudes of such bodies, long-term job security arrangements were not preferable to short-term, relatively higher, financial remuneration.

The Staff Committee, which represented the interests of the employees, decided to emphasize the question of basic salaries rather than the ancillary financial questions discussed by the Administration.[30] These latter questions, the Committee believed, could be handled more effectively by the Administration. Mr. R. Stinglhamber, the Chairman of the 1955 Staff Committee, made clear to the Group that the Committee felt that the International Staff/Secretariat should benefit from the general rise in living standards in member states which had resulted in part from higher wages. His memorandum concluded:

. . . there should be a total increase of at least 25% in the current overall emoluments of members of the NATO staff, in order to take into account the rise in the cost of living and the general improvement in the standard of living in NATO member countries.[31]

[29] 1955 Emoluments Report, par. 6.

[30] The Committee did, however, submit to the Administration its views about the provident fund. The Administration took these into consideration in formulating its proposals to the experts.

[31] NATO Doc. CP/55/56-N/48.

This attitude of the Staff Committee represented a fundamental difference in approach to the problem from that of the Group of Experts. For, although they produced a comprehensive plan for easing the financial burden of the International Staff/Secretariat, the experts did not provide directly for a substantial increase in the basic salary. Nor did they recommend an adjustment of expatriation allowance in the manner contemplated by the French delegation. The experts seemed to feel that their major contribution to the solution of the emoluments problem was to make some adjustments in policies and to recommend the institution of a new long-term personal security programme, thereby, to their way of thinking, relieving the pressure for higher salaries.

Whether, in fact, the experts had accomplished what they had been charged to do, and whether their recommendations would accomplish what they intended them to, were questions about which agreement was not unanimous. But the experts did not enter into these discussions; they disbanded immediately after submitting their report. Some criticism was made of this action as it meant that they were not available to defend their proposals. The Group thought, nonetheless, that since its members had been appointed as outside and disinterested experts it was fitting for its report to be submitted in that spirit: the report's reception should not be a matter which concerned them. It was submitted to the Executive Secretary, who forwarded it to the Secretary-General. It later went to the Civilian Budget Committee and then to the Council.

The report made eleven major recommendations. First, a provident fund should be established rather than a pension scheme.[32] The experts reasoned that NATO was an organization whose existence depended upon world political developments, and therefore it would not necessarily be permanent. A pension scheme required a more permanent organization. They said: 'This is a common characteristic of all international organizations, but it applies with particular force to NATO.'[33] They also noted that the age of many members occupying the lower grades precluded them from fulfilling the service requirements for pensions. In addition, many employees already drew

[32] 1955 Emoluments Report, par. 6.
[33] ibid. par. 53 (a).

pensions from other sources. Lastly, they pointed out that the majority of the stenographers and typists were not French and tended to resign after an average of three years' service, and that in the higher grades the employees who were seconded to the Organization returned to their national services after their tour of duty had been completed.[34] A large percentage of employees would thus not have served the period required for a pension.

The second recommendation was the elimination of the two cost-of-living allowances by their incorporation into the basic salary, and in addition a small increase in salary.[35]

Third, the experts suggested that a compensatory allowance should be granted in particular instances to avoid any undue hardship which might be caused by the application of the report.[36] The procedure according to which this allowance should be awarded was:

. . . that the Administration should be empowered by the Budget Committee in special cases arising in the officer grades, to advance an employee, as of the effective date of the changes in salary scales, to that step in the new range which is immediately higher than the step which he enjoys in the present scale. In such a case the employee should not be entitled to a further annual increment until the date upon which he would normally have qualified for it had no accelerated advancement in the range been permitted.[37]

The fourth recommendation was that expatriation allowance should be gradually reduced according to length of service.[38] The reductions were to level off when the allowance had been reduced to 25 per cent of the initial allowance for the heads of households and 35 per cent for other cases. The report said: 'It seems equitable to the Group of Experts that as years of service accrue, the initial rates of allowance should remain unchanged, seeing that stage by stage there should be a natural assimilation into the new mode of life and economy.'[39] On this view there was sharp disagreement and vigorous criticism by the Staff Association and the Administration.

[34] ibid. pars. 53 (a), (b), (c), (d).   [35] ibid. par. 11.
[36] ibid. par. 33.   [37] ibid.   [38] ibid. par. 39.
[39] ibid.

Fifth, the experts proposed a revised rental compensation scheme based on a quasi-mathematical formula rather than on a 'means test'.[40] Sixth, they favoured the continuation of the supplementary insurance scheme, except that, they said, the cost should be met out of interest earned by the provident fund.[41] This scheme had been instituted the previous year to supplement the French social security scheme with respect to illness, maternity, natural or accidental death, and temporary or permanent disability allowances. The insurance had been purchased pending the conclusion of the emoluments survey.

The Group's seventh recommendation was that the old-age pension section of the French social security benefits which had been available to the International Staff/Secretariat should be withdrawn. They felt that the provident fund provided adequate long-term security benefits.[42]

As their eighth proposal the experts redefined the grading system for certain officer grades. They inserted two grades into the system, 10A and 13A. Grade 10A was created to distinguish between administrative class people who had reached the limit of their chances of promotion and junior officers who were at the beginning of their careers. Grade 13A was created to distinguish between career officers and limited-term technical experts or seconded officers. The Group of Experts recommended a longer range of increments with smaller increases per increment for Grades 10 and 13 in order to encourage long-term employees who probably would not advance much farther, and a shorter range of increments with larger individual increases for Grades 10A and 13A, to compensate short-term employees or those who would probably continue to advance.[43]

Ninth, the experts recommended the abolition of interpreters' and translators' allowances. Their reason was: 'If the system of extra allowances on the grounds of specialist qualifications is allowed to continue a case might well be argued for

[40] ibid. par. 46. The housing problem is discussed fully in Ch. VIII.
[41] ibid. pars. 61, 63.   [42] ibid. par. 57.
[43] ibid. pars. 26–32. They further recommended that technical experts should be appointed at any step in the appropriate salary range instead of only at the beginning, which Article 6 (e) of the 1955 Staff Rules had stipulated.

its extension to other posts in the organization'.[44] These allow-ances were a carry-over from the practice begun in the 1920s by the League of Nations and other international organizations in order to encourage people to enter this type of work, because such qualified persons had been scarce.

The tenth recommendation favoured the retention of the installation allowance.[45] The last recommendation was that an organization and management study of the International Staff/Secretariat should be carried out before the report was put into effect.[46] On this point the experts felt quite strongly. At one place in their report they stated:

In endeavouring to compare the salary rates payable to members of the International Secretariat of NATO with those paid for comparable services in governmental and private employment, the Group of Experts have been seriously handicapped because there do not exist within the Organization clear-cut, written job specifications or statements of duties and qualifications of the various grades nor of the different types of positions lumped together within each grade.[47]

At another place they affirmed:

The Group of Experts cannot emphasize too strongly their re-commendation that arrangements should be made as soon as possible for a thorough examination of the organization and classification of the International Secretariat, making use of outside experts in organization, classification and method technique.[48]

The experts considered an organization and management study to be 'an essential preliminary condition' to the achieve-ment of a cohesive and comprehensive personnel classification and wages structure. Lastly, they viewed their report as an integrated plan, which should be adopted *in toto*.

A special working group was appointed by the Administra-tion to consider the report and make recommendations to the Secretary-General. This working group consisted of represent-atives from the Economics and Finance, and the Production and Logistics Divisions, the Deputy Executive Secretary, the

---

[44] ibid. par. 35.   [45] ibid. par. 44.   [46] ibid. par. 8.
[47] ibid. par. 14.
[48] ibid. par. 18. For the work of the Management Survey Team see Ch. VIII.

Personnel Officer, and the Financial Controller, who was appointed chairman. The Personnel Officer served as secretary. The Chairman of the Staff Committee was invited to observe. Although the working group did not approve of some of the anticipated consequences of the report, it recommended to the Secretary-General that the report be accepted as a whole.[49]

The Staff Committee, on its part, also decided to submit a memorandum to the Secretary-General presenting its views. This memorandum was quite critical of the report, and concluded with these proposals:

(*a*) that the Secretary General invite the Administration to define its personnel policy, particularly with regard to the recruitment and promotion of officers, the description of jobs and tenure of office, and that due consideration be given to the investigation now in progress in other international bodies; (*b*) that the Secretary General invite the Council to adopt the principle that the NATO Staff should benefit from the general rise in the standard of living of NATO countries, and to ensure that its implementation is not impeded by rigid budgetary considerations; (*c*) that the Staff's individual contributions to a Provident Fund should not entail any reduction in the present net salaries; (*d*) that pending the creation of a NATO Pension Fund, the Administration should maintain its contribution to the Social Security Pension scheme and to the supplementary insurance cover against risks of death from illness; (*e*) that consideration of the Experts' proposal regarding the Expatriation allowance be deferred until an enquiry has shown to what extent it is true to say that the expenses and commitments peculiar to members of the Staff entitled to an expatriation allowance, diminish in proportion to the number of years they spend abroad; (*f*) that the whole problem be treated as a matter of urgency.[50]

The Secretary-General's statement to the Civilian Budget Committee closely paralleled the memorandum of the Staff Association. The Committee, however, after refusing to investigate some of the criticisms made by the Administration, requested it to submit a document summarizing its minimum

[49] See 'Summary Record of a Meeting of the Working Group for Study of the Report of the Group of Experts on Emoluments of Members of the International Staff', 23 Nov. 1955; 'Minutes of Meeting of Working Group on the Report of the Experts on Emoluments', 22 Nov. 1955.

[50] NATO Doc. CP/55/56-N/48, Annex C, par. 9.

conditions of acceptability of the report. Apparently the Budget Committee did not want to reopen the issues which the experts had just examined. The Administration's conditions were:

(1) That the adoption of the report should not close the door to a later examination of salary scales and allowances, bearing in mind the points made by the International Staff with regard to the difficulties of recruiting and maintaining staff of the right calibre at the present rates of pay and allowances. (2) That notwithstanding the provisions of paragraph 57 of the Experts' report under which the Old-Age Pension portion of the Social Security benefits is to be terminated, a member of the staff so desiring may be given the option of having deducted from the contributions to his Provident Fund such sums as are necessary to continue the Old-Age Pension element of the French Social Security system; his final benefits under the Provident Fund being reduced proportionately. . . . (3) That placing a liberal interpretation on paragraph 33 of the Experts' report, no member of the present staff would have his net monthly remuneration reduced as a result of the change-over to the new system. Effect would be given to this principle by granting on a personal basis a compensatory allowance which would cease as further annual increments rendered it unnecessary. . . . (4) That no action to change the present system of expatriation allowance should be taken pending a thorough examination of the factors which might tend to justify the reduction of such an allowance after a lengthy period of service in Paris.[51]

The Budget Committee accepted all the qualifications made by the Administration except the one concerning the expatriation allowance. In this case the Committee stipulated that the phasing of the reductions in the allowance should begin after two years' service. The Committee's comment was: 'The Committee considers that the recommendations of the Group of Experts on expatriation allowance constitute an essential part of the Report, of which it is unanimous in recommending the acceptance as a whole.'[52]

The report, with these qualifications, then became the property of the Council, which approved it. The entire system it recommended came into operation on 1 July 1956. At its meeting on 16 May 1956 the Council had already decided to

[51] NATO Doc. BC-D(56)1.
[52] NATO Doc. BC-WP(56)1, Annex A.

bring into operation the major recommendations of the report, the provident fund which replaced the French social security provisions for old age pensions. It did not however replace the social security contributions for sickness, maternity, disablement, and death, and these continued. Employees were given the option of participating in either the French voluntary security old age scheme, or in the voluntary security scheme of their own country, if they did not want to participate in the NATO provident fund.

The life of the emoluments report was short, however, for in 1956 the Staff Association submitted a resolution to the Secretary-General:

[The Association notes] that since 1952, the monthly emoluments of the NATO staff have remained virtually unchanged, and recalls that the Provident Fund recently set up to offset the absence of a pension scheme, has not increased the current financial resources of the members of the staff.[53]

The Association had not wavered from its initial view that the problem should have been attacked directly through the basic salary rather than through ancillary programmes. The Secretary-General sympathized with the Association's complaint, and in October 1956 suggested that the Council should increase basic salaries further. A temporary increase amounting to 12 per cent of the gross salary received in June 1956 was authorized.

In reality, though, for a large number of members of the International Staff/Secretariat the increase amounted to only about 4 per cent after provident fund and supplementary insurance payments had been deducted from the gross sum.[54] The need for greater take-home pay led to expressions of disappointment by the Staff Committee and the Secretary-General. A Staff Committee Resolution passed on 17 January 1957 declared:

The Committee wishes to place on record the deep disappointment of the staff. The temporary measures which have just been taken constitute for most members of the International Staff only a

[53] NATO Doc. CP/56/57-N/37, par 10 and Annex II.
[54] NATO Doc. CP/56/57-N/37, par. 11.

very slight improvement, bearing no relation to the actual rise in the cost of living in France since 1952, nor to the general rise in salaries in the various NATO countries. The inadequacy of salary adjustments since 1952 has in fact amounted to a progressive down-scaling of grades. In any event, the Staff Committee considers that the NATO staff ought to have been granted the same net monthly increase as the OEEC Staff for corresponding grades and seniority. It deplores the confusion which has arisen between the monthly remuneration on which the purchasing power of the staff depends, and the Provident Fund from which members of the staff benefit only on leaving the Organization.[55]

Lord Ismay responded to this resolution with the following note:

1. Although thankful for small mercies, I am, as you know disappointed at the recent decision of the Council about staff salaries. However, we had to accept the views of the Budget Committee because the increase on which they agreed was the absolute maximum obtainable at the moment. In any case, it has been clearly stated that this was only a temporary measure pending a definite solution of the salary problem. 2. We have been in touch with the OEEC and the Council of Europe with a view to the rapid setting up of a group of experts to study on a broad basis the whole range of questions related to the emoluments of the staff of these organizations. 3. The terms of reference of this group have already been drawn up between us and will be submitted to the Council for approval in the near future. 4. There is, therefore, every reason to hope that the group of experts will be functioning in a few weeks' time, and that they will be able to place their conclusions before the Secretaries General by about the middle of the year. 5. It is likely—and for my part I shall suggest it to the experts—that they will, during the course of their study, ask for the views of the accredited representatives of the Staff Association.[56]

As this interchange suggests, the shadow of other events lay upon NATO's emoluments situation. One was the study which the Council of Europe had been making of the possibility of creating a European civil service. Although, as noted earlier, the Council had agreed that NATO's emoluments study should not await the result of the Council of Europe's study, nevertheless it was conceivable that action taken by NATO might

[55] NATO Doc. CP/56/57-N/37, Annex III.
[56] NATO Doc. CP/56/57-N/37, Annex IV.

be subject to a re-evaluation when the Council of Europe's report was produced.[57]

Also, in November 1955 the Council of NATO had approved the creation of a group of experts to conduct a management survey. This action was in line with the emoluments experts' recommendation, and contributed directly to the Council's reluctance to alter the salary structure drastically. Thus by late 1955 three different groups—the Council of Europe, a NATO Group of Experts on emoluments, and a NATO Management Survey Team—had been studying the general problem of providing adequate status and remuneration to personnel serving in European international organizations.

When the Management Survey Team reported in May 1956 it supported the contentions of the Staff Association and the Secretary-General. It said:

> . . . the Team recommends that the Secretary General and the Council consider an immediate further review of the emoluments of members of the International Staff. This recommendation is based on the following reasons: (a) Since the report referred to above was issued general pay increases in France and other NATO countries have occurred; (b) further pay increases are under consideration in France and other NATO countries; (c) in its survey, the Team came to the conclusion that additional grades within the present classification structure should be established . . . and that some of the present pay rates were inadequate to permit recruitment of satisfactory personnel and/or did not compare favourably with present local civil service emoluments.[58]

By May 1957—the month Lord Ismay retired—a second Group of Experts on emoluments had been authorized by the Council to make another study of the problem in the light of

[57] A conference on the organization of a European civil service had been held by the University of the Saar, under the auspices of the Council of Europe, in Nov. 1955. (See A. H. Robertson, *The Council of Europe* (London, 1956), p. 72.) A Committee of Experts on the European Civil Service was set up which sat at Strasbourg and was composed of representatives of the administrations of the European international organizations and their member governments. (NATO Doc. CP/56/57-N/37, Annex VI.) See also Université de la Sarre, *La fonction publique européenne*, Collogue de Sarrebruck, 7–10 novembre 1955 (Sarrebruck, 1956).

[58] General Report, par. 31.

altered conditions. This Group differed from the first one in that it consisted of experts working on behalf of NATO, the Council of Europe, OEEC, and Western European Union (WEU). Two of the five men named to this Group had served on NATO's 1955 Group: Mr. van Herwaarden of The Netherlands and Sir William Matthews of the United Kingdom. The second Group was given the same status as the 1955 Group: that is, it was charged to act in a personal capacity; and, with respect to the tasks assigned to it, it was to be independent of both the NATO organization and member governments.

This development was a step in the right direction; but, coming as it did at the conclusion of Lord Ismay's tenure of office, it left the general question unresolved for him; circumstances had militated against an immediate solution while he was Secretary-General. For example, the French government's initial request that NATO should adjust allowances rather than basic salaries in order not to embarrass the government's relations with its own civil servants, had complicated the issue from the beginning. Then the emphasis of the first Group of Experts on long-term financial security rather than on more direct short-term basic rises in pay to compensate for rising living costs had tended to frustrate the International Staff/Secretariat's demand for salaries and emoluments studies. Lastly, the broadening of the problem into a management survey and a combined international organizational study had led to hesitation and postponement in the short run although perhaps the ultimate outcome would be more desirable. In any event, for Lord Ismay, what was possible and what was desirable in terms of adequate and timely recompense could not be satisfactorily reconciled. But it is doubtful whether questions of salaries and emoluments are ever settled to the satisfaction of everyone in an international organization.

CHAPTER VIII

EFFORTS TO IMPROVE AMENITIES FOR THE INTERNATIONAL STAFF/SECRETARIAT

MANY of the personnel problems which beset Lord Ismay were also, of course, of concern to the Staff Association. The Association had been created shortly after the move to Paris, in response to this note from the Secretary-General:

> I feel that it might be the general wish to set up a Staff Association in the Headquarters of NATO, with the objects of protecting the professional interest of members of the Staff as a whole, and of making proposals to further the well-being of the staff, and suggestions for bringing the staff together in social activities.[1]

By December 1952 an *ad hoc* committee had been formed to work out the process by which elections to a permanent Staff Committee should take place. Qualification for candidature for the permanent committee required that an employee be under fixed contract, although members undergoing their probationary period were allowed to vote in the elections.[2] The permanent committee was to be elected by groups because 'groups of people who know each other in their professional surroundings [have] the advantage that they are likely to elect in the first place a representative whom they know personally and can rely on to support their interests'.[3] The Secretary-General, Deputy Secretary-General, Assistant Secretaries-General, Executive Secretary, Financial Controller and Personnel Officer were to be *ex officio* members.[4]

The first permanent Staff Committee was elected in January 1953. Its first action was to obtain official recognition of the Association from the Administration by gaining permission to have its existence acknowledged in the Staff Manual, as item

---

[1] NATO Doc. ON(52)84.
[3] ibid.

[2] NATO Doc. ON(52)132.
[4] ibid.

3000.[5] In 1955 this item became Article 40 of the Staff Rules, which read:

(a) There shall be a Staff Association consisting of all employees of the International Staff which shall, under a procedure approved by the Secretary General, elect annually a Staff Committee to serve as executive agent of the Association. (b) The Staff Committee shall; (i) protect the professional interests of members of the staff; (ii) make proposals to further the well-being of members of the staff; (iii) promote social, cultural and athletic activities among members of the staff; (iv) represent the personnel of the organization in relations with staff associations of other international organizations.[6]

For social activities the Association sponsored language classes, organized various clubs, such as ping-pong, riding, judo, and bridge, and arranged for evenings of bingo.[7] Other special facilities obtained by the Staff Committee for the Association were special price reductions on theatre tickets and skiing holidays, medical services available at the Palais de Chaillot, holiday camps for employees' children, and a lending library started from books contributed by members.[8] In January 1955 'thanks to the results of the bingo evenings, to the generosity of the Administration, and to the receipts from diplomatic petrol', a Christmas party was held for over three hundred children of members of the International Staff/Secretariat. This party became an annual event.[9]

One of the most widely-recognized projects in which the Association participated was the re-negotiation by the Restaurant Committee of the restaurant concession at the Palais de Chaillot. This Committee consisted of two representatives appointed by the Staff Association, one member appointed by the Financial Controller, one member appointed by the Secretary-General and, appropriately, a member of the French

---

[5] NATO Staff Committee Report, 1953–1954, par. 1 (a); NATO Staff Manual, 2 Feb. 1953, item 3000.

[6] NATO Staff Rules, 1 July 1955, Art. 40.

[7] Staff Committee Report, 1953–1954, par. 3. Lord Ismay became the Honorary President of the Ping-Pong Club.

[8] Staff Committee Report, 1953–1954, par. 2.

[9] NATO Doc. CP/54-N/26(Final).

delegation.[10] Complaints about the quality and cost of food and service were brought to the attention of the Committee.

In 1955 the Association issued its own magazine called the *NATO Staff Association Bulletin*. The *Bulletin* had only partial success owing to the lack of make-up and printing facilities and its numbers appeared irregularly. Nevertheless, it is an example of the effort which the Staff Committee made to bring the various parts of the International Staff/Secretariat closer together.

In 1955 several efforts were made to extend the relations of the NATO Staff Association with those of other international organizations. Building upon the already close functional association between OEEC and NATO, their Staff Associations exchanged information about their emoluments problems, including the study then being made by the NATO Group of Experts on emoluments and the pension schemes being considered by the two organizations. At the request of the NATO Staff Committee, the UNESCO Staff Association extended membership of the UNESCO Film Club to the NATO International Staff/Secretariat.

An investigation into the possibility of the Staff Association's joining the Federation of International Civil Servants Associations (FICSA) was only partially successful, because only Staff Associations of United Nations agencies were permitted full membership. NATO's Staff Association had to be satisfied with a co-ordinative relationship. The Staff Committee's report on the matter pointed out that the chief advantage of full membership was that member Staff Associations were entitled to legal defence before international courts free of charge. The report commented: 'Since, however, the NATO Staff Rules do not provide for the recognition by NATO of such courts, this advantage would not be enjoyed by NATO Staff.'[11]

However, a Committee for Co-ordination between the Staff Associations of European international organizations was established in 1956, with a representative from the NATO Staff Committee as its first Executive Secretary. The Committee

---

[10] NATO Doc. ON(53)35.
[11] NATO Doc. CP/55/56-N/48.

was composed of representatives from the Council of Europe, OEEC, the European Organization for Nuclear Research, and NATO. This committee helped to present the views of the various Staff Associations to the Group of Experts who were studying a European Civil Service.[12] It was also hoped that the Committee's work would lead eventually to closer relations with the FICSA.[13]

Both Lord Ismay and the Staff Association recognized that political pressures would inevitably arise over the appointment and use made of the NATO staff. These pressures were more likely to bear on the officer grades than on members of lower grades, such as clerks, guards and stenographers. Therefore, although at the time of his appointment Lord Ismay had requested the Deputies to give him a free hand in his selection of officers, he realized that he had to fit his appointments to the needs of geography and nationality.[14] This is a situation common to all international organizations. The Staff Association, although pressing constantly for a greater number of appointments and promotions according to the merit system, nonetheless recognized the political limitations of their policy.

The number of officers (Grades 10–15) in the International Staff/Secretariat never went above 200 during Lord Ismay's tenure of office, and many of these were technical experts, which tended to limit Lord Ismay's freedom in making appointments.[15] It was difficult to fit his wish to employ the best man available with the requirement of satisfying the wishes of the most interested and perhaps deserving delegations. Lord Ismay admitted this when he reported to the Council on the eve of his resignation:

It is perhaps not sufficiently realized that the NATO International Staff suffers from certain inherent handicaps . . . it is obviously desirable that all member countries should be proportionately represented on the staff. Consequently there can be no question of international competitive bidding for appointments. These have to

[12] NATO Doc. CP/56/57-N/37, Annex VI. See also Ch. VII.

[13] Purely within NATO itself, the Staff Committee maintained contacts with the military commands' committees, representing civilian staff interests. (NATO Doc. CP/57/58-N/9.)

[14] Interview with Lord Ismay, 28 May 1959.

[15] Speech by Lord Ismay, 5 Nov. 1954. (NATO Speech Series, No. 62.)

be allotted not to the best man available in the Alliance, irrespective
of nationality, but to the man selected by the government of the
particular country which, in the interest of proportionate representation, is asked to fill the appointment in question. . . .[16]

NATIONAL REPRESENTATION
INTERNATIONAL STAFF/SECRETARIAT[17]
(1954)

Member States	Officers down to and including Grade 10
Belgium	11
Canada	7
Denmark	4
France	61
Greece	2
Iceland	1
Italy	17
Luxembourg	1
Netherlands	9
Norway	4
Portugal	2
Turkey	2
United Kingdom	47
United States	21
TOTAL:	189

The general rule for the balance of nationality representation on the International Staff/Secretariat was that no single
nation should occupy a direct line of command. In other words,
if the top post was held by a Frenchman, then a national of
another State had to occupy the second-to-top post. Another
nation could register an objection and claim one of the positions
if this rule was violated. To keep himself informed of the
nationality distribution Lord Ismay had a monthly report sent

[16] 'Text of Lord Ismay's Report to the Ministerial Meeting of the North
Atlantic Council at Bonn, May 1957', as contained in the *NATO Letter*,
Vol. 5, Spec. Supp. to No. 6. He concluded: 'Thus there is little or no
prospect of substantial promotion within the International Staff.'

[17] *The Five Years*, p. 67.

to him by the Personnel Office. When he visited one of the member countries he took with him a chart showing the proportion of that country's representation in the International Staff/Secretariat. He also included in his annual report to the Council a general nationality distribution report. It is clear

OFFICER STAFF BY NATIONALITY[18]
(April 1957)

	Un-classified	GRADE						
		15	14	13	12	11	10	TOTAL
Belgium . .		1	1	6	2	1		11
Canada . .			1	2	2	2	1	8
Denmark . .				3	1			4
France . .	1	1	8	11	7		8	36
Germany . .			2	3				5
Greece . .						1		1
Iceland . .							1	1
Italy . . .	1		1	10	2		1	15
Luxembourg .					1			1
Netherlands .	1		5	3		2		11
Norway . .				3	1			4
Portugal . .							1	1
Turkey . .					1	3		4
United Kingdom	2	1	8	9	3		9	32
United States .	1¹	2	5	7	1		1	17
								GRAND
TOTAL .	6	5	31	58	23	6	22	194 TOTAL

The figures for interpreters, translators, and minute writers are not included in the above chart. They are as follows:

France					5	10	7	4	26
United Kingdom . .					3	7	6	1	17

¹ Appointment at present vacant.

that Lord Ismay never had far from his thoughts on personnel matters the nationality distribution of his International Staff/Secretariat.

During the early years the balance of national representation was estimated on a Divisional basis, which meant that each

[18] 'Text of Lord Ismay's Report to the Ministerial Meeting of the North Atlantic Council at Bonn, May 1957', as contained in the *NATO Letter*, Vol. 5, Spec. Supp. to No. 6.

Division was concerned only with its own pattern. When the Personnel Officer received a letter of resignation or withdrawal he wrote to the Assistant Secretary-General affected, requesting his suggestion for a replacement. The Assistant Secretary-General sent the Personnel Officer a job description, including qualifications required, and suggested which delegation—or delegations—should be approached. The Personnel Officer then sent out formal letters to these delegations, which could, if they wished, submit names of candidates. These names, together with personal data, were forwarded to the Assistant Secretary-General, who studied the information and returned a short list with his comments. The Personnel Officer occasionally found himself in an awkward position if the delegation subsequently asked why a nominee had been rejected, but he was not obliged to explain.

At any rate candidates on the short list were invited to come to Paris for an interview, or, if a senior officer was travelling in the country concerned, he would arrange to conduct the interview there. If a candidate came to Paris he first met the Personnel Officer for a preliminary interview at which the details of the job and the conditions of employment were discussed. The Personnel Officer wrote a summary of his opinion of the candidate and then arranged for him to be interviewed by a section head or other officer in the Division. After considering all the candidates, the Division indicated its choice and the Personnel Officer sent a preliminary letter of appointment through his delegation to a successful candidate. The candidate notified the Personnel Officer of his acceptance, again through his delegation, and the Personnel Officer arranged for his arrival date and final papers, including a security clearance. The security clearance could be accomplished only by the delegation concerned. Often, in order to avoid delay after the appointment, security clearances were initiated by the delegation at the time of nomination.

The general rule was that all recruitments to officer grades were conducted by the Personnel Office through the delegations. In practice the Personnel Officer was occasionally presented with a *fait accompli*. It sometimes happened that the Assistant Secretary-General went directly to the interested delegation, which made its selection of a replacement, to which the Assistant Secretary-General agreed. Then the Personnel Officer was informed of the impending vacancy and almost simultaneously the name of the new appointee was submitted.

Lord Ismay did not approve of these informal proceedings, and in 1954 he sent a letter to his Assistant Secretaries-General telling them that they should not make their own arrangements but should work through Commander de Vries, the Personnel Officer. The 'extra-legal' procedure was also objected to by the Staff Association,[19] and by the NATO Management Survey Team, which commented:

It would seem desirable that notices of vacancies in specialized posts should be published to give both qualified members of the Staff and the nationals of any member government the opportunity of applying for such posts. This practice, if adopted, would contrast with the present procedure under which a single country is asked to nominate candidates for a specific vacant post. . . . The Team also considers that the Head of Personnel should always be informed as soon as any senior officer post is about to become vacant. As a general rule, only the Secretary-General, his Deputy or the Head of Personnel should be authorized to approach Delegations and ask them to nominate candidates.[20]

The Team also wrote:

The recruitment of officers in the International Staff is complicated by requirements of geographical representation in these grades. The Team feels that this principle has perhaps been applied to over-small units and that it would be preferable for the Secretary-General and the governments to consider the Secretariat as a whole, without thereby disregarding the necessity of ensuring some geographical distribution in all sections of the Staff.[21]

This recommendation would presumably reduce the need to adjust recruiting needs at the Division level in order to satisfy requirements for representation by nationality. Lord Ismay agreed to the recommendation. After 1955 the Deputy Secretary-General received notification of a vacancy and indicated to the Personnel Officer which delegations should be

[19] See NATO Doc. CP/55/56-N/48, Annex C.
[20] NATO Management Survey Team, General Report, 1 May 1956, par. 38.
[21] ibid. par. 37.

approached. Then, after the interested delegations had responded, Lord Ismay decided on an International Staff/Secretariat-wide basis which delegation's nominee would be invited to accept the post. In practice the Assistant Secretary-General sometimes saw Lord Ismay about the impending vacancy before the Personnel Officer knew about it. The delegation and the Assistant Secretary-General were still able to work matters out beforehand, and the nominee for the replacement could still be named almost simultaneously with the notification that the vacancy would occur.

Lord Ismay was also sincerely interested in ensuring that the smaller Powers were not 'squeezed out' of the International Staff/Secretariat. He tried for several years to give appointments to the smaller Powers whenever possible, but he was not too successful in this endeavour, partly because the smaller Powers were not able to provide the men. Thus, although formally there were no 'entailed' posts in the International Staff/Secretariat, in practice there was a tendency for nationals of the same country to occupy the same posts consecutively. The Management Survey Team's suggestion that 'normally, to ensure a desirable degree of geographical balance and rotation as well as a cross fertilization of ideas, no two nationals of the same country should succeed each other in any of these policy positions',[22] could not be carried out during Lord Ismay's tenure of office.

Needless to say, the employees themselves were very much concerned about these personnel policies—especially promotion policies. The Staff Association accordingly took this matter up with the Administration in 1955. It received the following reply:

When an officer serving in NATO is interested in another section of the Secretariat, he usually puts in a request to the head of that section informing him that he would like to be counted among the candidates to be considered for any vacancy which may occur.[23]

This statement was somewhat in contradiction to Article 39(a) of the Staff Rules, which said:

. . . Heads of divisions and independent offices shall, in consultation with the Personnel Officer, review the qualifications of

---

[22] ibid, par. 33.   [23] NATO Doc. CP/55/56-N/48.

serving members of the staff in relation to vacant posts in their establishment before initiating recruitment outside the staff applicants.[24]

As the Staff Committee concluded: '. . . at present there is no official procedure to secure impartial application of the terms of Article 39(a) of the Staff Rules to officer grades.'[25] Lord Ismay, in his final report to the Council, confirmed the bleakness of the picture:

. . . the larger proportion of the more senior appointments of the Staff are held by officials who are seconded by their respective governments for a tour of service with NATO, and who are replaced on the expiry of that term by other officials similarly seconded. Thus there is little or no prospect of substantial promotion within the International Staff.[26]

Over this problem the Staff Committee had to rest content with the uncomfortable knowledge that promotions could not be separated from recruitment and emoluments problems, and that these could not be resolved by administrative means alone.

The Staff Committee received more favourable treatment for the Association on the subject of appeal rights and procedures. The policy for appeals followed from the policy for complaints, which was:

(a) A staff member should refer in the first instance any complaint affecting his work or conditions of service to his immediate supervisor, or, if necessary, through his supervisor to the Head of the Division or Office whom he has a right to see. (b) Alternatively, a staff member can at any time consult the Personnel Officer without reference to his supervisor. In the last resort he has a right to have the matter submitted to the Secretary General by preparing a memorandum stating his grievance. This memorandum will be forwarded to the Secretary General through the Personnel Officer.

---

[24] Staff Rules, Art. 39 (a).

[25] NATO Doc. CP/55/56-N/48. There was a clearly-defined promotion policy for the junior staff—Grades 8 and below—but promotion from non-officer to officer grades was very difficult.

[26] 'Text of Lord Ismay's Report to the Ministerial Meeting of the North Atlantic Council at Bonn, May 1957' as contained in the *NATO Letter*, Vol. 5, Spec. Supp. to No. 6.

At the same time a copy will be sent to the Head of the Division or Office concerned.[27]

The Staff Committee objected to the provision that the Secretary-General, after admitting the appeal, could either '(1) consider the appeal himself or dispose of it finally, or (2) appoint a panel of three members of his staff to consider the appeal and advise in its disposal'.[28] On 26 June 1953 the Committee was able to obtain the following revision:

When an appeal has been lodged with the Secretary General, he shall, within eight days, consult a panel of four members comprising: a Chairman, appointed by the Secretary General; a representative of the administration, also appointed by the Secretary General preferably from a division other than that of the appellant; a representative of the Staff Committee; a member of the staff, chosen by the Staff Committee from among members of the same grade as the applicant.[29]

The appellant still had the right to see the Secretary-General as a last resort.[30] Thus the Staff Committee was able to obtain greater 'worker representation' on complaint appeal boards.

Not once during Lord Ismay's tenure of office did he take issue with the findings of an appeals board, nor, except on one occasion when he upheld administrative action in terminating a contract, were any direct appeals made to the Secretary-General. Appeals which failed and which resulted in the dismissal of the appellant, occurred only three times. One of these appellants had been seconded and was removed by his government before the appeal judgement was made; the other two were permanent members of the International Staff/Secretariat.[31]

The principle behind the appeals procedure was that an international civil servant should deal with the Administration

----

[27] Staff Manual, item 2900. The only substantive change to this policy in the Staff Rules was: 'Except when complaints are based on purely personal grounds, they shall notify their immediate superior of their intention to state a complaint to the Personnel Officer'. (Art. 36.)

[28] Staff Manual, item 2910.

[29] Staff Manual, Corrig. 3, 26 June 1953; Staff Committee Report, 1953–1954.

[30] Staff Committee Report, 1953–1954.

[31] Interview with Miss K. Goddard, Assistant to the Personnel Officer, 28 July 1958.

and not with his government about such matters. In practice, especially if the individual was seconded, the government tended to become involved. There were plausible reasons for this. For one thing, a government naturally preferred its nationals to be above professional suspicion. And, if the dispute was personal, its existence, regardless of its outcome, could in the long run prove so injurious to the national's effectiveness that his usefulness both to the International Staff/Secretariat and to his government might be impaired.

In view of the variety of situations which could arise within an International Staff/Secretariat dealing with complex international problems representing many interests, the appeals record was very good. Doubtless this was due in part to Lord Ismay's good relations with the Staff Association.

The Staff Association, contrary to its wishes, could not carry any appeals to an international tribunal because, as mentioned earlier, it had no standing as an international body. The last resort for an appellant remained the Secretary-General. In broader terms, no memoranda or resolutions drawn up by the Staff Committee had any legal effect; the Committee could only point out certain conditions or recommend certain actions, which the Secretary-General could consider or ignore as he chose. The relationship of the members of the International Staff/Secretariat to the Secretary-General was unequivocally laid down in the Staff Rules: 'All members of the International Staff/Secretariat of NATO are subject to the authority of the Secretary General, will be assigned to their duties by him, and will be responsible to him for the performance of their duties.'[32]

In a larger sense, decision-making authority, especially if money matters were involved, lay with the Council. As the go-between or representative of the Staff Association's interests with the Council, Lord Ismay did what he could, but in such essential personnel problems as recompense and housing—both of which required positive governmental approval before any ameliorative action could be taken—the Secretary-General's effectiveness was limited. And in security matters the governments were supreme. They were not obliged to explain

[32] Staff Rules, Art. 2.

why a clearance had been withdrawn, and, *ipso facto*, an employee without a governmental security clearance was automatically dismissed.[33] The Staff Association could not defend the interests of its members by instituting a proceeding against a government. In other words, the Staff Association could negotiate but could not bargain. To bargain required an element of ultimate compulsion which could be exercised by either party; in the case of the International Staff/Secretariat there was no leverage for collective bargaining because there could be no strikes or appeals to an outside disinterested tribunal. Appeals and complaints were handled individually within the Organization.

In spite of its legal limitations the Association did have some freedom in its activities, due primarily to the fact that it could raise its own funds. These came from the profits made from bingo and the sale of waste paper, and also from the sale of liquor and petrol, which the Staff Association was permitted to sell at the diplomatic price plus a slight profit. This money was used to finance the Association's various social and cultural activities and also to provide for a loan fund which members could draw upon.

Here again however the Association had no right of distraint if a borrower defaulted. To overcome this difficulty the Secretary-General agreed that the borrower's standing in the provident fund could be used as a guarantee. An applicant agreed in writing, at the time he made his loan application, that the Administration could withhold his investment in the provident fund to the amount of the loan if he left the Organization without settling his indebtedness. The general policy was that a needy applicant should approach the Administration first for an advance or a loan, and then apply to the Staff Association for any balance he might need. The Association would also help in the repayment of a loan or advance made by the Administration.

The Administration charged interest on long-term loans but not on short-term ones. A short-term, non-interest bearing loan was defined as a loan not exceeding three months' emoluments per calendar year.[34] To cover this loan the applicant

---

[33] ibid. Art. 9.   [34] ibid. Art. 20.

was restricted from borrowing in excess of his provident fund holdings. The amount of a long-term loan was limited so that it:

. . . shall not exceed the separation benefits to which the staff member concerned would be entitled were he to resign from the Organization at the time when he applies for the loan (that is to say, at present, one month's emoluments per year of service). Interest on such loans shall be at 0·75% above the rate received by the Organization for its deposits in Paris at the time the loan is granted.[35]

These loans were chiefly intended to assist in the buying of housing accommodation. Thus the Administration and the Association, by co-operating, were able to work out loan systems which were complementary and which at the same time ensured the maximum amount of service with the minimum amount of risk.

Closely connected with the loan programme was the Association's interest in alleviating the International Staff/Secretariat's housing problems which had plagued it from the beginning. When the announcement that headquarters would be in Paris was made at Lisbon in February 1952 one commentator observed:

The choice of Paris as Atlantic Pact Headquarters will certainly rejoice the hearts of that city's landlords. Swarms of foreign officials are forced to outbid each other for furnished apartments. Some now cost as much as £150 a month or more. Already five major international organizations are struggling for space there—SHAPE, OEEC, UNESCO, the Mutual Security Administration, the Financial and Economic Board of NATO.[36]

In spite of assurances from the French government that it would facilitate the acquisition of suitable housing, the International Staff/Secretariat was without formal assistance of any kind for its first year in Paris. It was not until July 1953 that the Council recognized the housing difficulty. Then it approved the creation of a rental compensation fund which enabled the Secretary-General, under certain conditions, to grant financial

[35] ibid.   [36] *Daily Mail*, 26 Feb. 1952.

assistance for housing based on a scale commensurate with income.[37] An applicant to the fund had to be a permanent full-time member of the International Staff/Secretariat, who had been obliged to spend more than 20 per cent of his total emoluments in rent;[38] he must not own a habitable dwelling in the Paris area; he must not be on probationary status or under notice of departure,[39] nor in Grades 2, 3 or 4.[40] In Grades 10 to 15 he had to be recognized as the head of a household.[41] A general proviso stipulated that the applicant must have made every effort to obtain suitable accommodation at a rent lower than that put forward in his rental compensation fund claim. In special cases, however, where the applicant did not fulfil these requirements, he was permitted to make a request to the Secretary-General that he should recommend to the Advisory Committee on Rental Compensation that the application warranted consideration. The Advisory Committee consisted of a chairman nominated by the Secretary-General, two members—one belonging to the French delegation and the other to a delegation named by the Budget Committee, and the Personnel Officer. The Personnel Officer acted as secretary to the Committee and informed the Secretary-General of its recommendations. The final decision rested with the Secretary-General. In order to prevent duplication or over-payment an applicant was not given rental compensation if he was receiving either an installation allowance or a separation benefit. This scheme remained in effect until 1956.

The Staff Committee frequently registered its dissatisfaction with the scheme. In September 1953 it made some proposals to the Financial Controller to facilitate the purchase rather than the renting of housing. These proposals were 'that a

[37] NATO Doc. ON(53)56.

[38] 'Total emoluments' was defined as the gross salary including the basic salary, cost-of-living allowance, expatriation allowance, head of family allowance, children's allowance, and the translator's and interpreter's allowance.

[39] If his appointment was confirmed the rental compensation could be retroactively applied.

[40] Recruitment in Grades 2, 3, and 4 was restricted to residents in the Paris area.

[41] Staff Manual, item 2340.

NATO agency be set up with a view to: 1. providing information and advice on flat and house purchasing; 2. guaranteeing approved commitments of this kind by NATO personnel; 3. making loans to NATO personnel at lower than market rates for this purpose'.[42]

In 1954 the Committee circulated a questionnaire requesting such housing information as: the number of persons who purchased new or old houses, flats, or villas; the amount of deposit required for purchase; and the rent paid for similar accommodation. The inquiry revealed that about 30 per cent of the International Staff/Secretariat wished to buy their housing and that they were ready to pay annual instalments sufficient to cover mortgage charges.[43]

The crux of the problem seemed to be the 50 per cent initial deposit required to obtain loans from the *Credit Foncier*. To help solve this problem the Committee requested the Administration to grant medium-term loans of up to five years' duration. It also contacted the French Ministry of Reconstruction and the Director-General of the *Caisse des Dépôts et Consignations* in order to find out whether, under French law, it might be possible to arrange for the construction of new housing especially for NATO personnel. This project was unsuccessful, however.[44]

The Committee found that three categories of personnel were primarily concerned with housing: first, married officers, usually in Grades 12 and above, with two or more children; second, personnel in Grades 1–5 who were inadequately housed; third, single girls, mostly not French nationals, in Grades 7 and below.[45] Since it was just these categories that

---

[42] Staff Committee Report, 1953–1954, par. 2 (a).

[43] Report of the 1954/1955 Staff Committee, par. 8.

[44] A survey conducted in Oct. 1955, by the Staff Committee revealed that nearly all members of the International Staff/Secretariat living in unfurnished, over-crowded accommodation were Grade 1–5 personnel. These grades had been excluded from the rental compensation scheme because they were usually recruited from the Paris area and thus would have had no special housing difficulties directly attributable to their having been employed by NATO.

[45] Staff Committee Report for the Year 1955/56, par. 6.

could least afford the high down payments to purchase accommodation, in 1956 the Staff Committee decided to devote its short-term loan funds exclusively to housing. Because of the limited sum involved (1 million French francs), the Committee granted these non-interest-bearing loans for improvements in the home, such as alterations, papering, and painting.[46] The establishment of the provident fund in 1957 enabled the Committee to work out with the Administration the home purchase loan arrangements described earlier.

The Group of Experts on emoluments (1955) recognized this problem when they recommended a revised rental compensation scheme. In their report the experts estimated that the old fund was costing about 5,000,000 French francs annually. Their major criticism of the old scheme was that it had subjected the loan applicant to what they called a 'means test', which was administered by an Administration committee. It was a test of both the individual's ability to pay and his efforts on his own behalf to find housing. The experts felt that under these circumstances employees had shown a 'serious reluctance' to bring their applications for compensation to the Committee.[47] Apparently, besides causing personal embarrassment, the system had led to friction. As the Staff Committee commented:

> In connection with the Rental Allowance Fund, the Committee continued to think that, as allocated at present, instead of helping those with real difficulties in respect of accommodation owing to the low level of their salaries, its main result is to create ill-feeling among the staff owing to the absence of clear rules with regard to allocation and uncertainty with regard to the basic principles underlying it.[48]

The experts did not question the need for the fund; they even suggested that the Administration, with the co-operation of the French government, should take a more active part in helping the International Staff/Secretariat with its housing problems. The Group had been 'impressed by the real difficulties of the accommodation position in Paris at the present time'.[49] It recommended:

[46] Staff Committee Report for the Year 1956/57, par. 29.
[47] 1955 Emoluments Report, par. 48.
[48] NATO Doc. CP/54-N/26(Final).
[49] 1955 Emoluments Report, par. 46.

That a general rental subsidy be granted, consisting of one half of the amount by which the actual rent paid by a staff member exceeds 20% of his total NATO emoluments, the maximum subsidy not to exceed 5% of those emoluments in any one case. No subsidy to be payable except on certification by the Rental Committee that the accommodation occupied is not more elaborate than is appropriate to the grade, position and family circumstances of the employee.[50]

The Council adopted the recommendation, and the new scheme was published on 24 July 1956.[51] In effect, this formula provided graduated compensation based on the salary scale, which included, as appropriate, the head of household and children's allowances. The necessity for a restriction of the applicants to certain grades had been obviated because the percentage of allowance for the lower grades was so small in actual sum that it did not materially affect the rental accommodations which were deemed sufficiently elaborate for these grades.

The formula reduced the eligibility requirements for rental compensation as far as possible to a mathematical calculation. An applicant had only to be a full member of the International Staff/Secretariat, not on probation, not owning a habitable dwelling in the Paris area, and paying a rent exceeding 20 per cent of his total emoluments. To sharpen the calculation, rent was defined as 'the actual rent paid by the occupant of the accommodation, exclusive of all charges, such as heating, lighting, water, gas, electricity, service, maintenance, etc.'[52]

A reconstituted Advisory Board of Rental Compensation Allowance consisting of the Director of Personnel, the Financial Controller, and a member of the International Staff/Secretariat met upon the call of the Personnel Officer. This Board screened the applications, decided on retroactivity, and rendered the judgement.

This scheme and the loan arrangements were steps in the right direction, but they were far from offering a completely satisfactory solution of the housing problem. This was another of those situations where the sympathy and co-operation of the Secretary-General could obtain only limited support from

---

[50] ibid. [51] NATO Doc. ON(56)35. [52] ibid.

governments. Unless the Administration requested the French government to assist employees to procure suitable housing at manageable cost, either by sponsoring new housing construction or by establishing special arrangements for purchases or rentals, there was little else that it could do short of recommending the Council to commit its own funds to actual construction. This request would, however, have met with considerable opposition in the Civilian Budget Committee, if not in the Council. The upshot was that the Administration and the Staff Association had to work out matters as best they could.

Agreement between the Staff Association and the Administration was not as complete on the subject of the Management Survey. The Staff Association aligned itself with the governments' Civilian Budget Committee in supporting this endeavour. The Administration, on the other hand, was not as convinced of the feasibility of the study or of the appropriateness of its timing. Late in 1955 nevertheless the Council approved the idea and asked the governments to nominate three to five persons to the Management Survey Team. Three experts were nominated: Mr. G. Beaudry of Canada who became Chairman, M. R. Gaudriault of France, and Mr. W. O. Hall of the United States. Mr. E. G. Luff of the United Kingdom, a member of the International Staff/Secretariat, served as secretary. The team was directed to report to the Secretary-General rather than to the Council, which gave Lord Ismay discretion in accepting or rejecting its recommendations. This procedure was of some importance for, if the Council did not endorse Lord Ismay's recommendations, in effect it would have risked having taken a vote of 'no confidence' in the Secretary-General. The experts were authorized to study the:

(a) organizational structure for accomplishing work objectives; (b) operational procedures and methods throughout the International Staff/Secretariat, but with particular attention to the administrative and servicing elements; (c) size, organizational disposition and position classification of staff; (d) personnel practices, as they have a bearing upon the effectiveness of work accomplishments; (e) space layout and equipment requirements for the new NATO Headquarters, paying particular attention to scientific work flow and conservation of effort measures; (f) records management, both as to active current files in operating units and central records control and repositories, including the security aspects of records management.[53]

Lastly, they were asked to consider whether a permanent Management Analysis Unit should be set up within the International Staff/Secretariat.

The Team interviewed the majority of the members of the International Staff/Secretariat both orally and through a post description form which they requested each member to complete. The experts asked for an estimate of the percentage of his time an employee devoted to each of his tasks and the qualifications he felt were required for the duties he performed.[54] The interviewing phase of the project took over two months to complete, which pushed off the completion of the survey from an estimated three months to over four months. Even at that the Team pointed out that 'in the short time available, it proved impossible to examine in detail all of the procedures followed within the Organization, both in the functional and administrative fields'.[55]

Another weakness of the report was the fact that, as the Team said: 'Only a few delegations availed themselves of the opportunity offered to express their views on the organization and thus, what might be termed the "users' point of view" could not be fully assessed.'[56] The Team cited as an example of this, its inability to evaluate the effectiveness of certain projects in the information field, such as the *News Letter*, because the effect of such projects on opinion within NATO could not be measured.

The major structural alteration to the organization of the International Staff/Secretariat that the Team considered— the reduction of the number of Divisions by the creation of two Deputy Secretaries-General, one for Defence Planning and one for Co-operation in Non-military Fields—was never formally recommended.[57] The effect of this alteration would have been to divide the work of the International Staff/Secretariat among a larger number of Assistant Secretaries-General

[53] General Report, par. 1.

[54] In order to ascertain the views of the Secretary-General, the Deputy Secretary-General, and the Assistant Secretaries-General, without interfering with their normal activities, the Team interviewed them at lunch.

[55] General Report, par. 4.   [56] ibid. par. 5.   [57] ibid. par. 23.

heading reduced functional areas and reporting to one or the other of the Deputy Secretaries-General. One of the reasons which worked against this administrative proposal was that it would have left only three top posts in the International Staff/Secretariat—those of the Secretary-General and two Deputy Secretaries-General—as against the five already existing. This development would have run against the pressure to provide as much national representation as possible in the highest echelons of the Administration.

Another possibility considered by the experts was merely to enlarge the number of Assistant Secretaries-General by placing each one in charge of a more restricted field of activity.[58] The objection to this proposal was that it would have 'created difficulties by widening the chain of command'.[59] In public administration parlance, the Secretary-General's span of control would have been stretched excessively.

Accordingly the Team retained the concept of three Assistant Secretaries-General, each heading his own Division, and one Deputy Secretary-General. But it recommended a different division of responsibilities. Under the recommended organization there would have been an Assistant Secretary-General for Defence Production and Review, an Assistant Secretary-General for Infrastructure and for Emergency Planning, and an Assistant Secretary-General for Political, Economic and Social Affairs.[60]

This reshuffling of responsibilities, which would have down-graded the Information Division and the Annual Review function of the Economics and Finance Division and up-graded the Infrastructure function of the Economics and Finance Division, was never adopted. Lord Ismay resisted any changes in his organization which would have upset his established administrative pattern. For example, though the report compensated in part for the down-grading of the Information Division by recommending the appointment of a Public Relations Officer assigned directly to the Office of the Secretary-General, and this position would have been the logical place for Mr. Geoffrey Parsons, Lord Ismay's Press

[58] ibid. par. 23.   [59] ibid. par. 24.
[60] ibid. par. 27.

Chief and Information Director, it would have reduced Mr. Parson's part in those operations of the information side of the International Staff/Secretariat not connected with the press. If, under the proposed reorganization he had retained responsibility for both functions, he would have reported on press affairs to the Secretary-General and on other information affairs to the Assistant Secretary-General for Political, Economic, and Social Affairs. The fact that Lord Ismay had upgraded the Information Service into a separate Division in 1953, so that information and press matters under Mr. Parsons could be reported directly to him, underlined his reluctance to have either the Division or its Director subsequently downgraded.

The report also proposed to make the Controller for Infrastructure, who in Lord Ismay's arrangement reported to the Assistant Secretary-General for Production and Logistics, an Assistant Secretary-General in his own right. There was considerable opposition to elevating the Controller to this position (*see below* Chapter XII). Thus, when Lord Ismay said:

There are, however, a number of suggestions which do not, in my judgement, take sufficient account of the peculiar complications which confront NATO (such, for example, as considerations of political expediency and the novelty of the problems with which we have to cope) or of the impact of contemporary personalities. . . .[61]

he was in a way merely stating a truism upon which he had acted from the beginning. The Council, apparently recognizing this, rendered the following decision:

The COUNCIL: having discussed the report of the Management Survey Team and the Secretary General's comments and recommendations on this report (C–M(56)90), recognized the Secretary General's responsibility for the organization of the staff and took note that he would initiate action forthwith to implement such of the Team's proposals as seemed to him desirable and within his competence.[62]

With this 'vote of confidence' the Secretary-General was able to continue with his organization as he saw fit. He made

[61] NATO Doc. C-M(56)90
[62] Summary Record of a Council Meeting.

only two major adjustments: he separated the internal administrative or housekeeping functions from the Office of the Executive Secretary, creating a new Administration Division; and he brought the secretariats to all the policy-making committees under the Executive Secretary.[63]

Both of these changes involved the Establishment Committee. This committee had been set up in 1952 to supervise and control the Establishment Tables of the International Staff/Secretariat, which were submitted annually to the Civilian Budget Committee for approval.[64] It consisted of the Executive Secretary (or an officer nominated by him), the Personnel Officer, the Financial Controller, and such other members as were co-opted.[65] The Executive Secretary was chairman, although at times he delegated this duty to another senior officer, often the Deputy Executive Secretary. In the early days of the International Staff/Secretariat this committee worked without minutes. It met to consider the Estimates submitted by the Offices and Divisions, and sent its recommendations direct to the Deputy Secretary-General, who added his comments and forwarded the entire document to the Secretary-General. If an Assistant Secretary-General objected to a decision of the Establishment Committee he might take his grievance directly to the Secretary-General rather than request the committee to reconsider its decision. This procedure was discouraged by the Executive Secretary and the Financial Controller.

The Executive Secretary himself submitted Estimates for his secretariat, thus he straddled the budgetary fence. In addition, until the Management Survey was made, he was responsible, as was pointed out earlier, for the entire internal administrative side of the International Staff/Secretariat. This situation was resolved when the new Director of Administration became Chairman of the Establishment Committee, and was made

. . . responsible for the general administration of the International Staff: . . . responsible for the preparation and execution of the Budget, for the maintenance of accounts, and for the internal control of all expenditure.[66]

---

[63] See Ch. VI for a detailed discussion of these changes.

[64] Staff Manual, item 1130.   [65] ibid. item 1800.

[66] *The North Atlantic Treaty Organization* (Paris, 1957), p. 40.

With the anomalous nature of the role of the Executive Secretary resolved, the Committee was able to conform more closely to the procedure laid down in the Staff Manual:

All proposals for changes in the approved establishment in the course of the current financial year will, in the first instance, be submitted in writing to the Personnel Office with a detailed statement of the reasons for any proposed change. The Personnel Office will submit these proposals to the Establishment Committee, which will consider them in consultation with the Head of the Division or Office concerned. When the latter and the Committee do not agree, the matter will be submitted to the Deputy Secretary General for a decision. . . . At least once a year the Deputy Secretary General will chair a meeting of the Establishment Committee, at which the Assistant Secretaries General will be present, for the purpose of discussing general establishment matters, and, in particular, individual promotions.[67]

Another change took place in 1956. Whereas for several years the committee had drawn up the entire budget and not only that part dealing with Establishment Tables, under the new arrangement its duties were limited to considering strictly Establishment matters.[68]

The Executive Secretary had also been involved in the process of delegating authority and responsibility for budget expenditures before the appointment of a Director of Administration. In September 1952 the Secretary-General had delegated to the Deputy Secretary-General, who in turn had delegated to the Financial Controller, responsibility for the control and supervision of International Staff/Secretariat expenditures. Along with this, 'the Secretary-General and the Deputy Secretary-General also designate the Executive Secretary, subject to the rules that follow and to the general financial control of the Financial Controller, to incur commitments on behalf of the Organization'.[69] The Executive Secretary could delegate this

[67] Staff Manual, item 1130.
[68] The Committee had also been involved in loans and in revising the Staff Manual, both activities, technically speaking, lying outside its purview.
[69] NATO Doc. ON(52)96. Staff Manual, items 1100, 1101. These documents had superseded NATO Doc. ON(52)10, which had been drawn up prior to the reorganization in 1952.

authority to incur commitments in his name to two members of his staff. The authority for the Financial Controller to pay salaries and wages was granted under a written authorization signed on behalf of the Executive Secretary by the Personnel Officer.[70] The same procedure was followed for the payment of allowances. In effect therefore the Personnel Officer served as the agent of the Executive Secretary in the authorization of the payment of emoluments. In 1955 this salary commitment authorization power was granted exclusively to the Personnel Officer.[71]

It should be noted that the budget for the International Staff/Secretariat was but a part of the much larger budget of NATO. The general provision was: 'The Secretary-General, the Supreme Commanders and the senior responsible officers of other NATO organizations will annually, at the latest by 1st September, submit to the Council the budget estimates for the following year.'[72] The Council referred the budgets to the appropriate Budget Committee, i.e. civilian or military, which was required to submit its recommendations to the Council before 1 December together with a summary of the budget proposals. The Council's deadline for granting approval was 1 January. Thus, if all went well, the NATO budget year of 1 January–31 December would be provided for.

To preserve a proper check on accounts the Financial Controller was required to submit an annual financial statement to the Board of Auditors by the last day of May after the close of a financial year. This Board was composed of three audit officials from member governments and was appointed by the Council. Both the Auditors and the Financial Controller were appointed for three-year terms which could be renewed once.[73]

[70] Staff Manual, item 1101.

[71] Lord Coleridge was also responsible for ensuring that adequate records were maintained of expenditures for telephone calls, cables, and postages, for the rents, utilities, and maintenance of the premises at the Palais de Chaillot, and for the procurement of supplies and materials. (Staff Manual, item 1101.) These jobs were passed on to the Director of Administration in 1956 in conference with the provision quoted on p. 164.

[72] NATO Doc. ON(55)60.

[73] NATO Doc. ON(55)60, and Annex thereto. The Budget and Accounts Officer was made Deputy to the Financial Controller.

So that the Secretary-General could submit the International Staff/Secretariat's budget to the Civilian Budget Committee by 1 September, the Financial Controller issued his directives on the preparation of the Estimates to the Assistant Secretaries-General and the Heads of Independent Offices by 1 July. The main requirement was for detailed justifications to be furnished for any new activities and for all extensions or reductions of existing activities. These Estimates were examined by the Establishment Committee, as mentioned earlier, and then approved by the Secretary-General. From the Secretary-General, they were sent via the Council to the Budget Committee, which was the place where the budgetary requirements of the International Staff/Secretariat were reconciled with the governments' willingness to support them. If the governments delayed in agreeing to a budget, the Secretary-General was given the following authority:

(a) For the purpose of financing authorised expenditure required to be made in the following year, pending the receipt of contributions to the budget for that year, the Secretary-General may: (i) on making the final assessment of contributions to the budget for the current year, increase the amount due under Article 14 by the estimated total of additional funds required to meet such expenditure; (ii) in the event a budget cannot be approved by 1st January, call for advances to be made to annual contributions authorised under Article 7(b).

(b) Such increases and advances shall be carried as a credit to the individual member governments concerned.[74]

The Budget Committee's consideration was the culmination rather than the inception of the reconciliation, however, for from the lowest level to that (ultimately) of the Council, the budget process was subjected to various pressures. For instance, if a nation had a particular interest which it desired to have expressed in the budget, it could transmit this desire through one of its nationals on the International Staff/Secretariat, who perhaps would suggest that the item be included in his Division's or Office's estimate. If this method was not successful or

[74] NATO Doc. C-M(55)18, Annex A. The Information Division was allowed to buy direct from the suppliers; otherwise all requisitions had to be submitted through the General Services Section.

if the item was opposed at another stage—perhaps in the Establishment Committee—the government could work with the appropriate Assistant Secretary-General or Office Head, or even with an Establishment Committee member, to have it retained.

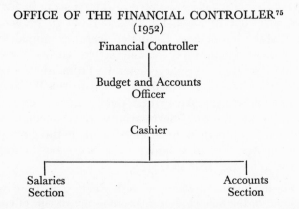

OFFICE OF THE FINANCIAL CONTROLLER[75]
(1952)

Financial Controller

Budget and Accounts
Officer

Cashier

Salaries   Accounts
Section   Section

If the Assistant Secretary-General supported the position of the interested government or if there was an item which he wished retained, he could either have one of his subordinate officers defend it before the Establishment Committee, or he could defend it himself, or he could wait until the budget had gone to the Deputy Secretary-General and exert his influence there. Lastly he could try to influence the Secretary-General.

If there was still resistance, the Assistant Secretary-General could attempt to convince a member of the Budget Committee —made up of national representatives—that the proposal should be reintroduced. A government likewise could reintroduce its suggestion on its own initiative in the Committee.

Occasionally in the Budget Committee a government made a reservation to an item in the budget, which it could either withdraw or press when the Council considered the budget. By doing this it obtained the time and the opportunity to 'lobby' for its point of view without directly obstructing the passage of the budget. Besides encouraging compromises over disputed items, this parliamentary device enabled the government to re-assess its interests until the last stage of the budgetary

[75] Staff Manual, 2 Feb. 1953, item 1017.

process. The budget was especially susceptible to this activity because it was drawn up, reviewed, and approved on a line-item basis, which required each item to be confirmed separately.

The Budget Committee possessed delegated authority from the Council to approve supplementary budgets, which widened the opportunity for giving expression to particular needs. The Management Survey Team criticized the excessive use of this authority when it said:

> The Team recommends that Budget estimates be prepared more carefully in order to avoid the need for having to reconsider two or three times during a period of four months, appropriations granted for a full financial year. The only normal justification for additional budgets should be important programme modifications or exceptional circumstances.[76]

In conclusion, as this discussion of the working problems and methods of the International Staff/Secretariat reveals, it was difficult to draw clearly the line between political needs and purely administrative needs. The two tended to become intertwined at nearly every point where policy played upon procedure.[77] The Secretary-General, the Staff Association, the Establishment Committee, and the Budget Committee all represented interests which at times coincided and at times did not. The work of the various independent Groups of Experts tended to soften these differences but by no means resolved them.

In the final analysis the governments, through their delegations, made the ultimate decision. But the requirement of unanimity in the Council and in Council Committees meant that the arts of compromise and adjustment had to be fully exercised in order to get policies adopted and the budget approved. As will be seen in Part IV, the same situation applied with equal validity to the so-called 'operating divisions' of the International Staff/Secretariat.

[76] This comment referred to items of equipment as well as to Establishment Tables. (General Report, par. 65.)

[77] For instance, when the German Federal Republic entered NATO, special consideration was given to placing German nationals on the International Staff/Secretariat. The politically important post of Deputy

ESTABLISHMENT—INTERNATIONAL STAFF/SECRETARIAT[78]
(1956)

Grades	Un-classified	15	14	13	12	11	10	8	7	6	5	4	3	2	Total
Secretary General Office	2		1		1			2	2						8
Executive Secretary		1	1			1			2						5
Secretariat			2	6					3	3					14
Conference Service			1	8	14	18	6	6	13	72		9	27		174
Registry				1			1	2	10	13	24				51
Building Section			1	1	1		7		1	1					12
Security			1	3		1		1	2	1		6	39		54
General Services				1	1		1	3	4	30	4		13	22	79
Personnel				1	1		2	1	8	9	2				24
Information Division			1	3	9	3	3	5	6	7	3				40
Statistics			1		4	1	5	6	3	4					24
Financial Controller			1	2	1	1	1	2	7	5					20
Political Division	1		1	2	3	2		1	3	2					15
Economics and Fin. Division	1		1	5	15	5	3	2	1	8	3				44
Prod. and Log. Division	1		2	20	26	6	2	3	17	14					91
Total	5	8	37	73	43	25	29	33	89	164	33	15	79	22	655

Executive Secretary happened to become vacant at this time and was offered to the German delegation. Priority of consideration for German nationals for posts in the Divisions as they became vacant was maintained until they were adequately dispersed.

[78] General Report, App. I. In 1954 the authorized strength was 627; the total number of appointments in all grades on 1 July 1954 was 596. (*The Five Years*, p. 67.)

PART IV

ADMINISTRATION OF
THE DIVISIONS OF
THE INTERNATIONAL STAFF/SECRETARIAT

'Making her debut at a NATO gathering, a young
matron sat silently through a two-hour discussion of the
Atlantic community. Afterwards, she thanked the
women to whose spirited pros and cons she had listened.
"I'm awfully glad I came", she said, "because I was
so terribly confused about the Atlantic community. Of
course", she confessed, "I'm still confused, but on a
much higher plane." '

Lester B. Pearson

'It seems clear that where the real driving force is a
political one, then economic considerations must take
second place. It is doubtful whether they have really
played much part in making up the minds of politicians
on an issue dominated by such questions as the sacrifice
of sovereignty, and the choice between supranational or
federal arrangements, or neither.'

A. M. Warburton and J. B. Wood

'Although NATO should be alert to seize every opportunity, however small, for augmenting its power and
authority, it should meanwhile only undertake in the
field of defence production, as indeed in any other field
of activity, that which it can successfully discharge
having regard to its *de facto* power and authority at any
time.'

Lieut.-General Sir Ernest Wood

'In infrastructure, member countries have worked together for the success of an enterprise which serves each
and every one of them. This is the very foundation of
the North Atlantic Alliance.'

Lord Ismay

CHAPTER IX

PRESS, PUBLIC, AND CULTURAL
RELATIONS

LORD ISMAY believed that one of his most important duties was to publicize NATO as much as possible. He felt that the Alliance could succeed only if the peoples of the member countries were convinced of its effectiveness and dedicated to its purposes.[1] He recognized that it was not enough continually to assure the Russians of the unity and steadfastness of purpose of the Alliance to resist aggression; it was almost equally necessary to convince the peoples of member countries of the existence of this unity and of the necessity for it. He said in 1952:

As I see it, one of the most important problems I have to solve is to give the average man and woman in Western Europe the conviction that if he or she will make certain sacrifices at this time, they can and will be defended in the case of attack, or better still that, if they will make these sacrifices, there will be no attack at all.[2]

He was very much aware that the general public in the member nations had only a limited knowledge about NATO. The findings of the International Press Institute at Zurich in 1954 confirmed his opinion. The Institute discovered that 79 per cent of the American people, 82 per cent of the British, 87 per cent of the Italian, and 89 per cent of the French had no idea what NATO was or what it stood for.[3] In May 1950, before the formation of the International Staff/Secretariat, the Council had agreed to establish an Information Service 'to promote and co-ordinate public

---

[1] Interview with Lord Ismay, 28 May 1959.
[2] *Daily Mail*, 16 Sept. 1952.
[3] Speech by Mr. Alastair Scott, officer in the Information Division, International Staff/Secretariat, 15 Nov. 1954. (NATO Speech Series.)

information in furtherance of the objectives of the Treaty while leaving responsibility for national programmes in each country'.[4] This arrangement remained unchanged throughout Lord Ismay's tenure of office. The actual carrying out of public relations projects rested with member countries.

On one level the Information Service had to seek publicity for Lord Ismay's own activities as Secretary-General. This chiefly involved relations with the press. On a different level there were the activities of the Information Division which worked under the direction of the Council Committee on Information and Cultural Relations.

The Director of the Information Service under the Deputies was a Canadian, Mr. Theodore F. M. Newton. He had been Consul-General for Canada in Boston before coming to NATO. He was a university professor who got into information work in Washington for the Canadian government during World War II. His Chief of Press and Public Relations was Mr. Geoffrey Parsons Jr., of the United States and his Chief of Editorial and Research, Mr. William Newton of the United Kingdom. Mr. Parsons had been Editor of the Paris edition of the *New York Herald Tribune*, and Mr. Newton, European News Editor for the BBC.

INFORMATION SERVICE[5]
(1952)

Director

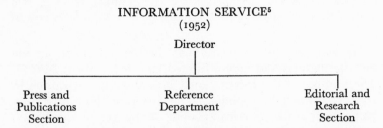

| Press and Publications Section | Reference Department | Editorial and Research Section |

This arrangement was carried over into the post-Lisbon organization except that the Information Service was placed within the newly-created Political Affairs Division.[6] After the departure of Mr. Newton in 1953, another Canadian, Mr. R. A. Farquharson, former editor of the magazine *Saturday Night*,

[4] *NATO Handbook* (London, Jan. 1952), p. 23.
[5] NATO Staff Manual, 2 Feb. 1953, item 1014.
[6] *The North Atlantic Treaty Organization* (Paris, Dec. 1952), p. 14.

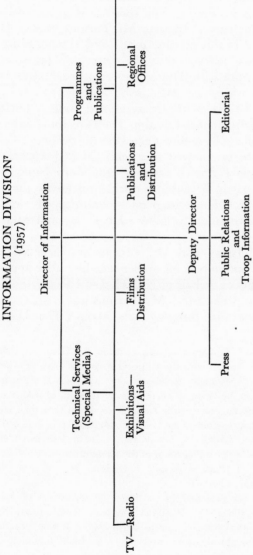

INFORMATION DIVISION[7]
(1957)

Director of Information

Technical Services (Special Media)

- TV—Radio
- Exhibitions—Visual Aids
- Films Distribution

Programmes and Publications

- Publications and Distribution
- Regional Offices
- Documentation

Deputy Director

Public Relations and Troop Information

- Press
- Editorial

[7] NATO Doc. ISM (57)4.

was appointed Director. Before Mr. Farquharson assumed the directorship, he made a report on information to Lord Ismay. All his recommendations were accepted. The Information Service was raised to the level of a Division, reporting directly to Lord Ismay instead of to the Head of the Political Division as it had done previously. The Director was also given direct access to Lord Ismay.[8] In 1954 Mr. Parsons became Director and continued in this position until Lord Ismay's retirement.[9]

Mr. Parsons believed that the Director's prime function should be to work with the press of member countries in order to obtain the widest and most favourable newspaper coverage possible for NATO. Lord Ismay agreed, and authorized the following steps to further this aim. The Director of Information would continue to have direct access to the Secretary-General[10] and he was to be allowed to attend Council sessions, partly because he spoke French fluently (and Lord Ismay was not fluent), and partly because he could thus advise the Council on its public relations and press programme. He would also be in a better position to know what to say and what not to say to the press.

Both Lord Ismay and Mr. Parsons also believed that, to reach the maximum possible audience in his public appearances and statements on behalf of NATO, Lord Ismay should himself become a 'personality'. Mr. Parsons was of great assistance to Lord Ismay in bringing this about. The Director of

[8] Under Mr. Farquharson's reorganization the Council's Information Committee was merged with the Cultural Relations (Art. II) Committee. The Canadian Permanent Representative was named Chairman and Mr. Farquharson, by virtue of his position as Director of Information, was appointed Vice-Chairman of the Committee. From that time on, during Lord Ismay's tenure of office, the Political Affairs Division had little control over information. Under M. Spaak, the Assistant Secretary-General for Political Affairs became Chairman of the Committee.

[9] Although Mr. Parsons headed a Division he was never made an Assistant Secretary-General.

[10] When it was proposed to continue the separation of information activities from the Political Affairs Division, the Assistant Secretary-General for Political Affairs was reluctant to agree. But he recognized that Lord Ismay thought the press and public relations function almost as important as the political affairs function.

Information thus became a very important person in the International Staff/Secretariat.

The result of the Director's work was that, from the relative obscurity of the Imperial Defence Committee and the British Cabinet, Lord Ismay, in the years he was Secretary-General, emerged as a familiar and well-liked figure on the international scene. He travelled a good deal and seized every appropriate opportunity to appear publicly while visiting member countries.[11] For instance, on a tour of Canada and the United States he travelled close to 7,000 miles, gave six public speeches (four of which were broadcast), two special broadcasts, eight press conferences, six off-the-record talks, and held seven official meetings.[12]

As to speeches, Lord Ismay was a warm, genial good-humoured, and informal speaker. He was fond of illustrating his points with anecdotes and finishing his remarks with a personal pledge of faith in NATO.[13] One of his favourite stories about the lack of knowledge of NATO was the following: 'At a party, the French Admiral, Georges Lemmonier, was pointed out to a guest as "Admiral NATO". "I say", said the guest, "I never saw a Japanese with such ruddy cheeks." '[14]

---

[11] Lord Ismay's travels took him to the following places during his first three years in office: *1952*: 18 July—Denmark; 22 July—Norway; 12 Oct. —Portugal; 16 Oct.—Italy; 25 Oct.—Holland; *1953*: 16 Feb.—U.K.; 4 Mar.—U.S., Canada; 11 May—Greece, Turkey; 14 Nov.—Belgium; 21 Nov.—Luxembourg; 6 Dec.—Big Three Bermuda Conference; *1954*: 24 Mar.—Belgium; 5 July—U.K.; 11 July—Iceland; 20 Sept.—Portugal. In July 1955 he made his first visit to the German Federal Republic. One observer commented: 'Ismay has emerged, even more than General Gruenther, as the real successor to Gen. Eisenhower as supreme figurehead and symbol of the Western Alliance.' (*Washington Post*, 15 Apr. 1956.) When the Secretary-General travelled, the host country handled most of his publicity.

[12] NATO Press Release, 2 Apr. 1953.

[13] His closing remarks were often: 'I believe with every fibre in my being that in the North Atlantic Treaty lies the best, if not the only, hope for peace. I believe that we are on the right road, and that we are gaining every day in strength, purpose and unity.' *Manchester Guardian*, 13 Mar. 1953.

[14] *Air Force Daily*, 22 Dec. 1953.

During his frequent trips, the need for constant affirmation of NATO's mission was repeatedly brought home to the Secretary-General. A story Lord Ismay liked to tell to under-score the continuing usefulness of NATO concerned a road outside a mountain village which passed a precipice with a sheer drop of 300 feet. The road at this point was so dangerous that the villagers had a wall built. Some years later a traveller returning to the village found that the wall had crumbled. He was told: 'It was unnecessary. There were no accidents.'[15]

In 1953 Lord Ismay announced that NATO had adopted a new flag which bore the four points of the compass against a circle, all of them in white against a blue background. Jokingly he said of this emblem: 'It enables me to have a flag on my car. I find that it makes an awful difference in a crowd.'[16]

In February 1953, in order to regularize his relations with the press and to encourage the distribution of NATO news, Lord Ismay inaugurated a policy of holding bi-weekly press con-ferences. The press commented at the time that these con-ferences 'should at least give an opportunity to clear up a lot of things for which NATO blames the press and the press blames NATO'.[17] Lord Ismay or his Deputy appeared before the assembled press representatives to make announcements, give statements, or answer questions. This procedure worked very well, partly because Lord Ismay briefed himself well on topics which might arise, partly because he used these occasions to underline positions which he felt should be emphasized, and

[15] *Daily Telegraph*, 31 Oct. 1956.

[16] *New York Herald-Tribune*, 29 Oct. 1953. Apparently several designs were considered, such as olive branches or shields, alone or in combination with the colours of the member nations. A member of the International Staff/Secretariat suggested a lighthouse, but later it was discovered that an insurance company was already using this emblem. Mr. R. A. Farquharson was chairman of the committee responsible for the NATO flag. He explained the flag's symbolism: the flag showed the four points of the compass, because the compass had led to the successful navigation of the Atlantic. The four points stood for NATO. The circle of unity around the four points of the compass star represented the Alliance. (Unpub. letter from Mr. R. A. Farquharson to Robert Jordan, May 1961.)

[17] *New York Herald-Tribune*, 20 Feb. 1953.

partly because he worked closely with his Director of Information.

One of the major difficulties between NATO and the press was the recurrent problem of getting news past the security barrier. The International Staff/Secretariat suffered in its public relations from rigid classification policies. The issue came to a head early in Lord Ismay's tenure of office. In October 1952 he wanted to release complete information about the airfield construction programme. He found to his annoyance that most of the information he would have used in speeches and press releases was classified. He suggested to the Council that security policies should be eased. He went on to say at a press conference: 'I well remember how when I was a technical intelligence officer I guarded my own secrets as a woman would her baby. But there can be too much of that.'[18] One final comment underscored his feelings about the matter: 'I confess to a sense of failure. And, if it is failure, the fault is my own—not the fault of my public relations staff. . . . Never in all the positions I have held have I felt so much in the dark.'[19]

Lord Ismay was in the dark in 1952 not only because of the classification problem but also because his relations with the Standing Group had not been clarified to the point where he knew exactly what the military side of the Alliance was doing,[20] and because there was a tendency at this time for member countries to deal bilaterally with one another rather than through the International Staff/Secretariat. Nevertheless the secrecy problem remained with him continuously. Security had to be constantly in mind when any public relations endeavours were being planned.

A significant concomitant to this situation was the fact that Lord Ismay had not only to convince the NATO military and civilian authorities of the effectiveness of a more generous approach to news but also to resist the reluctance of member governments to loosen up in this area. For it was the member

[18] *Manchester Guardian*, 30 Oct. 1952.

[19] *Daily Mail*, 9 Oct. 1952.

[20] In Oct. 1952 the Council authorized Lord Ismay to arrange with the Standing Group to provide the Council with more information about military affairs and to release more general military information to the public.

governments that looked with concern upon any policy that would bring to light information which they preferred to keep under their control. Thus, while the Secretary-General was attempting to get a freer flow of information to the public, member governments, through the Council, were resisting any loosening-up.

The normal pattern for the release of information—unless an Assistant Secretary-General gave a news conference—was for the Division or Independent Office to draft the news item, to clear it through the appropriate Assistant Secretary-General or Head of an Independent Office, and then to send it to the Information Division for final editing and release. But the most fruitful source of 'off-the-cuff' information for the press was often not the International Staff/Secretariat but the delegations. It was common knowledge that after a Council session the representatives of the press would be found, not in the NATO press room but in the lobbies buttonholing their contacts on the delegations. As one newspaper commented after a session of a Ministerial meeting:

The political discussion in the Atlantic Council was resumed this morning, when both Cyprus and the Middle East figured largely. The discussion was held in restricted session, and was supposed to be secret; but, with 80 people from 15 different nations present, secrecy is practically impossible to achieve, and reports of the debate, which appears to have been just as frank and outspoken as that of yesterday, are circulating here this evening.[21]

The methods of news-gathering from the delegations were many. There was of course the old temptation for the pressmen to play one delegation off against another. This was particularly effective when intra-NATO disagreements were under discussion. For instance, if the Greek delegation thought that the Turkish delegation was going to make a statement about Cyprus, then it might be tempted to rush a rebuttal into print. Or, perhaps, if a government thought that a proposal before the Council or a project under way by the International Staff/Secretariat, was opposed to its interests, but was reluctant to express its opposition publicly yet wanted to use public opinion to its advantage, it might find an appropriately-timed

21 *The Times*, 13 Dec. 1956.

'leak' the best way of accomplishing this objective. Or, if a smaller Power felt that one of the Big Three—or all of them—was pulling too much weight, it could object publicly and thus perhaps create a counter-pressure. Lastly the press could of course indulge in the age-old art of 'putting-two-and-two-together'. At all events, the locus of press information, if it was not with Lord Ismay, could more than likely be found with the delegations. Perhaps this by-passing of the International Staff/Secretariat was just another manifestation of NATO's non-supranational character.

Another reason for press reluctance to deal directly with the International Staff/Secretariat was its relative inaccessibility. Even the office of the Press Officer was located in the 'security area'. During working hours a journalist had to observe the following procedure if he wanted to see someone in Information:

All representatives of the press wishing to see a member of the Information Service will be directed by the Police to the entrance in the barrier on the Trocadero side [the 'back entrance' of the building]. At this entrance they will be admitted on showing their press identity card and will enter the fifth floor offices by the small door which gives direct access. Should it be necessary to conduct any member of the press or other visitor through the partition which separates the 'free' area from the restricted area on the 5th floor, a passport or identity document will be deposited with the Security Guard and a Visitor's Pass issued in accordance with the instructions laid down above.[22]

Any persons—including journalists—who desired to visit the office of a member of the International Staff/Secretariat had to undergo this procedure:

Visitors must always be escorted while within the restricted area of NATO Headquarters. When a visitor arrives at an entrance, the Staff at that entrance are responsible for telephoning the office of the staff member whom the visitor wishes to see, obtaining permission for the visitor to proceed to the office of the staff member concerned, and for escorting him to that staff member and handing the staff member the visitor's pass. At the conclusion of an interview, the staff member concerned is personally responsible for the visitor

[22] NATO Doc. ON(52)29.

until he is outside the security area. To ensure this, the staff member concerned should complete the visitor's pass, timing it and signing it, and then escort him to the entrance personally, or arrange for this to be done by another staff member or by *huissier*.[23]

These arrangements made the International Staff/Secretariat fairly inaccessible. The result was that the press library, which was outside the secure area became a reading room for the International Staff/Secretariat rather than a reception centre for the use of members of the press. It was more convenient and possibly also less compromising for a journalist to work with the delegations.

To safeguard documents each Division or Independent Office had an officer who was called the 'documents distribution officer' for his Division or Office. It was the duty of this officer to establish and maintain lists of persons authorized to receive certain categories of classified documents and to work in co-operation with the Head of the Registry and the Security Officer in implementing security regulations. The general rule was that documents should be distributed on a strict 'need to know' basis.

Only certain persons of the higher officer grades were authorized to originate the topmost security documents—in other words, to classify a paper as TOP SECRET or COSMIC TOP SECRET. This limited authorization was instituted in order to minimize the number of highly classified documents, because such documents were subject to special, and at times onerous, procedures of maintenance and distribution.

In 1957 Section Security Officers were appointed with the following duties:

The functions of the Section Security Officers will be mainly advisory rather than executive. Their duties, under the authority of their respective Heads of Division, will be: (*a*) to give advice to the staff within their divisions/sections on the application of the Security Regulations and procedures and to assist in the promotion of a high general standard of security. (*b*) In consultation with originators, to keep under review the classification of documents originated in their divisions/sections in order to ensure that this is neither too high nor too low. (*c*) To assist the Central Registry in

---

[23] NATO Doc. ON(52)108; NATO Doc. ON(57)58.

arranging periodical reviews of documents within their divisions/ sections with a view of downgrading or return to Registry. (*d*) To maintain liaison with the Security Bureau/Security Services on matters of security and to make suggestions for the improvement of security.[24]

To reduce the responsibility of possessing or storing classified documents, pleas and revised procedures were issued periodically encouraging their destruction. That this problem was never successfully overcome is clear from the fact that the pleas had to be reiterated and the destruction procedures altered.

Lastly, to discourage the circulation of unclassified documents, which, though raising no security problem, concerned administrative or other matters which it was inadvisable to expose to the comments of persons outside the Organization, a classification level called 'NATO UNCLASSIFIED—FOR OFFICIAL USE ONLY' was added to the five already in use— COSMIC TOP SECRET, TOP SECRET, SECRET, CONFIDENTIAL, RESTRICTED.

By and large these security regulations proved effective. It was especially important for them to be so, not only because of the aid and comfort secret documents would have given to any potential enemy of NATO, but also because of the distress a significant compromising incident would have caused in the Alliance. Apart from the work of the economic and logistic agencies in NATO, which were involved in the continuous interchange of information based on reports and questionnaires passing between the International Staff/Secretariat and member governments, the Alliance in its political aspect was especially sensitive to unauthorized leaks. Foreign Offices are notorious for their secretiveness, not only because they feel that it is important to safeguard the integrity of their participants in diplomatic negotiations but also because they do not want to embarrass their own or another government in its domestic political situation. For example, at times the Council discussed matters which could become the subject of partisan political debate within one or more of the member countries: the Cyprus problem, the siting of airfields or troops, or the length of conscription. If a security compromise was to occur,

[24] NATO Doc. ON(57)17.

members of the International Staff/Secretariat wanted to rest assured that they were not responsible. This extreme caution gave rise to jokes and cynical comments about NATO's 'secrecy phobia'.

The problem of security protection versus the need and right to promote an informed public opinion—a problem faced by every democratic country—was unresolved during Lord Ismay's tenure of office. And it is difficult to see how a really satisfactory solution could have been found to such an important and controversial matter. The diversity of interests was too great. The policy Lord Ismay adopted was that the Secretary-General, in co-operation with his Director of Information, should become the chief agent in generating public interest in and support for the Alliance, but at the same time he should enforce strict internal security regulations to prevent the unauthorized or careless compromise of information. He wanted the maximum information freed from security restrictions, but he also wanted strict control over classified information.

Lord Ismay believed in the desirability of sharing information about nuclear weapons. In this he was enthusiastically supported by the majority of the member countries. He consistently advocated the repeal or amendment of the American McMahon Act in order to enable the United States government to release to its allies more information about American atomic weapons research and the use of atomic weapons. He was signally unsuccessful, although the blame should not be laid at his feet. The problem was tied up as much with American domestic political predilections as with the needs of the Cold War.

Besides its press activities the Information Division had the responsibility of promoting NATO in the broad field of public and cultural relations. This responsibility was however restricted to 'working in cooperation with the national Information Services of member countries . . .'.[25] Although member governments recognized the need for liaison and co-ordination

[25] *The North Atlantic Treaty Organization* (Paris, 1956), p. 39. Those countries which were most insistent on distributing information exclusively through government channels (Norway and the U.K.), also had the better national programmes.

of information activities, this seemed to be as far as they cared to go; there was never any suggestion from the governments that these activities should be centrally executed or uniformly applied. The nearest they came to this position was in a recommendation made by the Council's Committee on Information and Cultural Relations in response to a Council Resolution that the scope of information about NATO in member countries should be enlarged:

The Committee therefore recommends that member governments should, by such means as they deem appropriate, ensure co-ordination of national activities intended to enlighten public opinion as to the aims and ideals of NATO and the dangers which the Organization was set up to resist, as well as to make the peoples of the Atlantic Community better known to one another. To this end governments who wish to ensure more effective co-ordination should establish a centre of co-ordination and/or one or more officials, to maintain liaison between national services on the one hand, and NATO on the other.[26]

When national information officers met together at the Palais de Chaillot, as they occasionally did, the variation in the diffusion of national responsibility among governmental bodies became manifest. For instance, a survey of the delegates to a conference held in January 1954, produced the following list: Belgium—the Chief of the Office of Information and Cultural Affairs in the Ministry of Foreign Affairs; Canada—the Chief of the Defence Liaison Division in the Department of External Affairs, the Head of the London Office of the National Film Board, the Public Relations Officer of the First Canadian Infantry Division, a Representative from the RCAF Air Division at Metz; Denmark—the Head and the Assistant Head of the Information Division in the Ministry of Foreign Affairs; France—the Director, Under-Director, and two officers of *secrétaire d'ambassade* rank of the Information Service in the Ministry of Foreign Affairs, four officials of the Information Service in the Permanent General Secretariat of National Defence, and seven officials of the Information Service in the Ministry of National Defence; Greece—the Director-General of Press and Information to the Presidency of the Council;

[26] NATO Doc. C-M(54)52.

Iceland—a member of the Icelandic delegation to NATO; Italy—the Chief of the Press Service in the Ministry of Foreign Affairs, the Chief of the Press Bureau to the Presidency of the Council; Luxembourg—the Assistant to the Director of Information and Press Service of Luxembourg; The Netherlands—the Director of Information in the Ministry of Foreign Affairs, the Director of the Army Information Service; Norway —the Head of the Information Service in the Ministry of Foreign Affairs, the Head of the Information Services in the Ministry of Defence, the Head of the Division for Cultural Affairs in the Ministry of Foreign Affairs; Portugal—the National Secretary for Information, the Chief of the Press Bureau in the Ministry of Foreign Affairs; Turkey—the Director-General of Press, Radio, and Tourism; the United Kingdom—an Under-Secretary of State in the Foreign Office, representatives from the Information Policy Division of the Foreign Office, from the BBC, and from the Central Office of Information; the United States—a Special Assistant from the Office of the Assistant Secretary of State for Public Affairs, a representative from the Department of State's Office of European Regional Affairs.[27]

With such a diversity of channels through which to work, it could never be easy for the International Staff/Secretariat to co-ordinate plans and projects. The Committee of Three on Non-military Co-operation in NATO made the following recommendations in an attempt to alleviate the difficulties:

In order to facilitate co-operation between the NATO Information Division and national information services, the following specific measures are recommended:

(a) an Officer should be designated by each national information service to maintain liaison with NATO and to be responsible for the dissemination of NATO information material;

(b) governments should submit to NATO the relevant information programmes which they plan to implement, for discussion in the Committee on Information and Cultural Relations. Representatives of national information services should take part in these discussions;

[27] NATO Doc. AC/87-D17. This list does not include representatives from the delegations or from the NATO military commands.

(c) within the NATO Information Division budget, provision should be made for a translation fund so that NATO information material can be translated into the non-official languages of the Alliance, according to reasonable requirements of the member governments;

(d) NATO should, on request, provide national services with special studies on matters of common interest.[28]

There were a number of reasons why the International Staff/Secretariat was not permitted to station NATO public relations and cultural officers in member countries. For one thing the governments felt that they were in a better position to judge the appropriateness or the emphasis of public relations projects. They felt that some information might appropriately be distributed by one country but not by another. This attitude stemmed partly from various national traditions about a government's engaging in domestic propaganda activities: for example, the United States Congress always resisted any tendency of the Executive Branch to engage in this 'non-democratic' activity.[29] The line between education—inform-ation—propaganda—counter-propaganda—political warfare—could be drawn differently according to a country's political traditions and foreign policies. Every government felt therefore that it should decide in which category a NATO information or cultural relations project should be placed.

There is also a natural tendency for governments to resist expenditures which are not deemed 'essential', which is another way of stating the truism that a government is not inclined to give to an international organization money which it could use for purely national purposes. Domestic expenditure can nearly always be more easily justified than expenditure incurred in foreign activities, and especially in those projects where control over funds has to be shared with other countries.

[28] 'Report of the Committee of Three on Non-military Cooperation in NATO', as reproduced in the *NATO Letter*, Vol. 5, Spec. Supp. to No. 1.

[29] In countries without government information machinery two other ways of promoting an effective NATO information programme were open: (1) to allow agents of NATO into the country; (2) to accept projects disseminated by a centralized domestic information service. Neither way was used. Another weakness was that Foreign Offices are unsuitable agencies to carry out domestic information programmes.

A further reason for the failure to develop a NATO-controlled public and cultural relations programme—and one which had been foreseen by the Committee of Three—was that, owing to the multi-lingual character of the Alliance, the risk of a misunderstanding of a phrase in translation, resulting in a change of meaning or implication was much greater if material was disseminated by a non-national office. It would also have been burdensome for NATO information officers if they had had to work in all the languages of the member countries.

A prime reason for the lack of consensus in public and cultural relations during Lord Ismay's tenure of office was the differing assessments by member countries of the nature of the Communist threat—apart from the actual armies of the Soviet Union. For example, the attitude towards Communism of Italy, where there was a large Moscow-subservient Communist party engaged in partisan political activity, differed from the attitude of Denmark, where the question of Communist activity in domestic politics was largely academic. In Denmark the Communist problem was seen in terms of Danish foreign policy towards Russia; in Italy it was seen in part as a domestic subversive issue. Whereas Italy, Greece, and Portugal wanted NATO assistance to counter subversive Soviet propaganda, the United States, the United Kingdom and France, all of which engaged in well-organized counter-propaganda operations of their own, were not interested.

In sum, many projects suggested by the Division were not carried through, owing to lack of money or of adequate terms of reference, or of domestic support and encouragement. Opposition came in either the Budget Committee, the Committee on Information and Cultural Relations, or the Council.[30]

Notwithstanding these difficulties the Information Division was able to embark on several worthwhile projects. One of the most successful and one which coincided with Lord Ismay's interest in good press relations was the tours for journalists drawn from member countries. The idea originated in 1952.

---

[30] Some members of the International Staff/Secretariat thought that the Budget Committee was the real master of the Information Division. It was at this point that the dual scrutiny of cost and policy coincided.

The host country drew up the itinerary, made all the arrangements, and paid the expenses of the tour within its borders. NATO paid travelling expenses to Paris (for general introductory briefings about NATO) and to and from the host country. In the host country the journalists met the leading political and public officials, visited various cultural, industrial, or topographic objects of interest, and inspected some NATO facilities. The Information Division provided an escort officer for the tour.[31] These tours were very favourably received by all the parties involved—the host country, the sending country, the journalists themselves, and NATO. In fact so many tours were made that, after the first few years of the project, governments had difficulty in nominating leading journalists who had not already been on a tour.

Another early project was the NATO Caravan of Peace. This Caravan was a mobile exhibit built around large truck-trailers which could be driven from town to town in the member countries and shown to local populations. It was financed primarily by the United States and was especially well received in Greece, Turkey, and Italy.[32]

The Division did not neglect the written word either. In 1953, after a conference of national information officers, it decided to publish a *NATO News Letter*.[33] This began life as a mimeographed document, but by 1956 it had become a printed multi-paged bulletin. Much of the news it contained was assembled from press clippings of subjects of interest to most of

[31] In 1955 the Information Division adopted a particular theme for each tour, e.g. agriculture in Denmark; communications and transport problems in Belgium, Luxembourg and The Netherlands. This idea did not work out very well, primarily because member governments nominated journalists who were not expert in the chosen theme. Another weakness of the programme was the host country's tendency to show too much. In some countries NATO paid *per diem*; arrangements for domestic costs varied according to country.

[32] The idea of the mobile caravan came from the Train of Europe, which had been used by OEEC. The entire information budget was supplied out of USIS funds until 1951 when the international budget was instituted. After that certain programmes were financed from ECA funds, such as the caravan, whose trailer-trucks were provided by ECA.

[33] The word 'News' was dropped from the title almost at once.

the NATO countries. The *Letter* was not the official mouthpiece of the NATO Council; rather it was a bulletin of the International Staff/Secretariat and its usefulness was as much documentary and archival as informational. Under Lord Ismay the International Staff/Secretariat was careful not to print stories which might offend any member country.[34]

The distribution of the *Letter* was handled in two ways. In Canada, the United Kingdom, the United States, the German Federal Republic, and The Netherlands, the national authorities sent it out. Bundles were made up by the International Staff/Secretariat and sent to the delegations. Thence they were forwarded to the appropriate agency in each country. For the other countries, distribution was direct from Paris on an *ad personam* basis. In May 1957 29,000 English and 4,000 French language copies were printed.[35]

Probably the most enduring of the Division's projects undertaken during Lord Ismay's tenure of office was the publication of the book *NATO The First Five Years 1949–1954*. The suggestion for the book came in 1953 from Mlle. Eve Curie, who at that time was an assistant to Lord Ismay. Lord Ismay took a strong personal interest in the book and considered it one of his best public relations achievements in NATO.[36] The non-military chapters were largely drafted by Mlle. Curie and Mr. John Vernon of the Information Division. The military chapters were drafted by officers attached from SHAPE and were reviewed by the Standing Group. The final writing was done by Lord Ismay and was based upon these drafts.[37]

[34] Only once, when the U.K. objected to an article about British arms shipments to Tunisia, did a delegation complain about a violation of this policy.

[35] The *Tass* and *Pravda* correspondents were included in the mailing list. The *Tass* correspondent once complained that the Polish news representative got his copies before he did, and implied that the West was trying to curry favour with the Poles. After M. Spaak became Secretary-General, the *Letter* contained articles of a more controversial and more analytical nature.

[36] Interview with Lord Ismay, 28 May 1959.

[37] At first he did this work at home in the evening, but later he took it to his office, to the consternation of those persons who wanted his attention for other matters.

The book had to be approved by the Council, so the Permanent Representatives were asked to comment on it. One major difficulty of co-ordination rested with the International Staff/Secretariat itself. Every Division or function of the International Staff/Secretariat discussed in the book wanted sympathetic treatment and the same amount of space. The book, being an 'agreed text', was a carefully-written factual account of the earlier years of the Alliance. It did not emphasize any particular aspect of NATO nor was it a critical survey. It was first available as a paperback in English and French. Later, Italian and Turkish editions were published, financed partly by NATO and partly by the governments concerned. It was issued free in large numbers to all NATO Staffs and Commands.

Another publication was the *NATO Handbook* which was brought up to date every year and reissued. There was also a NATO picture book, printed in The Netherlands in all the NATO languages.[38]

Motion picture publicity for NATO was handled for the most part on a decentralized basis. Most of the money for films was provided by the United States, and British motion picture specialists usually supervised their production. American MSA funds only were used to finance the film 'School for Colonels' (about the NATO Defence College), and the fifteen Atlantic Community Series of films. This series consisted of a film about each member country. Before a film was made about a particular country, that country reviewed the script.[39] Local film people were brought into the project as much as possible. The film 'Around This Table' (about the Council) was

---

[38] Just at the time the book was completed the final debate on EDC and its rejection by the French Parliament took place. This event temporarily disconcerted the planners of the book, for the International Staff/Secretariat could not know how so important a political development would affect NATO. After much discussion they decided to leave the book as it was and to add as supplementary appendices the documents of the London and Paris Conferences of October 1954, with no accompanying discussion.

[39] The Portuguese and Turkish governments especially wanted the films made about their countries to be written and produced according to their specifications.

financed two-thirds by United States MSA funds and one-third by NATO.

The best-known film made about NATO was 'Alliance for Peace' which was produced in 1949 under the auspices of SHAPE, and which gave an outline of the *raison d'être* of the Alliance. It has been re-edited three times. As 'Why NATO?' it was made in the languages of all the Alliance countries and shown to groups visiting the Palais de Chaillot as well as being widely distributed in every NATO country.[40]

The reception of visiting groups was one of the main functions of the Information Division. These groups ranged from youth organizations to trade union delegations. The total number of groups which visited the Palais de Chaillot in 1957 was 132, comprising 4,574 persons.[41]

Whenever possible Lord Ismay appeared before these groups to speak and to answer questions. He believed strongly that in the eyes of the visitor to NATO there was no substitute for the top man—even if he was not necessarily the best speaker available.[42] Very often the Director of Information or the Assistant Secretary-General for Political Affairs also appeared. When Mr. Parsons was Director of Information he tried to meet at least one out of four visiting groups. If there was a qualified national on the International Staff/Secretariat of the same nationality as the visiting group he was asked to meet the group. This variety of speakers—and variety of visitors—resulted in flexibility in presentation and by and large produced an intimate and personal approach which avoided the stiltedness of a uniform, set-speech reception. The appropriate delegation to NATO was notified of the scheduled arrival of a group from its country, and very often gave a cocktail party for the group. When dinners were given, informality was stressed and there was a minimum of protocol. Usually a tour was

[40] The third edition was made for the tenth anniversay of NATO, under the title 'The Atlantic Decade'.

[41] NATO Doc. AC/52-D(58)11.

[42] Interview with Lord Ismay, 28 May 1959. Partly owing to proximity and partly to the publicity given by the governments, most visiting groups came from the German Federal Republic, France, and the Benelux countries.

planned so that the group could visit not only the headquarters at the Palais de Chaillot, but also NATO headquarters at SHAPE and at AFCENT (Allied Forces Central Europe), and possibly the NATO Defence College.

The Information and Cultural Relations Committee thought that the reception of visiting groups was extremely valuable because this was the only point at which the International Staff/Secretariat met the people of member countries directly, and the only public relations activity which did not have to depend upon the intermediary action and support of member governments.[43]

Closely allied with the programme for the reception of visiting groups was the troop information programme which had been set up in response to a resolution of the committee made in 1954. The Committee decided that troop information and education should remain a national responsibility but that NATO should act as a clearing house for troop information publications and should supply the military forces with as much NATO material as possible. They also decided that the Information Division should conduct short courses for officers and senior non-commissioned officers.

The Officers and NCO's were nominated by their countries and drawn either from units in the field or from a staff position, whether from a unit committed to NATO or not. With the British Army of the Rhine and the United States Army, the quotas were supplied directly; otherwise, they were handled through the appropriate National Defence Ministry and in some cases through a NATO Command.

Two courses were offered. The longer course lasted four and a half days, and included visits to SHAPE and AFCENT, and a lecture by a representative from SACLANT. In addition a large number of military groups were sent for one-day briefings. These briefings were held for such groups as cadets from

[43] The only other project which brought nationals of member countries into direct contact with NATO—other than those in the Armed Forces— was the Fellowship programme. This programme began just before Lord Ismay retired, so at that date it had not had any appreciable influence on public and cultural relations. (Speech by Lord Ismay, 30 Sept. 1955. NATO Speech Series, No. 69.)

military academies, national defence colleges, and troop information or community relations officers.

Some courses were composed entirely of officers from a single nation; others were mixed. Most of the national courses were held for Canadian, German, American, or British officers. Up to 1960 these courses had a yearly annual attendance of 360 students. The average yearly attendance up to 1960 for courses composed of a multi-national selection of officers was 210. Between 1,100 and 1,200 persons a year attended the one-day briefings.[44]

In the field of radio the International Staff/Secretariat was not able to accomplish very much. Any direct radio activity was precluded through the restrictive policy on public information.[45] The only possibility open was for the Information Division to make up some 'canned' radio programmes for distribution in member countries, but this idea could not be carried out because European radio stations would not accept such programmes. The stations already broadcast the Voice of America and United Nations Information Service programmes of this type. The most the Division could do was to include radio journalists in the tours for journalists.[46] Efforts were made, however, to interest 'neutral' radio stations in carrying NATO public information material.[47]

Although the NATO library was not strictly a part of the Information Division, it came under this Division as much as any other. It was started in 1951 on a book grant given by the United States State Department. Most of the books were purchased from a list drawn up by the Information Service. When the unified budget was established the library was placed

[44] The only qualification for attendance made by NATO was that the student must have a working knowledge of one of the two official NATO languages.

[45] The only exception to this rule occurred during Ministerial meetings, when a direct broadcast was sometimes made from the Palais de Chaillot to member countries.

[46] The benefits from this activity were far from certain, because the journalists always reserved the right to write whatever they wanted to about NATO.

[47] The Information Division's radio, television, films, and exhibitions activities came under the Special Media section established in 1954.

under the General Services Section. After that, purchases were made partly in response to requests from the International Staff/Secretariat and partly from the usual book review notices.

In 1956 a Library Committee, upon which sat a representative from each Division, was formed to assist in this function. But the Committee's major work was to supervise the clipping library. Many of the requests for research materials made by the International Staff/Secretariat concerned subjects of a more contemporary nature than could usually be found in published books; therefore the clipping service became increasingly useful as the political activities of the Council grew. The service was instituted in February 1951, but it was not attached to the library until the end of 1956.

Closely connected with the clipping library was the day-to-day news summary which was taken partly from the teletype service of the major news agencies and partly from the daily newspapers. Mr. Parsons reviewed the news of the day and sent to Lord Ismay those items which he thought the Secretary-General should see.[48]

Although there were no official sub-libraries some of the Divisions collected their own specialized libraries. This could be done since, during Lord Ismay's tenure of office, the authority for the purchase of new books rested with the individual Divisions. The Economics and Finance Division, especially, found it useful to assemble a library which concentrated mainly on documents.[49]

The library was not involved in the mailing of the *NATO Letter*, nor was it responsible for supplying documents or copies thereof in response to requests either from within the International Staff/Secretariat or from journalists, scholars, or public servants in member countries. The mailing of the *Letter* was handled by the Information Division. Documents were supplied by the Registry.

In summary, the press and public relations functions of the International Staff/Secretariat during Lord Ismay's tenure of

[48] In particular, *The Times* had to be read, for Lord Ismay liked to 'keep in touch'.

[49] In later years the Political Affairs Division built up a documents file on political subjects.

office had to follow an uneven course.[50] The press function was largely conducted by Lord Ismay, working with his Director of Information within the limits placed upon them by the security policies of the Council. The information and public relations function had to be carried out on a pragmatic basis by the Information Division, depending upon a government's reaction to a proposal and its support of it.

The many-sided and paradoxical nature of NATO's military policies has generated a voluminous literature which is a form of publicity. A large part of this literature originated from private sources. It chiefly centres around questions of the atomic age and politico-military strategy. The extent to which this publicity increased the general public's awareness of what NATO was doing and how it did it was not accurately measured during Lord Ismay's tenure of office.[51]

If NATO's 'message' was not understood by the people of the world, the fault lay not so much with the efforts of the Information Division as with the international political facts of life. The Council increasingly became a bargaining agent in the Cold War; it took up such vital and encompassing issues as a German peace treaty, rearmament, disarmament, disengagement, economic prosperity, internal security, and aid to the under-developed areas of the world. These issues, the Council and the Secretary-General came to realize, could not be separated from NATO's interests. They were however issues which the International Staff/Secretariat had to handle very circumspectly. Agreement among NATO countries, if

[50] A lot of publicity has been given to the work of such extra-NATO organizations as the Atlantic Treaty Association and the NATO Conference of Parliamentarians. Strictly speaking, these groups did not come within the scope of the Information Division's public relations activities. The Division did, of course, co-operate with them as much as possible. The development of such organizations within the member countries was considered to be most valuable, in view of the limitations placed upon the Information Division. They were able to provide a service which NATO could not readily perform for itself.

[51] Public opinion polls conducted by the International Staff/Secretariat were ruled out as interfering too closely with domestic matters. The polls about NATO conducted within every country up to this time did not deal specifically with the effect of this literature on the public's understanding.

obtainable, was often only one step in the protracted process of negotiations either between East and West, or within the United Nations or some other grouping of nations. As Mr. Parsons rightly pointed out, information and politics could not be separated;[52] in fact information was a form of politics.

[52] Interview with Mr. Parsons, 22 Sept. 1958.

CHAPTER X

THE ECONOMICS AND FINANCE DIVISION

IN order to place the economic and financial functions of the International Staff/Secretariat in their proper perspective it is necessary to go back into the pre-Lisbon history of the Alliance. Although, on the military side, the planners of NATO had been able to draw upon the planning and staff work begun by the staff of the Brussels Treaty Organization (Western Union), no significant progress had been made toward reconciling military needs with economic means prior to the signing of the Treaty in April 1949.[1] By the following November, however, the Council had decided to set up a Defence Financial and Economic Committee, with a permanent working staff located in London and headed by a secretary.[2] The Committee was composed of national representatives of Ministerial or equivalent rank, who were to report directly to the Council. Its terms of reference were:

(*a*) To develop in co-operation with the Military Committee (including the Standing Group) and the Military Production and Supply Board overall financial and economic guides to and limits of future defence programmes, including military production programmes, which North Atlantic Treaty countries as a group and individually should undertake within available financial and economic resources.

(*b*) To appraise the financial and economic impact on member countries of major individual defence projects formulated by the Military Production and Supply Board or the Military Committee (including the Standing Group) including consideration of financing problems and availability of raw materials, capital equipment, and

[1] Ronald S. Ritchie, *NATO: The Economics of an Alliance* (Toronto, 1956), p. 36. The most significant economic work done by Western Union was in the field of Infrastructure. See Ch. XII.

[2] Final Communique of the North Atlantic Council Second Session, as contained in *The Five Years*, pp. 178–81; see Chart, p. 21 above.

manpower, and, on the basis of such review, make recommendations as to action on such projects.

(c) To recommend financial arrangements for executing military defence plans, and particularly financial arrangements for the interchange among North Atlantic Treaty countries of military equipment, surplus stocks, or materials, and equipment to be used in producing military equipment.

(d) To measure and to recommend steps to meet the foreign exchange costs of imports of materials and equipment from nonmember countries required by defence programmes under the North Atlantic Treaty.

(e) To consider, as may be found desirable and appropriate, plans for the mobilisation of economic and financial resources in time of emergency.[3]

In 1950 military events stimulated the Committee to come to grips with the very complex problems of multi-national financial and economic planning. Shortly before the outbreak of hostilities in Korea in June 1950 the Council had come to realize that, if the objective of 'balanced collective forces' was to be achieved, it would be necessary for 'the problem of adequate military forces and necessary financial costs [to] be examined as one and not as separate problems'.[4] But the practice of this principle came later. By September 1950 'The Council agreed upon the establishment at the earliest possible date of an integrated force under centralised command. . . .'[5]

In response to these actions the Council Deputies in October 1950 authorized the creation of an Economic and Financial Working Group:

. . . based upon the delegations to the Organisation for European Economic Cooperation of all NATO countries. This new working group, which, it is hoped, will hold its organisation meeting very shortly in Paris, will enquire how statistical information provided to the OEEC by NATO countries may be adopted so as also to serve the purposes of NATO. This working group will recommend what additional information should be furnished by NATO countries in

[3] ibid. p. 179. These terms of reference have been quoted at length because they were broad enough to cover the remaining history of the Division.

[4] Final Communique of the North Atlantic Council, Fourth Session.

[5] Final Communique of the North Atlantic Council, Fifth Session (resumed).

order to assess the impact of their defence efforts on their economies and also their relative abilities to carry the burden of expanded defence requirements. It will advise on measures necessary to ensure that the economic data submitted by NAT countries adequately reflects NATO defence planning. In this way, the Council Deputies hope to take advantage of the accumulated statistical background, the technical skills, and the habit and tradition of working together internationally in the field of economics that the OEEC delegations have developed over the past three years.[6]

Thus began a long and intimate association between NATO and OEEC. There were several advantages to be gained from this association. First, unnecessary duplication of effort in the economic field was avoided. Secondly, the participating nations were able to use OEEC's specialized staffs for NATO projects, thus reducing the strain on member countries' limited resources of economic specialists. Thirdly, it was possible to bring into NATO's calculations the potential contribution of the German Federal Republic to Western European rearmament, because in 1950 the German Federal Republic was a member of OEEC but not of NATO. Representatives of the United States and Canadian governments participated in meetings of the OEEC Council although neither country was a full member.[7]

By February 1951, from being an agency for facilitating the allocation of funds under the United States European Recovery Programme (Marshall Plan) for post-World War II economic recovery, OEEC had become an organization for protecting the economies of Western Europe from the threat of inflation due to rapid re-armament.[8] The outcome of this

[6] NATO Press Release, No. D-N/40.

[7] *The Organization for European Economic Co-operation* (Paris, 1953), p. 12.

[8] The 1951 report of the Secretary-General of OEEC to the OEEC Council listed five anti-inflationary recommendations: 1. Restriction of credit in order to make money harder to obtain; 2. Increase in coal and steel production; 3. Increase in European production of goods and 'feeding stuffs' otherwise imported, so as to conserve shipping space; 4. Increase in production, both in Europe and abroad, of such raw materials as sulphur, cotton, rubber, which were scarce; 5. Harmonizing of controls over the production of essential items. The report also dealt with the stabilization throughout the non-Communist world of prices of raw materials, which had been skyrocketing as a result of increased war production and stockpiling.

redirection of the American economic assistance programme was the creation of the Mutual Security Administration (MSA) as the successor agency of the Economic Co-operation Administration (ECA).

By May 1951 the economic and financial activities of the Alliance had grown so important that the Council authorized the establishment of a Financial and Economic Board (FEB), and at the same time incorporated the Defence Financial and Economic Committee into the Council. This Board met in Paris in order to be near OEEC and recruited an international staff under an international budget using as a cadre the staff of the Economic and Financial Working Group. Its duties were:

To examine economic and financial problems created by the joint defence effort; to advise on the equitable distribution of the burden arising from joint defence; and to advise the other organizations of the North Atlantic Treaty responsible to the Council of Deputies, and especially the Defence Production Board, on all economic and financial matters arising in the course of their work.[9]

M. Paul Leroy-Beaulieu, former economic and financial adviser to the French High Commissioner in Germany and an *inspecteur de finance*, was elected Chairman; Mr. Eric Roll, the senior member of the British delegation to OEEC and Minister Plenipotentiary, was elected Vice-Chairman.

The Board's first task was to assess the replies to extensive and detailed questionnaires which had been sent to every member nation by the Economic and Financial Working Group. These questionnaires dealt with such subjects as relative national and individual incomes, existing tax burdens, industrial capacity, and raw material resources. However, even this Board, with its international staff and its high-ranking membership coming directly under the Council Deputies, was unable to master the problem. The former Chairman of the Council of Deputies described the situation:

As the military plans were produced by the Chiefs of Staff and the Supreme Commander, and as the elaborate process of calculating

[9] *The Times*, 26 May 1951; see Chart, p. 25 above.

the costs of raising, maintaining and equipping the required forces was worked out, it became apparent that there was a *spread* or *gap* [his emphasis] between the forces and equipment which the member nations had planned to make available to NATO and the number of such forces and amounts of such equipment which were stated to be required by the military planners. The problem emerged in the summer months of last year, as a result of staff work by the military and civilian agencies of the Treaty Organization. It took on an aspect of overriding importance not only because of the very substantial figures involved and their impact on the economies of each member, but by reason, in particular, of the deterioration of the financial position of the two most important treaty partners on this side of the Atlantic [i.e. Great Britain and France]. Clearly, there had to be an over-all reconciliation of the claims of the military plans upon the economy of each member, of the most authoritarian sort. In effect, the combined military budgets and the costs of the military plans had to be brought into balance. On the one hand it was necessary to safeguard the economies of the treaty partners against greater defence burdens than they could bear, and, on the other, the commanders responsible for our protection had to be given definite assurance as to the forces and equipment to be made available to them.[10]

The FEB agreed with these points and recommended to the Council that the military and economic aspects of the question should not be considered separately, and that the analysis should not be made exclusively on a country-by-country basis, but that total costs should be assembled and applied against total resources.

It should be noted that during this period military requirements, both in men and equipment, had been the subject of protracted and detailed negotiations. The appointment of General Eisenhower as Supreme Commander, Allied Forces Europe, in January 1951, gave impetus to the drive towards a rapid build-up of forces-in-being under an international command. Member countries—as well as NATO—were finding it difficult to keep pace with the effect of this build-up on their domestic military and economic situations. It thus became ever more needful for NATO to improve its planning procedures.

[10] Speech by Mr. Charles M. Spofford, 20 Mar. 1952. (NATO Speech Series, No. 12.)

The Council came to grips with the problem in September 1951 at its Ottawa meeting. There the Foreign, Defence, and Finance Ministers first sat down to consider the problem jointly. On the one hand, they directed that the proposed military force and equipment targets should be weighed against the cost factor. They wanted to find out in economic terms, what the military planners were asking for, and then consider ways of cutting down the estimates if possible. On the other hand they wanted to assess the member countries' ability and willingness to support the military plans.

To reconcile the 'requirements of "fulfilling a militarily acceptable NATO plan for the defence of Western Europe and the realistic political-economic capabilities of the member countries" ' the Council appointed a highest-level *ad hoc* committee called the Temporary Council Committee (TCC).[11] It was in the work of the TCC that one of the most significant functions of the International Staff/Secretariat germinated.

On the OEEC side the importance of this situation was recognized when, in August 1951, the Foreign Ministers or their Deputies of the eighteen member nations of OEEC met to prepare a series of reports on the subject, which were presented at the Ottawa Council meeting.

The TCC—or the 'Twelve Apostles', as its members were called—consisted of Cabinet Ministers or Ambassadors of all the member countries and was the first committee which had been given the authority to negotiate directly with the Standing Group, the Military Representatives Committee, and the Supreme Commanders in one direction, and the governments in the other. It was asked to render a report to the Council at the Ministerial meeting to be held at the end of November 1951 in Rome.

At the inaugural meeting of the TCC Mr. Douglas Abbott, Canadian Finance Minister, nominated Mr. W. A. Harriman of the United States as Chairman; Mr. Eric Brofoss, Norwegian Minister of Trade nominated Mr. Hugh Gaitskell of the United Kingdom as one of the two Vice-Chairmen, and the Belgian Minister of Finance, M. J. van Houtte proposed M. J. Monnet

---

[11] *The Five Years*, p. 44.

of France as the other Vice-Chairman.[12] Two days later the three TCC officers were formally installed as the Executive Bureau (or 'Three Wise Men') which became the main operating agency for the TCC. Mr. Siverd Nielsen of Norway, a member of the Deputies' staff, was named administrative secretary. Then the TCC adjourned until 26 October to let the Three Wise Men go to work.

Although the FEB had an international staff upon which the TCC could have drawn, it preferred to assemble its own staff, mostly borrowed from the delegations. The United States in particular wanted a large staff, for it felt that the more thorough the job, the less likelihood there was that any one nation would be unjustly dealt with for lack of adequate information. The method which the TCC employed in some ways paralleled that of the FEB: questionnaires were sent out to all member countries requesting detailed information, to cover the next three years, on their re-armament programmes and their industrial and financial capacity to support these programmes.

The TCC wanted to know about the numbers of regular and reserve groops countries were proposing to raise, the state of their training, the types of equipment available for future defence production and the plans for using it. Questions were asked about the cost of defence programmes, their impact on all sectors of the economy, the measures which were being taken to meet this impact, and additional measures which could be taken by the countries, acting together, to strengthen their economies.[13]

As the replies came in the staff of the Executive Bureau studied them and assembled them into a form useful for further individual and comparative study. Then each country had its reply appraised by a committee of experts and by the Bureau. When a particular country's programme was considered, the representative of that country on the TCC sat with the Execu-

[12] A general election was imminent in the U.K. and Mr. Gaitskell, as Chancellor of the Exchequer, felt he could not serve actively, so he was represented by Sir Edwin Plowden. *L'Humanité* headlined the election of Mr. Harriman as Chairman: *'Harriman, dictateur atlantique va decider les affaires françaises.'* (10 Oct. 1951.)

[13] *The Five Years*, pp. 44–45.

tive Bureau. The Bureau could add other members when it felt that they were needed, which was especially the case when the programmes of the United States, the United Kingdom, and France were under consideration.[14] When this process had been completed the full TCC met in order to make a final examination of the work of the Executive Bureau.

This examination was characterized by a frankness on the part of the delegations which was unusual in such delicate matters, invading as they did the innermost recesses of a nation's national existence. But neither the Bureau nor the TCC had been empowered to take decisions; they could only make recommendations to the Council.

Working parallel with the Executive Bureau's staff was the Screening and Costing Staff headed by General Joseph T. McNarney of the United States and including representatives from Britain, France, and Belgium. Their task was to screen the military inventories and estimates drawn up by the NATO Commands in order to pare them down as closely as possible. The relative opulence of the American army made this task particularly important. For instance, the fact that an American division cost approximately 100 million pounds a year to maintain, and a Turkish division approximately 7 million pounds a year implied that not all of the extra 93 million pounds for the American division was being spent as frugally as possible, although doubtless much of the difference was due to greater mechanization and higher American pay levels.[15]

It was also pointed out that 'General McNarney's former command, EUCOM, still lists 626 officers, including 21 generals and 120 full colonels, although many of its responsibilities had been taken over by the U.S. 7th Army. EUCOM

[14] The U.S. was represented at its interrogation by Mr. Frank Pace, Secretary of the Army, Mr. Richard Bissel, acting ECA Administrator (in place of Mr. Harriman), Dr. Fleischmann, Head of the U.S. Defence Production Board, and Mr. Frank Nash, Assistant Secretary of Defence; the U.K. by the Chancellor of the Exchequer, Mr. R. A. Butler; and France by a strong delegation of six Ministers, including M. René Mayer, Minister of Finance, M. Georges Bidault, Minister of National Defence, and the Chiefs-of-Staff.

[15] Anne M. Warburton and John B. Wood, *Paying for NATO* (London, 1956), p. 37.

headquarters at Heidelberg are sometimes referred to as "Pentagon on the Neckar".[16] But the argument lay not entirely against the Americans. A case was reported of one member country listing among its equipment shortages enough vehicles to give each of its divisions twice as much wheeled transport as had been included in the Tables of Equipment of a United States division.[17]

The Screening and Costing Staff also examined every nation's over-all military production programme. In doing this it had the support of NATO's Defence Production Board (DPB) and the help of the research it had accomplished. The Staff was organized into four teams: force analysis, logistics, budget study and cost analysis, and co-ordination.

The Executive Bureau worked toward a deadline of 24 November, the date set for the Rome meeting of the Council, but delays kept occurring which threatened to prolong its work beyond that date. For example, by 3 November only four countries had replied to the questionnaires—Britain, which was the first, followed by The Netherlands, Belgium, and Iceland.[18] France had delayed its submission pending notification by the American government of the amount of aid it would grant her. The French economic situation was so perilous at that time that this assistance would determine whether she could or could not undertake certain commitments. By 10 November only three countries' programmes had been examined by the Bureau—those of The Netherlands, Norway, and Iceland. The following days were devoted to the United States, Britain, and France.

As the work progressed, delay became certain for two reasons. The first was a disagreement among the members of the Executive Bureau as to the proper approach to defence planning. M. Monnet argued that it was not possible to consider long-term planning goals, stretching out into 1953 and 1954, as anything resembling definite commitments. He based his opinion on two factors: the inability to assess the Russian threat so far in advance; and the inability of nations, e.g.

---

[16] *New York Herald-Tribune*, 27 Oct. 1951.

[17] *New York Times*, 3 Dec. 1951.

[18] *Financial Times*, 3 Nov. 1951.

France, to plan their defence programmes so precisely, especially when United States aid was an integral part of them.[19] Mr. Harriman and Sir Edwin Plowden, by contrast, wanted to plan over a three-year period, aiming toward a maximum force of complete readiness by 1954.

The second reason for the delay was the complicated nature of the assignment. It was not possible to pull together all the pieces into a comprehensive report by the time of the meeting. When the Council met in Rome, instead of considering the full report, they heard a progress summary. The Council's communiqué stated tersely:

> The Chairman and one Vice-Chairman of the Temporary Council Committee informed the Council of the progress of the Committee's work directed toward the reconciliation of military requirements with political-economic capabilities. They stated that the Committee's final report and recommendations would be presented early in December for the consideration of member governments and the Council at its next session.[20]

Accordingly, the full interim report was circulated to the member governments in December. Mr. Harriman hailed it as a milestone in the association of the Western Powers. He called it 'the first comprehensive review of how the resources of the member countries under peace-time conditions can best be employed in the interests of common security'.[21]

The report was divided into four parts: first, a preamble which gave a synthesis of the work and the general principles underlying the project; second, a general discussion of the military and economic problems involved and the achievement goals proposed, concentrating primarily on 1952; third, a breakdown of each nation's position in the programme, prepared on an individual basis; and, fourth, the proposals for reorganization. Separate annexes took up in detail each nation's condition, with observations thereon.[22]

---

[19] American foreign aid was authorized and appropriated on an annual basis, in spite of frequent assertions both at home and abroad that the Administration should be given authority to enter into longer-term commitments.

[20] Final Communique of the North Atlantic Council Eighth Session.

[21] *The Times* and the *Manchester Guardian*, 19 Dec. 1951.

[22] *Financial Times*, 11 Dec. 1951.

The report had found eight countries deficient in some way —France, Belgium, Canada, Denmark, Italy, Luxembourg, Norway, and The Netherlands. Only three were judged to have been making a military effort commensurate with their capabilities—the United States, Portugal, and Britain. (Iceland was not considered because it did not have any military forces.) The Finance Ministers who assembled at the December meeting of the TCC to receive the interim report agreed that they should transmit it to their governments before registering official reactions. None of them was willing to accept without reservation the new burdens envisaged in the annexes. They decided to meet again in January to prepare 'a supplementary report for the Council meeting at Lisbon based on comments by governments and NATO agencies on the Report just completed'.[23] The reconciliation of the governments' policies— political as much as economic—could then be made by the Council. It was necessary for the governments to assess not only the equitability of the report, but also the extent to which they could convince their respective parliaments of the need to act upon it. In some cases this was no easy matter, because the NATO assessment represented almost the entire defence budget and involved almost the whole of the armed forces.

The reaction of some governments to the findings of the report—and especially to the annexes—was sharp. The Belgian government thought that the recommendation that Belgium ought to devote 8 per cent of its gross national product to defence during 1952 was unfair. It would increase Belgium's defence spending by over 35 per cent. It was reported that 'the executive bureau's conclusion was rejected outright in an angry reply that challenged its statistical information, procedure, method, judgement and competence'.[24]

The report suggested that Belgium's surplus industrial capacity should be used to assist in the re-armament of other allied countries. The financing of this undertaking could come from credits voted by the Belgian government. But the Belgians pointed out that it was impossible for them to extend

---

[23] Statement by Mr. Harriman, Chairman of TCC, 18 Dec. 1951. (NATO Press Release, No. 28.)

[24] *New York Herald-Tribune*, 1 Feb. 1952.

financial facilities, either by grant or by loan, beyond the credits granted and the commitments still to be honoured by Belgium in the European Payments Union (EPU) where its credit standing was very high.[25]

The initial French response, as made by M. Monnet at the TCC Committee meeting, was to accept an increase in defence spending. But later M. Monnet's action was disavowed by the Cabinet. The French government encountered difficulty in expanding its defence effort by the recommended 5 per cent because the National Assembly had just substantially reduced the amount of the tax yield which the government had sought in order to cover the expenditure in the budget originally contemplated, and because the government was still waiting to find out how much financial assistance it could expect from the United States.[26]

The Italians objected to their treatment and claimed that the cost of repairing the damage caused by recent extensive floods would limit the financial resources available for defence.

Although the United States escaped criticism, the report suggested that it should buy more finished products from Western Europe for its own defence programme in order to help solve the balance of payments problem of its allies; and also that it should pay for these 'off-shore purchases' through the EPU, thus strengthening the EPU's ability to facilitate currency reconciliations. The report also recommended that the United States should distribute aid on a multilateral basis through NATO rather than on the usual bilateral basis.[27]

[25] The same suggestion had been made to Belgium at an OEEC Council meeting.

[26] See Dorothy Pickles, *French Politics* (London, 1953), pp. 117–37 for a description of events leading up to the 1951 French budget crisis. For a very readable account of the relationship between NATO policies and French domestic politics during this period, see Alexander Werth, *France 1940–1955* (London, 1956), Pt. V.

[27] In fact, the combined military budgets of France, the U.K. and the U.S. represented about 90 per cent of the total military expenditure of the Alliance. Therefore, although the smaller Powers might have balked at an upward reassessment of their share because of the domestic economic impact, in global terms the issue was not as significant as it otherwise appeared.

General Eisenhower, the best-known and most influential military leader in NATO (and it was the high military estimate that had provoked the economic crisis), was careful to avoid giving the impression that the report was intended to compel governments. He emphasized that 'it is up to each country to decide what it can do. I am sure that each will make the best effort'.[28] He refrained from endorsing any of the specific recommendations for increased defence expenditure. In addition he admitted that the build-up plans for defence would still apply even if some governments felt that they could not meet the goals set by the report.

At the pre-Lisbon meeting of the TCC in January 1952 Belgium, Canada, Denmark, and Norway submitted supplementary replies, which 'helped to affirm an atmosphere of basic agreement on objectives'.[29] The TCC for its part progressively reduced the earlier estimates of defence spending and produced a combined 'supplementary report' to the interim report, in which the United States government agreed to 'expand its off-shore purchasing programme, the Canadian and Belgian governments agreed to make an additional effort to finance re-armament, and the Norwegian and Danish governments agreed to extend their national military service from twelve to eighteen months.[30] On the military side the Defence Ministers met to consider the estimated strength goals, with a view to perhaps readjusting them.

Another complicating factor which emerged was the reluctance of the government of the German Federal Republic to agree to an estimate of its share of defence costs. If the German government refused to make this contribution, the calculations of the TCC would be upset, and a larger contribution would have to be made by the other countries. The problem was resolved when the Executive Bureau consented to make an estimate of what they believed the contribution ought to be and submit it to the Council meeting at Lisbon.[31]

[28] *Sunday Times*, 16 Dec. 1951.

[29] *New York Herald-Tribune*, 9 Feb. 1952.

[30] One of the Belgian government's objections had been that Belgium was the only country with a twenty-four month conscription period.

[31] The need for this action arose when the Allied High Commissioners in Germany were unable to come to an agreement with the Chancellor,

When the Council met at Lisbon it 'took detailed and comprehensive action based on the recommendations of the Temporary Council Committee'.[32] It agreed that the principles of work applied by the TCC should be incorporated into the Council's normal working methods and should be carried out in the newly approved International Staff/Secretariat. At the time Lord Ismay took office the Council issued the following policy statement:

The Council and the International Secretariat should in particular be so organized as to perform the functions of reconciling the NATO programmes with politico-economic capabilities. The precise method by which the Council and the International Secretariat should be organized to carry forward this task on a continuing basis will be determined by the Council in the light of the TCC recommendations and with the advice of the Secretary-General. However, the following steps appear to be required: (a) Continuing screening and costing of military plans. This may require a section of the International Secretariat organized and technically equipped for the purpose. This Section should work closely with the military agencies of NATO; (b) Annual review of economic capabilities. For their work in connection with this review the International Secretariat may require to be temporarily augmented by analysts and experts in the economic, military and other fields, as appropriate; (c) Final determination by the Council of annual programmes, including force targets and programmes required for the supporting build-up of forces.[33]

The Council thus deposited on the International Staff/Secretariat a problem which had vexed the Alliance almost from its beginning, and which had reached such proportions that it had been lifted out of the regular context of Alliance activity and organization and incorporated into a 'crash' operation of

---

Dr. Adenauer, who had insisted that his country's ability to pay should be assessed not by the High Commission but by NATO. The U.S., the U.K. and France agreed on two conditions: the right of the three countries to ask for financial support for non-European army divisions stationed in the German Federal Republic must be acknowledged; detailed negotiations must be left to the officials of the High Commission and the German Federal Republic.

[32] Final Communique of the North Atlantic Council, Ninth Session.
[33] NATO Press Release, 4 Apr. 1952.

the first magnitude. The nagging pre-occupation of the Council Ministers with this unresolvable dilemma, and the semi-public Debates which had paced each new development, were bequeathed to Lord Ismay to bring under control. This was by far his greatest responsibility during his first year in office.[34]

A helpful event which coincided with the Lisbon decisions was the OEEC Council's decision made at its meeting held in March 1952, to expand OEEC's activity in complementing NATO's economic and financial functions. The Council approved two resolutions; the first proposed that OEEC should undertake an annual review of the economic position and prospects of its member countries, and invited the United States and Canada to participate; the second proposed a general examination of the internal financial situation of member countries.[35]

The exact division of work between the two organizations was indicated by NATO's Assistant Secretary-General for Economics and Finance:

> For the performance of its economic functions, NATO makes use of basic statistical data supplied by the OEEC. But many elements of the defence programmes are of an extremely secret nature, and their economic implications can only be examined by the NATO services. The latter endeavour to evaluate for themselves the economic and financial position of member countries.[36]

The Council provided that NATO's Annual Review should establish firm goals for the following year, provisional goals for the second year, and planning goals for the third year. Then, at the end of a year, the provisional goals would be reviewed

[34] Interview with Lord Ismay, 28 May 1959.

[35] There was some talk at this time of curtailing OEEC's operations and staff considerably, and lodging NATO's economic and financial needs exclusively with NATO. The opposition, led by France and the U.S. preserved OEEC's role. The neutral nations—Switzerland and Sweden—supported the contention that NATO and OEEC should remain separate. The British were the prime movers in reducing the scope of OEEC's activities, and, largely on their insistence, OEEC's budget (and therefore its staff) was nearly halved in 1952–3. It was also suggested that OEEC should become the economic arm of the Council of Europe.

[36] Speech delivered by M. René Sergent, undated. (NATO Speech Series, No. 13.)

before becoming firm goals, the planning goals would be reviewed before becoming provisional goals, and so on.[37] A country was formally committed in any year only to the firm goals.

The fiscal year for NATO was set from 1 January to 31 December in line with the following reasoning:

The ideal would be for all the NATO partners to have identical fiscal years. This, of course, is not the case. Six member governments operate on a calendar fiscal year; four have fiscal years commencing within three months after the beginning of the new year; and the other four governments, including the United States, operate on a July–June fiscal year. At the same time, the calendar year basis is not inconvenient for the United States since the President traditionally submits his budget message as early as January: A Review that is concluded in November or December enables the United States to take account of the plans and commitments of its allies in developing recommendations on its vitally important aid programme. It has been agreed that NATO should, for its own planning, work on the calendar year basis.[38]

With the setting up of the International Staff/Secretariat not fully completed until May 1952, and recruiting for most of the positions not finished until July, it was imperative for action on the 1952 Annual Review to be started as soon as possible in order to meet the December deadline. The Economics and Finance Division had acquired many of the expert personnel who had worked with the former FEB, but it should be recalled that the FEB's staff had not been used to the fullest by the TCC which had used its own staff in large measure. Therefore, with the co-operation of OEEC, the Division had to undertake this initial, precedent-setting review with a relatively inexperienced permanent cadre. To help overcome this deficiency and to provide the additional staff needed, experts were loaned to the International Staff/Secretariat.

General supervision of the operation was provided by the Annual Review Committee, a Council committee presided over by the Deputy Secretary-General. In the absence of the Deputy Secretary-General, the Assistant Secretary-General for Economics and Finance acted as chairman.[39] The most

---

[37] *The Five Years*, p. 90.   [38] ibid. p. 92.
[39] In 1955 the holder of this office was appointed Chairman.

important question, in terms of method, which the Annual Review Committee had to decide at the outset, was how to co-ordinate all the various parts of the review process. The process, in brief, was:

> January–March—drafting of the Questionnaire in the light of previous experience and agreeing on a modified procedure for the Review; March–July—issue of planning guidance by Supreme Commanders, visits to each capital by special military teams, and completion of the Questionnaire by member governments; July–October—analysis and discussion of national programmes and drafting of final report; November—consideration of report by governments, followed by Council meeting at Ministerial level for adoption of force goals.[40]

The Annual Review Committee agreed that a steering committee should be formed to provide co-ordination. However there was disagreement as to the character of the committee. One proposal was for a steering committee composed of seven members of the Annual Review Committee, which would act as its executive agent, but which would be unable to take separate decisions. Countries not represented on the steering committee would be free at all times to participate.[41] A variation on this proposal was the suggestion that the committee might consist of, first, a small number of representatives nominated by the Annual Review Committee, who would be under an obligation to attend all meetings of the committee, and who would bear the responsibility for the work of the Annual Review; and, second, representatives of any other country wishing to participate.

There was strong opposition to the creation of a steering committee whose membership was restricted in any way, and it was proposed that the seven-man limit should be regarded as a definition of a quorum rather than of a fixed composition. In this way all countries would be on the same footing, since the division of members into categories of obligatory and optional attendance would be avoided. It was felt that many decisions which would be taken during the process of the

[40] *The Five Years*, p. 92.
[41] The equivalent body to the Steering Committee in the TCC operation was the Executive Bureau.

Annual Review would be of a political nature, and therefore it would be unwise to exclude any countries from the steering committee.

The upshot of this discussion was agreement to maintain the Annual Review Committee in its entirety for the over-all supervision of the Annual Review, and to create a steering committee composed of members of the International Staff/ Secretariat to conduct the day-to-day co-ordination and supervision. The Annual Review Committee, on behalf of the Council, would make only a general statement as to the objectives of each Annual Review and the points in which the Committee was especially interested, and would leave the responsibility of working out detailed procedure with the steering committee.

All in all, as the review process worked itself out, the bulk of the planning, supervision, and execution of the Annual Review rested on the International Staff/Secretariat. At first the co-ordination and execution of the Annual Review were carefully maintained on a formal basis, but after 1953, with the growth of confidence in the procedures and people, more informal relations grew up among the various parties. This tended to give more flexibility to the activities of the steering committee and to allow more initiative to the International Staff/Secretariat.

The Deputy Secretary-General was named chairman of the steering committee; he was assisted by the Assistant Secretaries-General for Political Affairs, Production and Logistics, and Economics and Finance, the Head of the Office of Statistics, and the Standing Group Liaison Officer. The Deputy Executive Secretary served as secretary, and was made responsible for co-ordinating the activities of the secretaries assigned to the various technical teams and working groups.[42]

The first step in the Annual Review was the issuance of the questionnaire according to which the countries would:

. . . describe their defence efforts along the following lines: the actual programme in military terms of the forces they propose to raise; the material which is expected to be available, whether from

[42] Interview with Lord Coleridge, 2 Aug. 1958.

home production, foreign purchase or mutual aid deliveries, and steps being taken to fill any deficiencies; the financial aspects of their plans and their relation to the economic capabilities of the country.[43]

The 1952 questionnaire consisted of two parts and five sections. Part A was devoted to the defence effort of the country and contained four sections. Section I was the Defence Report, which dealt with such questions as the forces available to meet force goals at selected dates; the other forces available for defence of the NATO area; and the strength and composition of the total armed forces.

Section II listed required and planned expenditures, which included, for the first Review, actual expenditures to 30 June 1952, required expenditures to 31 December 1953, and planned expenditure to June 1955, for both personnel and material. In order to arrive at these figures all countries' defence budgets were consulted because they contained actual or contemplated defence appropriations and expenditures. Thus there grew up a direct relationship between the national budgets and the replies to the NATO questionnaires.

Section III of the questionnaire set forth equipment requirements and resources. In calculating these, countries had to describe their defence production policies and programmes. The major subsections were: deficiencies, requirements, and resources of selected major items of military equipment; production of major material under off-shore procurement contracts; self-financed and planned deliveries; deliveries under MSA. The information was categorized by armed services and items of equipment. Section IV dealt exclusively with NATO Common Infrastructure. In this Section countries could only estimate their share roughly because the actual 'slice' which was to be common funded had not by then been agreed upon and therefore the allocation of the shares had not been made.[44]

Section V was contained in Part B, Economic Considerations, and consisted of supplementary economic tables. The figures

---

[43] *The Five Years*, p. 93.

[44] NATO Doc. ARQ(52). The common funding process for Infrastructure is discussed in Ch. XII.

were given in national currency units. Part B was to be completed in conjunction with the economic questionnaire which had been circulated separately by OEEC. The information required for this part was not detailed, because of national differences and because the OEEC questionnaire went into detail. Members of NATO's International Staff/Secretariat were directed to study the OEEC replies, to attend OEEC country examinations, and in general to bring to NATO the knowledge of the economic situation of member countries which had been acquired by OEEC.[45]

In Part B governments were asked to explain the differences between the December 1953 force levels and the higher Lisbon goals set up in February 1952. They were also asked to discuss the political and economic impact of the new goals as well as their financial and balance of payments positions.

The forms themselves made only a small part of the questionnaire—there being about sixteen of them in all. The bulk of the questionnaire—approximately 200 pages—was devoted to instructions and definitions in order to ensure that information which could be collated was received from each country. It was highly necessary to ensure consistency among the replies, and to facilitate this certain basic definitions had to be arrived at.[46] The first requirement of course, as mentioned above, was the establishment of a uniform fiscal year for NATO. In addition a standard definition of defence expenditures was adopted which applied to both NATO and OEEC: only those expenditures made, required, or planned by national governments which could be identified and justified specifically to meet the needs of the armed forces could be included in the questionnaire. Defence expenditures could be classed under

[45] The close co-operation between NATO and OEEC was affirmed when the first Assistant Secretary-General for Economics and Finance, M. René Sergent, resigned in March 1955 in order to become Secretary-General of OEEC, replacing M. Robert Marjolin. M. Sergent was replaced in NATO by M. Fernand-Didier Gregh of France, formerly Director of the Department of Operations for Asia and the Middle East in the International Bank for Reconstruction and Development.

[46] NATO Doc. ARQ(52). These definitions were first worked out by DFEC and FEB.

five headings: military personnel; major equipment; military construction; operations and maintenance; other defence expenditure.

Certain specific sub-definitions were laid down. These were: A—expenditures for 'security forces' could be listed only if the forces had been trained in military tactics, equipped as military forces, and in war would be used under military authority; B—the same qualifications as in 'A' above applied for colonial forces; C—expenditures for stockpiling could be listed only if they were directly connected with the military side of the economy; D—civil defence expenditure could not be included; E—retirement pensions and war damage payments could not be included; F—research and development in military technology could be included; G—economic aid could not be included; H—expenditure for end-item assistance (i.e. finished products, or 'hard goods') could be listed by the donor country, but not by the recipient country; I—reimbursements and occupation costs could not be included.[47]

At the same time that the countries were drawing up their replies to the questionnaire, the Standing Group was establishing firm force goals for 1953 (including costing estimates), provisional goals for 1954, and targets for planning purposes for 1955, with detailed tables of priorities. The Group's statement on these subjects was submitted to the Chiefs-of-Staff of the member countries, and to the Supreme Commanders for their comments, and then sent to the Military Representatives Committee, where it was reviewed, revised, and issued. To assist in the proper balancing of the military estimates with the member nation's budgets, special teams of military experts visited every country to help work out any problems or differences that arose. In this way maximum co-ordination at the planning and estimating level was achieved.

The International Staff/Secretariat estimated that the average reply would be at least 300 pages in length. In other words, the International Staff/Secretariat would receive approximately 4,000 pages to be reproduced and distributed, totalling over 1,000,000 reproduced pages. This was a formidable challenge to the International Staff/Secretariat's repro-

47 ibid.

duction and distribution services, especially as the need for these papers was immediate.

As replies came in they were distributed to all the other delegations, to the Standing Group and Supreme Commanders, and to the appropriate Sections of the International Staff/Secretariat.[48] Specifically, they were considered by five technical teams, who were responsible for analysing and making recommendations in their respective fields. These were a military considerations team, under the supervision of the Standing Group Liaison Officer; a defence expenditure team, under the Assistant Secretary-General for Economics and Finance, and consisting of one officer each from the Production and Logistics Division, the Office of Statistics, and the Standing Group together with experts on costing and military budgets loaned by the delegations; an equipment and production team, under the Assistant Secretary-General for Production and Logistics, and including one officer each from the Economics and Finance Division and the Office of Statistics, three from the Standing Group, and experts on equipment planning; an infrastructure team under the Assistant Secretary-General for Production and Logistics, which worked in conjunction with the Council's Infrastructure Committee and included one officer each from the Economics and Finance Division, the Office of Statistics, and the Standing Group; an economic capabilities team under the Assistant Secretary-General for Economics and Finance and including one officer each from the Political Affairs Division, the Office of Statistics, and the Production and Logistics Division, together with consultants.

The development of 'country studies' assembled from the national replies to the NATO and OEEC questionnaires was carried out by country working groups composed of representatives from the delegations and members of the International Staff/Secretariat. These groups were chaired by either the Assistant Secretary-General for Economics and Finance or the Assistant Secretary-General for Production and Logistics, or their Deputies. The International Staff/Secretariat membership of the country working groups was determined as follows:

[48] *The Five Years*, p. 93.

[Members] would be drawn from the five technical teams at the determination of the chairman of the technical team in each instance. Any particular examination of a country on sections of ARQ(52) would be conducted by the working group with the appropriate technical team sitting in. In practice, because several working groups may be sitting at one time, it will be necessary for the chairman of the technical teams to designate the individuals to meet with each working group.[49]

A timetable for processing the replies was drawn up. It was estimated that the technical teams would take three days to examine and analyse a reply. Therefore, on the fourth day the Chairman of the appropriate working group was to assemble his group to 'review and relate the analyses which have been made, and to determine a programme of future work'.[50] The technical teams were then given several days to clear up with the delegations any points which needed clarifying, but the teams could only work directly with a government if that country's working group agreed. The working group was the primary point around which the technical teams, the International Staff/Secretariat, the Standing Group, and the delegations operated. After several days had elapsed the working group reassembled to draft a synopsis of the country's reply and a list of questions on further matters gathered from the comments of the Standing Group, the delegations, and the technical teams.

These questions pointed out problems for solution and they were thus limited largely to general policy matters. This was not as true for the first Annual Review as for subsequent ones. In 1952 the questionnaires and country programmes were drawn up in much greater detail than was considered necessary for the Reviews that followed. For instance, one list of questions submitted by a delegation ran to 125 pages. The countries were frankly curious as to how their allies were conducting their military programmes. Another reason for this detail was that the United States Military Assistance Advisory Groups (MAAGs) also used the information to plan the level of American Mutual Defence Assistance to support the Review. This information was used both in the allocation of funds and in the justification to Congress of the Administration's request for annual authorizations and appropriations. After 1955 the MAAGs requested their information directly from each country, thereby obviating the necessity for extensive detail in the Annual Review. By 1955 the following policy had been established:

The Report should present to the Council the main military issues, and an estimate of countries' capabilities to face these issues in a form suitable for discussion by Ministers during a short session. By this stage in the process of the Review the mass of detailed information should have been set aside—those points of principle should be brought out which are the individual and collective concern of the responsible Ministers.[51]

It thus became the duty of the country working groups to bring out the main points of policy which needed to be clarified and discussed, and to examine the major problem areas arising from the military force estimates, the Annual Review questionnaire, the OEEC economic questionnaire, and the replies to them.[52] From this fund of information the working group drafted the country study. The country study was submitted to a final examining session scheduled by the Annual Review Committee. This was the point where all the drafting and coordination which had taken place was brought to the formal attention of the country concerned. The questions asked, however, would already have been co-ordinated with the country informally. It was provided that 'the basis for this examination will be the questions put forward by the International Staff, concluding the country study, and additional questions, if any, circulated after the informal meeting with Examining Delegations'.[53]

The examining session was truly multilateral. Any country had the right to be present just as all the replies and briefs which had gone into the preparation of the country study had been circulated among the delegations. As it worked out, certain countries always appeared to examine certain other

[51] NATO Doc. SC(55) Gen.-D/2.
[52] NATO Doc. SC(55) Gen.-D/2. Compare NATO Doc. ARQ(57) with NATO Doc. ARQ(52) for the change in emphasis between specific detail and general problem areas and deficiencies.
[53] NATO Doc. SC(55) Gen.-D/3 (Revised).

countries until an annual pattern had been set which was more or less followed each year.[54]

The session took place around a large square table. On one side sat the examined delegation; opposite to them sat the chairman of the Annual Review Committee. On the other side sat the examining delegations, opposite to which sat a panel of experts representing the economics, financial, infrastructure, production, and military planning functions of NATO. The questions were brought forward, discussed, and resolved if possible. There was a free and frank interchange among all the participants, which was a notable development in the history of international relations. As Lord Ismay said:

Here are fourteen [later fifteen] member countries voluntarily exposing to the scrutiny of fellow members the details of their individual defence efforts and budgets, and then explaining and defending their plans in open discussions with their colleagues. As a result, all member governments are acquiring the habit of working together on a very intimate basis and learning to appreciate their respective problems.[55]

The session was purposely held at the level of senior officials instead of at Ministerial level, as had been the case with the TCC.

After the conclusion of the examining sessions the International Staff/Secretariat completed the final draft of the Annual Review report, wrote the general chapter which introduced it, and prepared to submit it to the Council.

From this point onwards, the work of an Annual Review is focused on the physical result of the exercise—which is the voluminous report submitted to governments. The 1953 report contained some 360 pages of typescript, and was divided into three main parts. Part I was a short introduction and summary, designed to highlight the major considerations which emerged from the Review. Part II, some 50 pages in length, consisted of a series of chapters on the NATO-wide aspects of different topics which appeared of special importance. For example, one chapter was devoted to military

[54] This followed the example of OEEC which selected small panels of countries to conduct the separate interviews, though reserving the right for any delegations which so desired to attend. (NATO Doc. AC/19-R/5.)

[55] *The Five Years*, p. 97.

problems, another to major equipment deficiencies and a third to the long-range problems of the maintenance of NATO forces. Part III consisted of fourteen country chapters describing the defence effort, the unsolved military problems and the economic situation of each country, and concluding with a series of recommendations.[56]

In 1954 the Council approved a Resolution which provided that member countries should furnish a brief written statement by 15 April of the following year on their progress in implementing the recommendations made in the previous year's report. This procedure did not work out too well, primarily because not enough time had elapsed since the completion of the review for a country to have carried out the recommendations. Progress could be assessed, nevertheless, in the military Commanders' comments on the military estimates, in which they gave details of the implementation of the previous year's recommendations, and in the examining session, where references could be made to past reports.

The first Annual Review was by far the most difficult. After the International Staff/Secretariat, the military planners, and the delegations had become acquainted with their tasks and with each other, after procedures had been worked out, and after the mass of information had been sifted and analysed, subsequent Reviews became increasingly more routine. The questionnaires were progressively reduced in length and complexity.[57]

Lord Ismay singled out this progress for mention in his last report to the Council:

. . . there has been a steady improvement in working relationships, formal and informal, between the NATO military authorities and the civilian International Staff. Mutual confidence and respect between civil and military staffs, though a basic condition of sound defence planning, is not easily or rapidly brought about in a new setting, with new men and new problems, even on the national plane. Nevertheless, thanks to the readiness of national delegations to accord increasing responsibility to the International Staff,

[56] *The Five Years*, p. 96.
[57] See NATO Doc. ARQ(57) in contrast to NATO Doc. ARQ(52). The substance was the same, but the format became much simpler.

collaboration between the NATO military authorities and the Staff has developed in the most encouraging fashion.[58]

The pressure to complete the first Review was so great that the Annual Review Committee had to meet late into the night so that the report could go to the December Ministerial meeting of the Council. Even at that, it was not possible to complete the report on schedule. Important policy issues were submitted to the Council at its December meeting, but the force goals were not finally agreed upon until the Ministerial meeting in April 1953, and it was not until the 1954 Review that procedure had become sufficiently regularized to allow completion under the annual time-table without undue pressure.[59]

One continuing reason for delays was that often elections and new governments interfered with a prompt submission. The replies had to be signed by the Ministers responsible. The Ministers, therefore, wanted them to be carefully developed and closely scrutinized. This took additional time if a change of government occurred—or even threatened to occur—midway through the review.

Another reason for delays was the reluctance of governments to conclude considerations for new defence programmes. The technological race constantly imposed pressure to continue with research and development rather than to commit planning programmes to production. The rapid obsolescence of new projects contributed directly to soaring defence budgets. Therefore, where a nation's budget year coincided with NATO's, there was a tendency for delay in submission according to NATO's 'budget schedule' because of delay in bringing to a conclusion decisions on new defence programmes. The age of missiles and rockets did not lessen the problem.

[58] 'Text of Lord Ismay's Report to the Ministerial Meeting of the North Atlantic Council at Bonn, May 1957,' as contained in the *NATO Letter*, Vol. 5, Spec. Supp. to No. 6. Members of the International Staff/Secretariat first met with the Standing Group planners in Washington in 1954; in 1955, for the first time, they accompanied the military Commanders' teams on their visits to NATO capitals. In 1956 they worked with the military planners on the review of the broader implications of the military recommendations to member countries, and on the general report to the Council at the end of the year. (ibid.)

[59] *The Five Years*, p. 92.

As pointed out earlier, the brunt of the burden of conducting the Annual Review was borne by the Economics and Finance Division, which had been divided into the following Sections: Reconciliation, General Economic Studies, Economic Mobilisation, Finance, and Costing and Screening. Some of these Sections performed tasks which were not directly related to the Annual Review and others found their functions becoming less important.

ECONOMICS AND FINANCE DIVISION[60]
(1952)

Assistant Secretary-General for
Economics and Finance; Deputy
Assistant Secretary-General

Reconciliation Section	General Economic Studies Section	Economic Mobilisation Section	Finance Section	Costing and Screening Section

For instance, the Costing and Screening Section was originally set up to carry on the work of the McNarney Committee. But the McNarney staff had made a fresh beginning and had accumulated a vast amount of information. It was now not necessary to receive that amount of information every year, since the MAAGs asked detailed questions about costs. Therefore this function received decreasing emphasis in the International Staff/Secretariat.

The General Economic Studies Section, on the other hand, became more important. Its function was to prepare 'information papers' which were devoted chiefly to the analysis of general economic conditions. In February 1953 a committee to study Soviet economic policy was established which prepared papers on Soviet economic conditions, including economic aid programmes. By 1956 the research work of the Section had become so important that the Council created a Committee of Economic Advisers which was placed under the chairmanship of the Assistant Secretary-General for Economics and

[60] *The North Atlantic Treaty Organization* (Paris, Dec. 1952), p. 33; Staff Manual, item 1016.

Finance and which reported to the Council. This Committee supervised the work of the Soviet economic policy committee.[61]

An effort to redirect the economic activities of the Alliance into less restrictive channels was made by the 1956 Management Survey Team. As noted in Chapter VIII, the Team recommended the abolition of the posts of Assistant Secretary-General for Economics and Finance and Assistant Secretary-General for Production and Logistics and their replacement by an Assistant Secretary-General for Political, Economic and Social Affairs, and an Assistant Secretary-General for Defence Production and Review. These officers would have had the following duties:

The Assistant Secretary General for Political, Economic and Social Affairs would be responsible for cultural co-operation, for public information, for following political trends throughout the world, for assessing the economic position of the members of the North Atlantic Community and relating it to other countries of the world, and for performing economic and social functions as assigned. The functions which he would perform are directly related to Article II of the North Atlantic Treaty.

The Assistant Secretary General for Defence Production and Review would be responsible for the Annual Review of military programmes and for the exchange of production and technical information between members of the Community. The work with expert technical bodies and committees is recognised as more limited than was originally conceived. The Team also recognises that the main responsibility rests with National Governments in the person of experts sent to Headquarters for relatively brief periods. It is the view of the Team that preparation of papers and other technical material is primarily the responsibility of national experts, although continued impetus in that field as heretofore would have to be given by the International Staff.[62]

Despite the good intentions and the possible validity of these recommendations, Lord Ismay decided not to change his organizational structure so drastically.[63] Nonetheless, at the

---

[61] The creation of a Committee of Economic Advisers had been recommended by the 1956 Committee of Three on Non-military Co-operation. (*The North Atlantic Treaty Organization* (Paris, 1958), p. 71.)

[62] General Report, par. 27.

[63] For some reasons, see Ch. VIII.

time he retired, the balance of work of the Division had become so altered that it was found necessary to have only three Sections: Finance and Defence Budget [Planning] to conduct the Annual Review; Economic to produce research papers for the Committee of Economic Advisers; and Statistical to do the work formerly done by the suppressed Office of Statistics.[64]

ECONOMICS AND FINANCE DIVISION[65]
(1957)

Assistant Secretary-General for
Economics and Finance; Deputy to
the Assistant Secretary-General

Finance and Defence Budget [Planning] Section	Economic Section	Statistical Section

Mr. Charles Spofford, the former chairman of the Council Deputies, summarized the underlying reason why the economic functions of the International Staff/Secretariat had evolved as they did during Lord Ismay's tenure of office:

An important factor limiting NATO's economic activity has been that significant negotiations have been taken outside the NATO framework. To some extent this has been inevitable, since the North Atlantic area is not a natural and self-contained trading unit. In part it is due to the fact that the major economic problems turn upon the relations of the principal Treaty partners, notably Britain and France, to the United States, which have been dealt with through bilateral talks. In part it has been due to the special position of the United States and its pattern of administering the aid programs separately with each of the Treaty partners. But although NATO has done little on the positive side to eliminate competition in the economic policies of its members or to encourage economic collaboration between them (in the words of Article 2 of the Treaty)

---

[64] *The North Atlantic Treaty Organization* (Paris, 1959), p. 88. The diminishing importance of the financial and economics side of the International Staff/Secretariat's functions was reflected in the fact that, whereas the first Deputy Assistant Secretary-General for Economics and Finance provided by the U.K. was a very high Treasury official, his two successors were of progressively lower rank.

[65] NATO Doc. ISM(57)4.

it has done the necessary to see that the military commanders have the common facilities they have asked for, and its broad-scale venture into the economic analysis of the rearmament effort has put the military commitments into better perspective and has acted as a safety valve in pointing out in time and in economic terms the danger points resulting from the military build-up.[66]

By the time M. Spaak became Secretary-General the nature of the Russian threat, which included Chairman Khrushchev's definition of peaceful coexistence, presaged greater diversity for NATO's financial and economic functions. But this diversity lay as much with political as with military factors, as Lord Ismay well knew when he retired.

[66] Speech delivered, 26 May 1953. (NATO Speech Series, No. 39.)

CHAPTER XI

THE PRODUCTION AND LOGISTICS
DIVISION

WITH the possible exception of the Standing Group, no other Alliance activity could trace its beginnings more directly to the Anglo-American co-operative endeavours of World War II than the Production and Logistics Division.[1] The activities of the various Anglo-American Combined Boards, the most relevant of which was the Combined Production and Resources Board, provided a precedent which carried over into the post-World War II era. As one official who participated in this area of wartime co-operation has observed:

The combined boards of World War II have now been dissolved for a considerable period, but the combined process has not been abandoned. The post-war international scene finds the existence of organs of collaboration and economic forms of cooperation in many fields. . . . Various efforts at inter-nation economic co-operation which have been tried under the European Recovery Program as well as those undertaken by the North Atlantic Treaty nations fall into a similar category. In these as in other contemporary international undertakings it is interesting to note both combined board influence and the participation of former combined board personnel.[2]

The major aspects of the pattern of inter-governmental co-operation developed by the Combined Boards were fourfold.

---

[1] Some students would trace it back to World War I and the creation of various inter-Allied administrative bodies, the most famous of which was the Allied Maritime Transport Council. An authoritative American government officer has stated: 'As need for Anglo-American cooperation became more evident during World War II, both Englishmen and Americans turned to the Allied Maritime Transport Council as a model upon which inter-nation organization might be based.' (S. McKee Rosen, *The Combined Boards of the Second World War* (New York, 1951), p. 100. See also Sir Arthur Salter, *Allied Shipping Control* (London, 1921.)

[2] Rosen, p. 270.

16

First, the international agencies should not displace national authorities, but their purpose should be to facilitate direct contacts between the responsible officials concerned. Second, they should facilitate the exchange of information. Third, they should enable participants to consult, to focus the issues involved, and to come to decisions. Fourth, the recommendations made should be implemented by national agencies upon approval of the governments.[3] To a great extent this has been the pattern worked out within NATO to carry on its production functions. But there was much discussion before it was evolved.

To trace this evolution it is necessary to recall the organization called the Western Union Defence Organization (WUDO), set up under the Brussels Treaty of 1948, for here was the genesis of the NATO International Staff/Secretariat. Lord Ismay recognized this relationship when he said:

For rather more than the first two years of NATO, the work of defence production planning was carried out under a committee system. The Military Production and Supply Board (MPSB), established in November, 1949, was the first of these NATO committees. It closely resembled the former Western Union Board and worked in a similar way. The heads of national delegations to the MPSB met in committee at frequent intervals and each head of delegation made members of his staff available for *ad hoc* study groups. When highly technical studies were required, each delegate obtained qualified representatives from his country to serve on special sub-committees. This was the beginning of the system of 'groups of experts'. . . .[4]

This was in essence the procedure which was developed by the Combined Boards. Gradually, however, the techniques and initiatives were refined and diversified according to the programme needs of the International Staff/Secretariat.

The Military Production and Supply Board's (MPSB) precursor, the Western Union Supply Board, was established in October 1948, and consisted of the Ministers of the five member nations or their representatives. The day-to-day operations of the Board were carried out by a Supply Executive Committee which was in continuous session and which was

[3] ibid. f. 12.
[4] *The Five Years*, p. 12; see Chart, p. 21 above.

served by the Western Union Military Supply secretariat. The secretariat was made up solely of seconded persons since WUDO never had an international budget.[5] It was this secretariat which, alone of all the civilian bodies in WUDO, was integrated into NATO, being carried over into the MPSB secretariat when it was organized a year later.

Until July 1951, when the international budget of NATO was instituted, the head of the MPSB secretariat had to wear two hats: those of MPSB and the Western Union Military Supply secretariats. After July 1951 the latter was allowed to go out of existence along with the Western Union Supply Board, although they were never formally dissolved. A number of the expert working groups referred to above by Lord Ismay were carried over *in toto* into the MPSB.

The MPSB was set up under the Defence Committee in accordance with a decision of the Council rendered on 17 September 1949. The Defence Committee issued the following terms of reference to the MPSB:

. . . The following general provisions shall govern the operation of the North Atlantic Military Production and Supply Board:

1. The North Atlantic Military Production and Supply Board shall be composed of a representative at the sub-ministerial level from each signatory country. It shall report directly to the Defence Committee.

2. The Board shall establish and maintain close working relations with the appropriate military bodies set up under the Defence Committee. It shall look to them for information on military requirements and work to insure that, insofar as feasible, the military production and procurement programme supports defence plans effectively. The Board shall also work in close co-ordination with the military bodies on the promotion of standardisation of parts and end products of military equipment, and provide them with technical advice on the production and development of new or improved weapons. To facilitate the fullest co-operation and exchange of information between them on matters of joint interest, the Board shall

---

[5] Interview with Dr. H. West-Burnham, former Head of the Western Union Military Supply secretariat, later Head of the Infrastructure Secretariat Section of the Production and Logistics Division, 25 Aug. 1959.

establish and direct a suitably representative liaison group on a working level in Washington to work with the Standing Group.

3. The Board shall maintain close working relations with the finance and economic machinery to be established by the Council, and look to it for guidance on all relevant economic and financial factors.

4. The North Atlantic Military Production and Supply Board is responsible to the Defence Committee for the performance of the following functions, having regard for the principle of self-help and mutual aid in the field of military production and supply.

(a) The review of the military supply situation on the basis of data to be secured from the appropriate military bodies on military material requirements and on the current availability of military material to meet such requirements.

(b) The recommendations to the Defence Committee of ways and means of increasing available supplies where they fall short of requirements, either from production, surplus equipment or equipment economically capable of rehabilitation. In preparing such recommendations, account shall be taken of strategic factors, of physical capabilities of individual countries to produce military material, of the importance of securing maximum efficiency and integration of production, and of the guidance furnished by the finance and economic machinery with respect to financial and economic considerations.

(c) The promotion of more efficient methods of producing military equipment and of the standardisation of parts and end products of military equipment, including conservation in the use of strategic and critical materials, and including advice to the appropriate military bodies on the production problems involved in proposed new weapons or modifications in existing weapons.

· · · · · · · · · · ·

6. The Board shall provide itself with such subordinate bodies and staff assistance as may be necessary to carry out its functions. In particular, there shall be, in addition to the liaison group in Washington, referred to in paragraph 2, a permanent working staff in London, composed of qualified personnel representing interested countries, to carry on the day-to-day work of the Board. The Board shall have a

Secretary, with suitable assistance, to perform secretarial administrative functions.[6]

The secretariat of the MPSB was known as the permanent working staff (PWS).

It was clear that the MPSB could carry out its duties only with the help of the Council Deputies (set up in May 1950), the Standing Group (set up in September 1949), and the United States Military Assistance Advisory Groups (MAAGs). To accomplish its mission the MPSB set the following conditions. First, the Standing Group should draw up a list of types of equipment which were militarily acceptable. Second, the needs of the forces should be compiled. Third, the countries for whom the armaments produced were destined should be named so that the producer governments could place the production contracts. Fourth, the monetary and financial problems relating to the exchange of armaments should be solved. Much research had to be done and much information assembled before any decisions could be made.

In addition a note of urgency was injected into the situation by the outbreak of hostilities in Korea in mid-1950. In response to this the Deputies inaugurated a High Priority Production Programme. As discussed in Chapter X this rapid rearmament brought on the severe economic problems which beset NATO from 1950 to 1953.

At its meeting in Copenhagen on 12 July 1950 the MPSB agreed that nine task forces should be established, to be assisted by the PWS, which was to be composed of senior production experts from member countries. These task forces would visit the producing countries to confer with the national authorities and to examine facilities in order to draw up a series of objective reports in which recommendations would be made as to means of increasing production in the fields where the deficiencies were greatest. The task forces would base their inspections upon military requirements data given them by the Standing Group, and would take into consideration such factors as unit costs and production time-lag.

---

[6] *The Five Years*, pp. 180–1. These terms of reference remained as the basic charter for all NATO's defence production activities. The alterations made were of emphasis more than of substance.

Consequently there was pressure from the outset on the military and economic agencies of NATO to produce comprehensive, timely, and accurate information. In the opinion of the MPSB and the PWS this information was slow in coming and was not suitable when it did arrive. These deficiencies were partly attributable to the size and scope of the over-all planning required in 1951 to bring the Alliance into a state of military and economic effectiveness, and partly to the kinds of questions which were asked. The PWS and the task forces were confronted with such knotty problems as: the final disposition of approved items; the method of approval of militarily acceptable types of equipment; the receipt of manufacturing licences, if such were required; the reception of raw materials and machine tools to facilitate production of finished products; the choice of recipient countries for the placing of contracts; the allocation of raw materials and machine tools, and of the finished delivered products; and the precise definition of that part of production retained by the producing country for its own use.[7]

In addition the PWS had to examine such ancillary matters as the standardization and choice of armaments (in liaison with the Standing Group and the Regional Planning Groups); the distribution of surplus armaments stocks; the existence of customs duties on imports essential for defence production; the relation of the MPSB with various NATO bodies; and the transfer of the Western Union Supply Board subcommittees to the MPSB.[8]

The MPSB met periodically; the task forces, subcommittees, and the PWS were all seconded. It was soon discovered, as Lord Ismay said:

. . . that this committee system did not permit sufficient continuity, a proper division of labour, or effective forward planning. Delegations had to represent not only their own national point of view but also an impartial corporate international point of view. The duality of their functions meant that collective recommendations might not always be entirely objective.[9]

In line with this view the MPSB recommended to the Council at its Ministerial meeting in December 1950 that the

---

[7] NATO Doc. D-C/321.   [8] ibid.   [9] *The Five Years*, p. 128.

PWS should be allowed to engage in bilateral negotiations with member countries in order to facilitate the exchange of military equipment to meet military requirements. This would give the seconded staff of the PWS a direct authority previously reserved to the subcommittees of the MPSB.

The semi-executive functions which the MPSB recommended should be given to the PWS were: to extract those task force recommendations which appeared to be acceptable, and then to ask the appropriate national authorities of the countries concerned about carrying them out; to examine the task forces' reports and take note of the Standing Group priorities, the national replies to each report, and the task force comments on difficulties; and to name the recipient country for each item to be produced, upon agreement with the Standing Group.[10]

The Council agreed that the MPSB had not been able to fulfil its purpose, and in its final communiqué made the following announcement:

The Council, desiring to simplify the structure of the North Atlantic Treaty Organization in order to make it more effective, asked the Council Deputies to initiate appropriate action. In this connection the Defence Committee, meeting separately on 18th December, had already taken action to establish a Defence Production Board with greater powers than those of the Military Production and Supply Board which it supersedes. The new Board is charged with expanding and accelerating production and with furthering the mutual use of the industrial capacities of the member nations.[11]

In accordance with the Council's directive the MPSB met on 11 January 1951 and agreed to the following arrangements: first, that all the functions and responsibilities of the MPSB and the PWS should be assumed by the Defence Production Board (DPB); second, that the PWS, task forces and subcommittees of the MPSB should continue their activities under the guidance of the DPB; third, that the foregoing arrangements should continue until the DPB had the opportunity to establish its own organization and to appoint its chief executive officer, who

[10] NATO Doc. D-C/321.

[11] Final Communique of the North Atlantic Council, Sixth Session.

would be known as the Co-ordinator for Defence Production and would be a non-voting member of the Board.

The two major improvements upon the MPSB organization were the creation of the post of Co-ordinator for Defence Production and the constitution of the DPB in such a way as to ensure that the heads of delegations to it would be continuously available for meetings in London. The mandate given to the Co-ordinator was to:

> . . . head the unified international staff which is charged with coordinating and expediting the programmes and policies recommended by the DPB. The Coordinator will organize and direct the DPB staff and will make recommendations to fulfil the objectives of the Board, which is set up to augment and expedite the production of defence equipment by the North Atlantic Powers. The Coordinator will also be responsible for establishing liaison, as appropriate, with the other NAT agencies, and will represent the DPB before other NAT and non-NAT agencies.[12]

Mr. William R. Herod of the United States, who was appointed Co-ordinator on 15 January 1951,[13] was given the rank of Minister and was authorized to approach governments directly. He headed an organization that, by the time of the Lisbon Ministerial meeting, numbered about 137 persons, 30 of whom were officers.[14]

The DPB was organized into two parts: a Production and Programmes Division to carry on the work of the MPSB;[15] and an Analysis Division to draw up the list of military requirements and correlate and analyse the information gathered for the use of the DPB and other interested agencies.

The major achievement of the DPB was to continue the process initiated by the MPSB of gathering information and

[12] NATO Press Release, 27 Feb. 1951.

[13] Mr. Herod had been President of the International General Electric Company before going to NATO.

[14] As of 7 June 1951 there were 48 persons in the DPB; as of 30 June 1951 there were 119; as of 31 Dec. 1951 there were 137. (Interview with Lieutentant-General Sir Ernest Wood, K.B.E., C.I.E., M.C., former Chief-of-Staff to the Co-ordinator for Defence Production, 15 Jan. 1959.)

[15] The only change made in this respect was to reduce the nine equipment categories of the MPSB task forces to six technical sections.

issuing reports. These reports 'covered artillery and infantry support weapons, tanks, transport vehicles, engineering equipment, escort vessels and minesweepers, and recommended production additional to that already planned by the countries themselves'.[16] This achievement fell far short of what Mr. Herod had thought that his office and organization should have accomplished.

Apparently Mr. Herod believed that he would have strong executive authority to co-ordinate the placing of production orders among the various countries, the allocation of deliveries, and the development of a system of common funding to pay for orders. If he had been able to work out the functions of the DPB in this way, he would have become the strongest single administrator in the pre-Lisbon civilian organization. He would also have been a truly international administrator—even supranational. Because the performance of the Co-ordinator and the DPB did not match Mr. Herod's expectations, it is appropriate to consider in further detail the duties which were placed upon the DPB during its fourteen months of life.

The Council Deputies defined the general task of the DPB as: 'To achieve the maximum production of military equipment in the most efficient manner, at the least cost, in the shortest time, to meet the military material requirements of NATO.'[17] Further, the DPB was instructed to 'concentrate its activities upon those aspects of military production and procurement which involve major problems of NATO international cooperation'.[18] Specifically, the DPB had fifteen duties: (1) to keep the over-all production situation under constant review; (2) to keep availabilities of supply under constant review; (3) to recommend external aid for production projects where eligible; (4) to recommend suitable solutions for [supplies of] machine tools, raw materials, etc., where they are insufficient for the fulfilment of military needs; (5) to co-operate in achieving standardization; (6) to facilitate the exchange of drawings, patents, 'know-how', etc.; (7) to study and recommend the substitution of non-critical for critical materials, where it proved appropriate; (8) to encourage and assist in the planning of industrial mobilization on a co-ordinated NATO basis;

16 *The Five Years*, p. 128.   17 NATO Doc. D-D/205.   18 ibid.

(9) to co-ordinate national defence production programmes; (10) to plan integrated production programmes; (11) to recommend the allocation of production tasks between member countries; (12) to arrange that national production programmes conform to the supply priorities of the armed forces; (13) to recommend the allocation of civil capacity to military production; (14) to recommend the creation of new capacity where necessary; (15) to consider how the production capacity of non-NATO countries could help the rearmament effort.[19]

In a nutshell the question was: Given the international climate in which the DPB had to work, was it possible for it to achieve its goals? The Chief-of-Staff to the Co-ordinator for Defence Production answered this question and offered a reason for his answer. He said:

The agency has failed to fulfil all the tasks set out in its charter. It has failed not because the charter is defective, but because it is inappropriate to the present stage of the development of NATO itself. A charter of such all-embracing character could only be fully discharged where the organization uniting a confederation of nations is itself as strong or stronger than its constituent parts. The NATO organization will only reach such a position when the individual NATO countries have, bit by bit and over a considerable period of years, made what in total amounts to a surrender of national sovereignty sufficient to establish such a balance of power.[20]

In the opinion of the Chief-of-Staff the last seven duties listed above should not have been laid on the DPB unless the member countries had been willing—or able—to make the requisite adjustments in their national policies to enable their accomplishment. As he observed: 'It is just these and similar powers which the architects of EDC propose shall be transferred by the contracting countries to the EDC Defence Commissioners. The creation of a common EDC budget will automatically bring such result. Therein lies the key. Power and authority in defence production resides with the authority controlling the funds'.[21]

Originally both the Defence Production Co-ordinator and the Chief-of-Staff had strongly favoured the establishment of a common defence budget for NATO, which would have resulted

---

[19] NATO Doc. PL/EW/243.   [20] ibid.   [21] ibid.

in the common funding of defence production with all the attendant controls and authority which go with the power of the purse.[22] This course was discussed at length during 1951 and 1952, but it failed of adoption. Instead the Annual Review system was developed which was nothing more nor less than co-ordination in the drawing-up of each member nation's defence budget.[23] The Annual Review was an assessment made entirely on national lines, with no hint of supranationality.

Closely related to common funding was the idea of arranging for the production of items in one country for the use of others. But, as the Chairman of the Council Deputies admitted in May 1951: 'While the production of each nation for its own forces has moved ahead, production by various member countries for use by others has been a problem which has not yet been solved.'[24]

An additional budgetary factor which coloured all of these considerations was the predominant economic influence which the United States exerted in the Alliance. American contributions both in kind (end-items or 'hard goods') and in money

[22] They were not the only prominent NATO officials who favoured common funding. For instance, M. van Zeeland of Belgium, a former Chairman of the North Atlantic Council, wrote on 30 June 1951: 'Might it not be best to replace the existing system—whereby each country makes its own voluntary contribution—by a fair sharing of the military charges based on quotas determined in common agreement from standards of allocation deeply studied and accepted by all?' (*The Times*, 1 Dec. 1951.)

[23] For a full and lucid exposition of the concept of common funding see Anne M. Warburton and John B. Wood, Ch. II. Their conclusion parallels the Chief-of-Staff's: 'NATO was not intended to be a supranational authority; it has never tried to raise an international army; nor has it attempted to become a gigantic procurement agency. . . . Even though it may be admitted that the NATO system, based as it is on national armies financed at the discretion of national parliaments, loses some economic advantages which a common defence budget would have, we do not think it useful to present this choice as though it were purely an economic one. To get the full economic advantages offered by the common defence budget system, all member countries would have to agree to submit themselves to a supranational authority and to disband their armies in favour of an international army.' (p. 16.)

[24] Speech by Mr. Charles M. Spofford, 10 May 1951. (NATO Speech Series, No. 2.)

(off-shore procurement (OSP)) had a direct bearing on a recipient nation's defence production plans. Because the United States could commit these Mutual Defence Assistance Funds for only one year ahead, the recipient countries were never in a position to plan their rearmament programmes over a long period, and in many cases they found it difficult to 'compartmentalize' the production of military equipment into fiscal years.

In any event, during most of Lord Ismay's tenure of office the relationship of the European and North American members of NATO was that of recipient-donor. Nations tried to estimate what proportion of their defence needs would be covered by the United States and then estimated their defence budgets accordingly. The United States in its turn tried to estimate the size and destination of equipment or OSP orders. Here again the Annual Review served to facilitate this exchange of information but could not solve the problem.[25]

---

[25] That this situation was not new can be seen from a statement by Mr. Milton Katz, U.S. Executive Officer of the Combined Production and Resources Board during World War II. He wrote: 'An international organization designed to carry out a defined mission through the combined efforts of its members is unlikely to achieve its purpose unless the contributions of the members toward the common objective bear some relationship to their respective shares in the authority exercised. Membership in the Board had originally been limited to the United States and Britain on the theory that all others of the United Nations required assistance to meet their requirements for weapons, equipment, and supplies, and that only the United States and Britain had the capacity to produce for others as well as for themselves. This was true of the United States. It was true of Britain only in a limited sense and only in relation to nations other than the United States. In her economic relations with the United States, Britain was primarily an applicant for aid. The British members and staff of the Board were unremitting in their efforts to achieve the objective of combined production planning. But, because of the underlying economic relationship, the various British national departments and agencies tended inevitably to regard this as incidental. Their preoccupation was with the need to satisfy British deficiencies out of American production.

'For the same reason, the interested departments and agencies of the United States found it difficult to grasp the Board's basic mission. In the confusion between the concept of the United States as the arsenal of democracy and the concept of pooled resources and combined programming, there was some puzzlement among American national agencies at

The result of all of these factors was a gradual realization that the DPB—and especially its Co-ordinator—had been saddled with a task which could not be completely fulfilled. Defence production in NATO had to be geared to the realities of international life. Therefore, when the Deputies and the Temporary Council Committee drew up the plans for the reorganization of the civilian side of the Alliance, they recommended that the DPB be transmuted into a Division of the newly-integrated International Staff/Secretariat. Opinion on this proposal was not unanimous however. For example, the Executive Secretary of the Deputies' organization felt that he could not recommend the transfer of the DPB to Paris because he could not see any usefulness in such a Division without common funding.[26]

Even Lord Ismay believed that those production activities that were possible should be handled exclusively by the delegations, using the International Staff/Secretariat in a purely secretariat capacity, and not having any experts serving as international civil servants.[27] As this approach had not been seriously considered by the Council, Lord Ismay, after several months in office, decided to form a Production and Logistics Division with an American at the head, who would be assisted by a military-type chief-of-staff. The Division consisted of two branches: a Production Branch headed by a general production expert who would be Assistant Secretary-General for Production and Logistics; and an Infrastructure Branch headed by a specialist in either finance or civil engineering.[28]

---

what sometimes seemed to them to be a 50 per cent voice of the British in the distribution of predominantly American resources. In the main, they tended to regard the Board merely as a convenient forum through which to work out *ad hoc* adjustments with their British counterparts, and they resisted or sought to circumvent its endeavours to discharge its central mission.' ('A Case Study in International Organization' (*Harvard Business Review*, Autumn 1946, p. 17).)

[26] Interview with Dr. West-Burnham, 25 Aug. 1959.

[27] Interview with Lord Ismay, 29 May 1959.

[28] Mr. Herod remained with NATO for only ten months, although he had been appointed for a two-year period. There was never any question of his becoming the first Assistant Secretary-General for Production and Logistics. As was noted at the time of his resignation: 'NATO officials in

The Secretary-General assigned a threefold function to the Division (hereafter called the Production Branch): first, planning production programmes; second, acting as the 'expert broker' for exchanging information and guiding technical studies; and, third, participating in the Annual Review by assisting in the formulation of equipment levels and specifications and in their correlation with national defence budget planning.[29]

The prognosis of the Chief-of-Staff to the Co-ordinator for Defence Production who subsequently became the chief executive officer for the DPB after the Co-ordinator's resignation in November 1951, and who for a time was Deputy Assistant Secretary-General for Production and Logistics, thus proved to be accurate. He said, at the time of his departure in September 1952:

> The lessons of the past give clear indication that in present circumstances the functions of the NATO production agency should be advisory rather than of an executive character. Where executive action is needed it should be fulfilled through Council action. Executive production powers should not reside in the PL Division, and much less in individual Sections save insofar as power and authority have already been specifically entrusted by the NATO countries, as in the case of Infrastructure.[30]

During the period immediately after Lisbon and before the appointment of the first Assistant Secretary-General for Production and Logistics, a special study was made of the organization and management of production and logistics. In view of the confusion over the definition and implementation of the defence production programme, it was felt that some

---

London are reticent about the reason for Mr. Herod's resignation, but the short period which he has held this appointment has given rise to speculation that a policy disagreement lies behind his decision.' (*Daily Mail*, 16 Nov. 1951.) The announcement of his resignation was made at the Rome Ministerial meeting of the Council, in Nov. 1951. By then the TCC had been appointed and was undertaking its 'crash' programme which culminated in the Lisbon Ministerial meeting and the reorganization.

[29] *The Five Years*, pp. 128–9. For a detailed discussion of the Infrastructure Branch see Ch. XII of this study.

[30] NATO Doc. PL/EW/243.

administrative order should be introduced, and that the transfer of the DPB to Paris provided a suitable occasion to do so. Lord Ismay asked Mr. William Batt of the United States to perform this task.[31]

Mr. Batt recommended the reduction of the staff from its former number of well over a hundred to about eighty persons.[32] He also recommended the formation of ten Technical Sections: review and liaison, production co-ordination, aircraft, ammunition, vehicles, shipbuilding, infrastructure, spare parts co-ordination, armament, and electronics.[33] The Infrastructure Section became the Infrastructure Branch in 1953.

By 1956 the number of Technical Sections had been reduced to four: aircraft, ammunition, electronics, and engineering, and there was one General Section—formerly the Review and Liaison Section.[34] The General Section was made 'responsible for the political, economic and administrative aspects of the work . . . including the co-ordination of the work on problems affecting more than one Technical Section.'[35] In other words, where necessary, they co-ordinate the work of their more technical colleagues, and help to channel it in a manner best calculated to accomplish desired results. The reduction of the number of Technical Sections meant only that some sections had been combined, thereby adjusting to changes in activities. Broadly speaking, except for the rapid growth of the

[31] The idea was first broached by the U.S. Mr. Batt had played a prominent part in the work of the Anglo-American Combined Boards. He had served on the U.S. Defence Advisory Commission, as Deputy Director of the Production Division of the U.S. Office of Production Management, as Vice-Chairman (International Supply) of the U.S. War Production Board, as the American Member of the Combined Raw Materials Board, and as Representative to the Combined Production and Resources Board. At the time of his appointment to NATO he was Chief of the U.S. Mutual Security Agency Mission to the U.K.

[32] Interview with Lieut.-General Sir Ernest Wood, 15 Jan. 1959.

[33] NATO Staff Manual, 2 Feb. 1953, item 1015.

[34] NATO Doc. ISM(57)4. The General Services Section was the result of a suggestion made by Mr. Batt, who had envisaged a type of cabinet empowered to take strong decisions. (Interview with Dr. West-Burnham, 7 Aug. 1958.)

[35] Speech by Mr. J. Murray Mitchell, Assistant Secretary-General for Production and Logistics, 1 Oct. 1956. (unpub.)

Infrastructure Section into the Infrastructure Branch, the organizational structure did not change significantly from the DPB period.

Mr. Batt, in his report to Lord Ismay, envisaged three general purposes for the Division. He hoped, first, that it would co-ordinate production as new weapons were developed and introduced; second, that the concept of common funding would become more attractive to the member governments; and, third, that the Division would contribute to the exchange of technical information and 'know-how'. As it turned out, only Mr. Batt's third hope was realized during most of Lord Ismay's period in office, for, as will be seen, it was not until late 1956 that the movement to co-ordinate and share in new weapons production techniques began to make headway. Common funding was never seriously considered after its rejection in 1951.

PRODUCTION AND LOGISTICS DIVISION[36]
(1952)

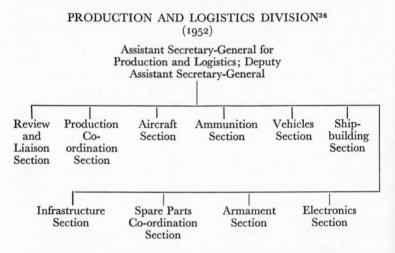

Assistant Secretary-General for
Production and Logistics; Deputy
Assistant Secretary-General

| Review and Liaison Section | Production Co-ordination Section | Aircraft Section | Ammunition Section | Vehicles Section | Ship-building Section |

| Infrastructure Section | Spare Parts Co-ordination Section | Armament Section | Electronics Section |

The Assistant Secretary-General for Production and Logistics underlined the lack of progress in fulfilling Mr. Batt's first two purposes in a speech delivered in October 1956. He said:

. . . although one might jump to the conclusion that the way to organize the defence production side of an Alliance is (1) to draw up an agreed list of all the defence items required, and (2) then

---

[36] *The North Atlantic Treaty Organization* (Paris, Dec. 1952), p. 33; Staff Manual, item 1015.

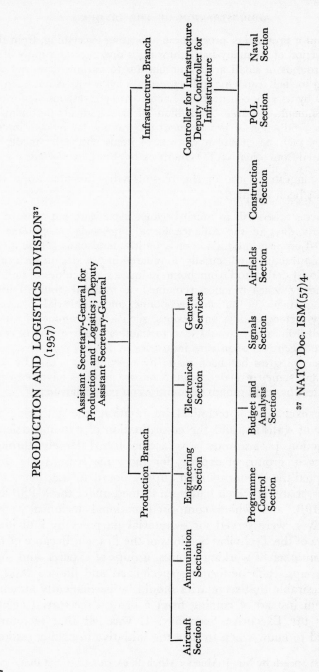

PRODUCTION AND LOGISTICS DIVISION[37]
(1957)

Assistant Secretary-General for
Production and Logistics; Deputy
Assistant Secretary-General

Production Branch

Infrastructure Branch

Controller for Infrastructure
Deputy Controller for
Infrastructure

Aircraft Section

Ammunition Section

Engineering Section

Electronics Section

General Services

Programme Control Section

Budget and Analysis Section

Signals Section

Airfields Section

Construction Section

POL Section

Naval Section

[37] NATO Doc. ISM(57)4.

17

work out a production programme allocating everything, from the construction of so many battleships right down to the supply of so many rounds of small arms ammunition to various countries according to their capacity and resources, such a way is not open to NATO by its very constitution. Each country is responsible for the establishment, execution, and financial arrangements pertinent to its own production or procurement programme for its own forces, whether such procurement consists of items nationally made, or purchased from other NATO countries, or elsewhere abroad. . . .[38]

He suggested some of the reasons why the first approach had not been adopted:

I have stressed this so much because ideas were put forward in the early days of the Alliance for a large-scale programme of NATO-European production on a multi-lateral basis. These ideas, though attractive intellectually, foundered in practice on such reefs as national desires to favour home industries, difficulties of finding the money when finance remained a national responsibility, differing stages of national economic and industrial progress, security factors, and so on. Besides, such a programme, if super-imposed from above, would tend to smother the free play of competitive incentives of private industries in NATO countries. . . . however, progress has been made by working on a case by case basis, and some correlated production programmes have been put into effect by small groups of countries on particular items.[39]

The exchange of technical information, the gathering together of statistics, and the co-ordination of national defence production programmes was accomplished largely through the use of groups of experts, for the same reasons that had prompted the Western Union Supply Board to use them. The groups, many of which had been formed under the MPSB and the DPB, and which comprised national technical representatives, were served for secretarial purposes by individual officers of the Technical Sections of the Branch. Because of the large number of working groups, groups of experts, and their sub-groups, each performing specialized and limited tasks, it was desirable that secretaries should be permanently attached to them instead of coming from a central secretarial agency under the Executive Secretary. It was felt that secretaries needed to know when to take the initiative in calling sessions,

[34] Speech by Mr. J. Murray Mitchell, *op. cit.*   [39] ibid.

how to write minutes and reports in the appropriate vocabulary —in two languages, technical vocabulary problems became considerably greater—and when and with whom to co-ordinate a group's work. The secretary could stimulate his group and prompt further initiatives if he had technical knowledge of the subject area of his group. Therefore, only the secretariat to the Council Committees and their working groups, as distinct from these technical groups, were placed under the Executive Secretary. This action conformed to the policy recommended in 1956 by the Management Survey Team that all secretariats to the policy-making Committees of the Council should be within the office of the Executive Secretary, who was responsible for providing for the Council's secretariat needs.

The groups were the focal point for 'doing business' in the Production Branch; therefore, it is appropriate to examine their status and functioning in detail. The convening of persons of specialized skills and/or experience to perform a specific task and then disband had long been recognized as a useful practice in conducting international affairs. As pointed out earlier, the Combined Boards in World War II, constantly did this.[40]

[40] See Rosen, *op. cit.* NATO's associated international organization, OEEC, used groups of experts in a similar manner, although adapted to its own purposes. Mr. A. H. Robertson, in *European Institutions* (London, 1959), described their use: 'In accordance with the provisions of Article 15(c) of the Convention, the Council has set up a large number of Committees, each competent for the detailed study of a particular sector of economic activity. The primary division between these Committees is into "horizontal" and "vertical". . . . The task of the Horizontal Committees is the general study of a given economic problem common to all Member States. . . . The Vertical Committees are more specialised, being concerned with the study of specific products or services, such as the Coal, Iron and Steel, Maritime Transport or the Textile Committees. . . . The Vertical, or more specialised, Committees normally meet from two to four times a year, staffed by experts appointed by their governments, but usually coming from the home departments or from industry itself. The Horizontal, or more generalised, Committees meet more frequently, being attended for the most part by members of the permanent delegations resident in Paris. The function of both is to give expert opinions on matters within their competence and to reach the maximum possible agreement on the issues under consideration; where differences remain, it is for the Executive Committee or the Council—as political organs—to settle them.' (Pp. 36–37.)

Experts were brought together to dispose of an intransigent administrative or technical problem, to conduct preliminary negotiations before passing a matter on to higher bodies, to serve as the receptacle of a problem found irreconcilable at a higher level, or to exchange information.

When national defence policies are involved, however, many types of private and public interests can be brought to bear on a question. For this reason one of the major problems of the Production Branch was to see that the groups of experts were created and used effectively. This was of course a matter of policy as much as of administration, and therefore a matter which was in the final analysis, handled by the Council through its Committees. It was officially laid down: 'The members of Groups of Experts created by any of the Committees of the Council remain national representatives and act within the framework of the directions given by their own governments. They have no international status.'[41] The experts were paid by their respective governments.

The relationship of the groups of experts with the International Staff/Secretariat was carefully delineated:

The Chairman may be chosen by the Group of Experts or by the Secretary General or by the parent body which created the Group, according to the decision taken by the authority which approved the terms of reference of the Group.

The International Staff provides a secretary to the Group who is responsible, under the Chairman's instructions, for convening meetings, the preparation of agendas and, in some cases, papers connected therewith, the issue of minutes and for all other secretarial duties.

The International Staff is also so organized that there is an appropriate Division or Expert Section to support the work of Groups of Experts, to undertake research, to provide statistical services, to supply advice when requested, and to prepare papers for the Groups' consideration.[42]

[41] NATO, General Guidance for NATO Groups of Experts (Paris, 1955), p. 5.

[42] ibid. p. 6. In 1956 the NATO Management Survey Team recommended: 'In staffing for Working Groups and Committees concerned with the exchange of technical data, the division should use the technical experts as Chairmen of Committees, and members of the Executive Secretariat as Secretaries of Committees.' (NATO Management Survey Team, General Report, 1 May 1956, Annex I, par. 84.)

A group of experts could establish sub-groups or working parties from its own membership whenever the group found it necessary in order to subdivide its work or to expedite it.[43] But a group was not permitted to set up sub-groups which branched out into subject areas not specifically provided for in the group's terms of reference or which could not be construed as a logical extension of these terms. By 1956 there were over thirty groups, with memberships varying from four or five countries to twelve or thirteen, depending upon the subject and upon the interest of the countries. With a few exceptions (in the Production Branch, groups dealing with matters restricted to patentees or licensees), membership of the groups was open to those countries interested in participating.

It had been expected that the work of the various groups engaged in production activities could be suitably controlled by having them operate under the rubric of the Production Branch. They used the research and statistical facilities of the Branch's Technical Sections and were dependent upon its secretariat service. But less than two years after the creation of the Production and Logistics Division it became necessary to consider measures for tightening up the Council's control over the groups. On 12 February 1954 the Belgian delegation, in agreement with a memorandum previously circulated by the International Staff/Secretariat, suggested that a high-level permanent Council Committee should be established for this purpose. Each delegation had on its staff a production adviser, usually of the rank of Counsellor, who headed the production activities of the delegation and was thus responsible for its representatives to the groups of experts; it was now suggested that these advisers should meet as a committee to co-ordinate production matters and to discuss their problems.[44]

Another motive for the creation of this committee was the fact that the Annual Reviews (two had been held by early 1954) had revealed production lags; it was felt that further co-ordination would shorten delays because the committee could handle some of the production problems which the Annual Review brought to light.[45]

---

[43] General Guidance, p. 7.
[44] NATO Doc. (Belgian delegation letter) AR/101/54.   [45] ibid.

The Belgian delegation's proposal was sent to the Assistant Secretary-General for Production and Logistics, who forwarded it to Lord Ismay. On 3 March 1954 Lord Ismay presented the idea to the Council in the form of a suggestion that a Working Group on the Formation of a Production Committee should be created. This suggestion was adopted. The Group amplified the Belgian proposal in only two respects: it recommended that the committee should be concerned not only with the industrial aspects of production but also with standardization, and that is terms of reference should be short and general.[46]

At its Ministerial meeting in April 1954 the Council approved the terms of reference for the Defence Production Committee (DPC) on the lines proposed earlier. The Committee, composed of the defence production advisers from the delegations, was authorized to serve as the general advisory body to the Council on all defence production questions; it was also given authority to appoint groups of experts, to fix their terms of reference, and to forward the reports of the groups of experts, together with its own recommendations, to the Council. The Council invited the Secretary-General to nominate the Assistant Secretary-General for Production and Logistics as Chairman and to request a report from the Committee in six months' time.

The DPC submitted its first report to the Council in October 1954, as instructed. It dealt with such questions as the maintenance of equipment of North Atlantic origin (spare parts), the preservation of an industrial base for war-time production in the member countries, and the development of advance plans for industrial mobilization. But the main emphasis was on supervision of the groups of experts.

The DPC had come to play a central role in the life of the groups of experts; it could be either a help or a hindrance to their activities. If the Committee approved of a new project, for instance, it could if necessary push it through the Council and authorize the appointment of a group of experts to work it out. If the DPC disagreed with a proposal, it could either

[46] NATO Doc. AC/71-R1, Annex II. DPC also assumed responsibility for the work of the Working Group on Co-related Production Programmes in Europe.

not take implementary action, or suppress the group working on that subject, if one already existed. An underlying reason for the Committee's hesitation in creating a group was that expenses would automatically be incurred by the governments providing the membership. Travel fees and *per diem* payments would have to be met, and an additional expense would be incurred indirectly because the International Staff/Secretariat budget would have to provide facilities for meetings, secretariat services, etc.

Initiatives favouring the alteration of a group's status, or its creation or suppression, could come through several channels. Governments could make the proposal through their delegates on the Committee, and thence to the International Staff/Secretariat, or through their Permanent Representatives to the Council and thence to the DPC and the International Staff/Secretariat; the International Staff/Secretariat could initiate a proposal to the Assistant Secretary-General, who could introduce it in the DPC; or the Assistant Secretary-General could pass the proposal to the Secretary-General, who in turn could introduce it into the Council and thence to the DPC. In practice, as far as production matters were concerned, the Council seldom acted without having referred the matter first to the DPC.

As for the Assistant Secretary-General, his occupancy of two positions—he was Head of the Production Branch of the International Staff/Secretariat and Chairman of the DPC, a Council Committee—did not create difficulties. As long as a group of experts was working within its terms of reference he was not directly involved. Only if a matter of policy arose, such as the introduction of a new subject or the redirection of a subject, would he take part. In both his capacities he could contribute to whatever considerations or decisions were taken. In addition, as Head of the Production Branch, he was able to work out suitable adjustments with the Executive Secretary if secretariat duties were not being carried out properly. It was obvious, however, that the balance of power lay on the side of the delegations.

As mentioned earlier, the specific question to which the DPC addressed itself during its first six months—and indeed for two years thereafter—was what exactly were the groups of experts doing and to what extent were they working within their terms of reference. To get rid of any misconceptions about the organization of a group the Committee laid down this policy:

Each Group of Experts is attached, for the provision of the various facilities necessary for the execution of its work, to the appropriate technical section of the Production and Logistics Division.

Subject to the confirmation by the Defence Production Committee, Groups of Experts will choose their own chairman—either one of the members of the group, or the head of the section concerned. In the absence of the elected chairman, the head of the section concerned acts as temporary replacement.

When a chairman other than the head of section concerned has been appointed the latter will assist him and help him guide the Group in the performance of its duties.

The secretary to the Group will be provided by the International Staff and will normally be an officer of the technical section concerned.[47]

As far as the role of the experts was concerned, apparently the DPC wanted to make sure that they were competent from both a technical and a national viewpoint, for the Committee provided:

In arriving at conclusions, it is expected that the Groups of Experts will primarily give consideration to the technical aspects of the problem rather than to the national preferences of their individual countries. However, it is recognized that the individuals composing the groups must keep in mind, as a secondary consideration, their countries' preferences, since, in the final analysis, it will be essential for NATO nations to approve the solution before it can be made effective. It will, therefore, be necessary for each individual of a group of experts to familiarise himself with the national position and preference of his own Government.[48]

Certain controls over the activities of the groups were instituted by the DPC. The most far-reaching was the requirement that draft agenda, reports of meetings, and an annual report be submitted to the DPC. By imposing this requirement on the groups the DPC ensured that the entire process of their

[47] General Guidance, p. 9.   [48] ibid.

activities, including the work of the International Staff/Secretariat, was tightened up.[49] At first the DPC saw all the reports rendered by the various sub-groups and working groups, as well as those of the main groups. But this proved to be too burdensome, so a modified procedure was approved:

The Chairmen of the sub-groups and special working groups will normally submit reports to or seek instructions from their main Group, but where necessary the Defence Production Committee can be informed directly in cases where presentation by the main Group would cause serious delay.

The Chairman of the main group, or failing him, the head of section concerned and/or the Secretary, will attend meetings of the Defence Production Committee when questions of interest to the Group, and in particular the annual report presented by it are being discussed there, in order to give any detailed information required and to answer any questions the Committe may wish to put.

Each Group will submit to the Defence Production Committee once a year, before 30 September, a progress report for itself, its sub-groups and special working groups, covering the preceding period 1st August–31st July.[50]

To tighten up the day-to-day work of the groups and their subsidiary bodies the DPC required that after each meeting of a main group it should draw up a programme of further activity to be undertaken by itself or by its sub-groups or working groups before the main group's next meeting. Then, on the basis of this tentative programme the secretary of the main group could prepare a composite draft agenda for submission to the DPC for approval.[51]

As regards location of meetings, in March 1956 the Civilian Budget Committee approved a policy statement which precluded excessive travel on the part of the International Staff/

[49] The policy paper by which the DPC controlled the groups of experts was NATO Doc. AC/74-D/122(Final). The electronics groups were not examined closely until Apr. 1956. The final paper on control of the electronics groups was not issued until Autumn 1956 when twenty-odd groups were reduced to about four.

[50] NATO Doc. AC/74-D/250. This policy was laid down a year after Lord Ismay retired, but its purpose and intent had been developing during his tenure of office.

[51] Quoted in NATO Doc. AC/74-D/250.

Secretariat. Doubtless this statement was a reaction to a tendency some groups of experts had to assemble in places convenient for reasons other than the performance of their duties. The Committee:

> . . . recommended that the meetings of Groups of Experts should be held as far as possible in the Paris district, on the understanding that if a meeting was held elsewhere at the request of a particular country, the latter should be made responsible for the cost of any travel on the part of members of the International Staff; on the other hand, if the decision to hold a meeting outside France was taken by a NATO Committee or by the International Staff, and not as a result of an invitation from one of the member countries, it should be left to the Financial Controller to decide whether it was necessary to send members of the International Staff to such meetings.[52]

Requests to hold meetings in places other than Paris had to be submitted through the DPC for the approval of the Secretary-General.

Another vexing problem was whether and under what conditions industrial representatives should be allowed into meetings. The implications of this problem are obvious when it is considered that information exchanged about production plans might result in the placement of competitive orders. To prevent any unauthorized or inadvertent disclosures of information the DPC followed a rigid policy, the main provisions of which were:

> . . . that on the occasion of the consideration by the Defence Production Committee of a given Group of Experts' agenda, the decision shall be taken as to whether industrial experts should or should not be admitted to the proposed meeting of the Group or to meetings of such Sub-Groups as may be directed to deal with any one of the items on the agenda, and such decision shall be duly recorded;

> that in the event of a decision that industrial experts are not entitled to participate, the approved agenda shall bear an appropriate indication to this effect, which shall be similarly borne on the Sub-Group agendas;

---

[52] NATO Doc. ON(56)14.

that when a Group of Experts proposes to the Defence Production Committee the creation of a Special Working Group to deal with a particular item, the Committee shall decide whether or not industrial experts may take part in the work of such a Group, and such decision shall be duly recorded;

that industrial experts shall be defined as persons employed in privately-owned industrial or commercial enterprises;

that in all cases, whether of Groups of Experts, Sub-Groups or Special Working Groups, the Chairman concerned shall ensure that members of the Group are formally introduced at the beginning of each meeting and their status announced.[53]

In December 1956 the DPC approved a draft statement submitted by the Working Group on the Protection of Proprietary Technical Information which was intended to give general guidance to the groups.[54] This statement, together with the restrictions placed upon the presence of industrial representatives, went a long way to ensure confidence in the integrity of the work of the groups of experts.

From this exposition of the work of the DPC it would seem that the Production Branch's achievements were rather limited. Limited or not, the Branch's efforts were considerable. Throughout the period under discussion it concentrated its efforts mainly on the co-ordination of production programmes. In the five years of Lord Ismay's leadership, however, there were alterations and fluctuations in emphasis which could be roughly identified with the tenures of the various Assistant Secretaries-General, and which arose from the Alliance's changing economic and political situation.

From 1952 until 1956 the emphasis was on the creation of military industrial production capacity in Western Europe, on the build-up of the planned forces-in-being, and on the standardization of equipment. From late 1956 the emphasis shifted to maintenance of the production base which had been created and to adjustments to meet the altered conditions presented by

[53] Quoted in NATO Doc. AC/74-D250, Annex. App. A.

[54] Quoted in NATO Doc. AC/74-D250, Annex. App. B. The statement applied to patented, unpatented, patentable, and unpatentable technical information, and to the relevance of technical information which had been security classified by a government.

the advances in military technological research and development, especially in the atomic field.[55]

The first Assistant Secretary-General—appointed in June 1952—was Mr. David Luke Hopkins, an American business executive and philanthropist. Mr. Hopkins had a twofold purpose: to build up both the military stocks and the productive capacity of the European members of the Alliance. To accomplish this dual task he set about encouraging the development of what he called 'co-ordinated production'. By this he meant the voluntary pooling by member nations of information about production plans, including the utilization of production facilities.

Under Mr. Hopkins the International Staff/Secretariat ascertained the production positions of member countries, what stocks they had on hand, and what their needs were (this was done partly through the Annual Review). Then the Branch applied against this information equipment needs for the contemplated military forces (force goals). The International Staff/Secretariat had to perform such tasks as estimating the tonnage of stocks on hand and the consumption rates over a given period of time, and evaluating the efficiency of a production capacity which produced specified goods at a certain rate.

Although this was important work—especially in the fields of ammunition, propellents, and explosives—it was not the

---

[55] This does not mean that there was consistent leadership in the Branch for the entire period of Lord Ismay's tenure of office; nor that the Branch was necessarily either engaging in new activities or neglecting old ones during any particular period. In the first instance, there were extensive periods when the post of Assistant Secretary-General was vacant because the U.S. was tardy in naming a replacement. Thus the shifts in emphasis did not coincide exactly with the terms of office of each Assistant Secretary-General. Rather, each Assistant Secretary-General tended to become identified with these emphases, owing partly to the circumstances in which he worked and partly to his own interpretation of his mission. In the second instance, the work of all the Technical Sections of the Branch went on regardless of whether there was an Assistant Secretary-General or not. M. Alain Moreau of France, Deputy Assistant Secretary-General from May 1955, and his predecessors, functioned as Acting Assistant Secretary-General during the intervals.

co-ordinated production programme originally envisaged. Paradoxically, Mr. Hopkins found that he was severely limited in his endeavour by the overwhelming impact which his own country's production and supply policies had on the Alliance. He was faced with the same situation that had confronted the Co-ordinator for the DPB. In 1952 the European member countries were just recovering economically from the ravages of World War II. Their production capacity was still limited, and their reserves or stocks of military supplies and equipment were virtually non-existent. Therefore, the United States had to provide the bulk of the equipment in order to rearm NATO's forces, and at the same time to encourage the build-up of the member countries' productive capacity in order to avoid throwing them into economic chaos.

For these purposes the United States instituted the Mutual Defence Assistance Programme (MDAP) which was administered bilaterally. A Military Assistance Advisory Group (MAAG) was situated in each NATO country to collect its own information about the country's needs. Reports were sent to Washington where they were compiled and made into a single comprehensive programme to be submitted each year to Congress. From 1952 to 1956 it could be said that the Production Branch (and also the Economics and Finance Division) of the International Staff/Secretariat had to work in conjunction with the United States; there were few signs of a co-ordinated, multilateral effort.

Lord Ismay recognized this when he said:

United States aid to Europe . . . has been furnished on the basis of bilateral agreements negotiated between the United States and the individual recipient countries. The level and the nature of the military aid given to NATO member states is based on the military force goals agreed upon in the course of the Annual Review, the recommendations of the NATO military authorities and the ability of the recipient country to utilize the aid effectively.[56]

By April 1954 the value of equipment furnished by the United States to its NATO partners had reached about $15,000,000,000.[57] Of this aid $1,700,000,000 had gone toward

---

[56] *The Five Years*, p. 136   [57] ibid.

OSP. The OSP programme in effect, tended to pre-empt the second part of Mr. Hopkins's objective, just as bilateral direct assistance had pre-empted the first part. Nonetheless OSP provided advantages:

. . . it enlarges the European military production base, reduces the dependence on North American sources of supply, and fosters the development and maintenance of modern military production techniques and special skills. In certain instances, it prevents existing European defence production capacity from deteriorating or going out of use;

supply lines are shortened, with consequent easing of logistical problems;

European unit costs are lower in some instances than United States costs, and packing and shipping charges are smaller; it is therefore possible for a given expenditure in dollars to procure more equipment;

the scheme lends general support to the economy of the European member nations by providing not only a means of earning dollars but also employment for many European workers;

it is easily dovetailed in with the NATO correlated production programmes for Europe and these two concepts are being developed along lines mutually beneficial and stimulating.[58]

The distribution of commodities obtained through OSP was controlled by the United States. It was possible, therefore, for a NATO country to manufacture equipment on behalf of the United States for delivery to a non-NATO country, but the bulk of such procurement was delivered either to the manufacturing country's forces or to another NATO country. However, the fact that control was held by the United States did not add to the authority of the Production Branch nor did it encourage the development of co-ordinated production.[59]

One of the biggest steps toward furthering the build-up of European capacity through OSP was the placing of orders for

[58] ibid. pp. 137 and 139.

[59] For example, the Pentagon was strongly influenced by costs, which meant that a country with no productive capacity was less likely to get an order than a country with plant, raw materials, or technical skills. Ideally, perhaps, from a NATO-wide viewpoint, productive capacity should have been developed in the country with little or none.

aircraft. The Aircraft Section of the Production Branch played a useful part in this. The International Staff/Secretariat had its first opportunity to promote the co-ordinated production of aircraft in June 1952 when the United States announced that, if a sound plan could be devised for European aircraft production, it would be willing to place OSP contracts to help the cause of co-ordination. The International Staff/Secretariat made a study of the situation and recommended that military aircraft be produced in Belgium, France, Italy, The Netherlands and the United Kingdom. With the International Staff/Secretariat's report as a starter, the countries concerned engaged in bilateral negotiations with the United States (and here the system lost its 'co-ordinative character') which culminated some ten months later in the signing of contracts worth some $550,000,000.[60] Mr. Charles E. Wilson, United States Secretary of Defence, echoed the sentiments of his NATO colleagues, when he said:

We hope that the International Staff, with the full support of all NATO nations, will soon be in a position to provide other co-ordinated procurement plans for achieving a strong and unified Europe. This will be far more efficient and far less costly than the past efforts of individual European nations to achieve complete self-sufficiency in all branches of arms and military supplies. I believe the aircraft procurement programme initiated by the NATO International Staff is a symbol of the progress being made in our collective efforts toward achieving military unity within the structure of the North Atlantic Treaty Organization.[61]

One weakness in this idea of co-ordinated production was the fact that, just as the Annual Review was sometimes held up until countries ascertained what part of their defence budgets would be augmented by United States Mutual Defence Assistance funds, so each country viewed production co-ordination in terms of its chances of obtaining contracts from the United States rather than from one another.

All these considerations began to have their effect by mid-1953 when Mr. Hopkins was succeeded by Mr. Lowell P. Weicker, an American manufacturer. Under Mr. Weicker

[60] Statements by Lord Ismay, 23 Apr. 1953, (NATO Press Release.)
[61] Statement made 23 Apr. 1953. (NATO Press Release.)

defence production assumed a different emphasis. The change was toward increased standardization of items of equipment. It was felt that, with the greater flow of equipment into the hands of the military forces and the gradual dispersal of capacity to produce equipment, it would be useful—indeed in some instances essential—for all nations to be using similar types of equipment and ammunition, produced according to the same specifications. The idea went back to the earliest years of the Alliance, but it had become especially appropriate by 1953. This was true both in regard to the American equipment being introduced or locally produced, and to new items appearing as the result of research and development.

The Production Branch helped this effort by assisting in the creation of groups of experts to consider specific items which lent themselves to standardization. A large number of such groups were brought into existence in 1953. The groups ascertained whether the manufacturing techniques applied to production of the items under consideration were aimed at reducing costs and duplication of research and development. They pooled their information in order to arrive at a situation conducive to agreement on uniform specifications.

It was necessary to build up extensive stocks-in-being of ammunition almost from nothing to have on hand for immediate expenditure if war broke out. But, because of the high rate of consumption of ammunition in war-time, it was also necessary to establish a strong and secure production base which could work to full capacity when needed. During Lord Ismay's tenure of office, therefore, standardization was applied most fully to the production of ammunition.[62]

One of the most promising groups was the Group of Experts on New Ammunition Manufacturing Techniques, which inquired into the results of the research and development of new weapons, new explosives, and propellents, and into the plans for the adoption of standard ammunition for conventional weapons. It also worked out such problems as how to produce

[62] Other notable areas of standardization were electronics—resistors, capacitors, tubes, etc.; and armaments—towing hooks and braking systems. An example of the limitations on standardization of ammunition stockpiling was the necessity to conform to the various national laws regarding the handling and storing of ammunition.

stocks of ammunition at the lowest cost and how to store them.

The Ammunition Section of the Production Branch played a major part in the development of 'new ammunition (as in the case of the 40/70 ammunition); the components of ammunition (as in the case of propellents and propagols); new techniques (as in the case of steel cartridge cases, sintered driving bands); new methods of packaging ammunition; and radiac and anti-gas equipment'.[63]

The Branch did important work in handling the testing and specifications made necessary by the decision to adopt a standard round—the 7·62 mm.—for rifles and machine guns. It was not intended that all NATO countries should use the same rifle, but it seemed eminently reasonable that all troops should fire the same bullet. Common range facilities for testing weapons and ammunitions were also set up. Two Regional Test Centres were equipped, one in the United States and the other in the United Kingdom. The Ammunition Section of the Branch was the clearing-house for both these Centres and the repository for the test records.[64]

Considerable interest was shown in the Bofors anti-aircraft gun and ammunition developed and manufactured in Sweden, which was not a NATO country. But restrictions limited the use of information about Bofors weapons to Bofors licensees so that it was necessary to compose special groups of experts, called panels of experts, consisting only of representatives of those countries which were licensees. These panels were not placed directly under the DPC. As an indication of how one project could lead to another, the work done with Bofors led to the development of relations with the International Civil Aviation Organization in order to investigate the possibilities of standardizing a ballistics meteorological message.[65]

These activities of the Branch were dovetailed to a large degree into the work of the Military Agency for Standardization. This Agency, which came into existence early in 1951, was located in London and came within the ambit of the Standing Group rather than of the Secretary-General. The Agency was responsible for negotiating agreements to comply with a particular standardization project among those parties

[63] NATO Doc. AMM/1-1-01/2341.   [64] ibid.   [65] ibid.

who wished to participate. The draft STANAG, as the Standardization Agreement was called, set forth the terms of agreement and the technical specifications. Drafts were circulated to the governments and after ratification were issued as STANAGS.[66] If a proposed STANAG was highly technical the Agency requested the appropriate group of experts in the Production Branch to work out for it the specifications, standards, and other provisions. Thus, although a requirement for standardization usually originated on the military side of the Alliance, much of the initiative for a project and its technical arrangements were provided by the Production Branch.

When Mr. Weicker relinquished his post in 1955 the emphasis began to shift from standardization toward the concept of the 'maintenance of the production base'. By 1956, when Mr. J. Murray Mitchell, an American banker who had served as Assistant to the Head of the United States Office of Defence Mobilization, became Assistant Secretary-General, the OSP programme had begun to run out, which meant that factories in Europe were being converted to the production of consumers goods. Prosperity in Europe was creating a demand for more factory space and the leverage toward military production which the United States had exerted in channelling production activities was reduced as her expenditure became less liberal.

Another reason for the shift of emphasis was the changing nature of the Alliance's defence needs: in 1956 there was a distinct movement away from the policy of training and equipping large standing armies towards that of having smaller, more highly trained units, equipped with atomic weapons and possessing greater firepower per man.[67] It was argued by some persons that, if atomic war were to come, it would last only about thirty days; therefore, why maintain a large military production base which would not have an opportunity to be used? This argument encouraged the member countries' natural tendency to use their productive capacity for civilian purposes or to let it lie idle rather than burden their defence budgets further than was minimally necessary. The

[66] Speech by Mr. J. Murray Mitchell, 1 Oct. 1956. (unpub.)

[67] The basic policy decision announcing this change had been made in 1954 but its effects were not felt until 1956.

encouragement given by the Production Branch to maintain the production base was intended to counteract this tendency.

The redefinition of the nature of NATO's military forces resulted in a transformation which brought into play administrative concepts and agencies which had not been foreseen. The first of these new agencies was concerned with spare parts. The need for it arose because the European allies found themselves relying on military equipment which was rapidly becoming obsolete in the United States. For, as the Americans moved away from the use of conventional weapons, they became increasingly reluctant to continue to manufacture those items of conventional equipment which were still needed for replacement purposes for the forces of the Western European nations.

To resolve this problem the Council decided to establish a NATO Maintenance and Supply Service Agency—commonly referred to as the Spare Parts Agency. The Agency came into existence late in 1957. It was almost a commercial enterprise, for it was authorized to buy from its own funds spare parts in quantities justifying the placing of economically feasible production orders, and, as requisitions came in from the member countries, to sell them. Till then groups of experts working with the Spare Parts Co-ordination Section within the Production Branch had done this work but, as the need grew so large and the financial implications became obvious, recourse was made to this modified common funding scheme and the Section was dissolved. The agency was not placed within the International Staff/Secretariat.

Lending increased recognition to the changing technological situation, the Council, at its Heads of Government meeting in December 1957, approved the creation of a Science Committee of the Council and the appointment of a Science Adviser to the Secretary-General.[68] The basic scientific research aspects of defence production were lodged with the Office of the Science Adviser, leaving pre-production research and development to be dealt with by the DPC (renamed the Armaments Committee).

With these new developments, which underlined the opening-up of new possibilities for co-operation in the field of

[68] Final Communiqué of the Heads of Government meeting of the North Atlantic Council, Dec. 1957.

defence production, the Production Branch found its relationship to other NATO bodies changing, but it continued to provide useful assistance both through the research and co-ordinative work of the technical sections and groups of experts, and through the taking of whatever initiatives it felt would contribute to the solution of complex new problems which arose as a result of technological developments.[69]

[69] The creation of an Agency for the Control of Armaments, within the framework of WEU in Oct. 1954, produced a situation in which one European international organization was working toward the limitation of armaments while another was trying to build them up. (See *The Five Years*, Suppl. App. for the Agreements bringing WEU into being.) WEU's Standing Armaments Committee from 1956 onward played a significant role in the defence production policies of the European members of NATO. The dichotomy between NATO and WEU in this respect was not as great as might appear, for the same national representatives who sat on NATO's DPC also sat on WEU's Standing Armaments Committee. In 1958 the DPC was renamed the NATO Armaments Committee and given slightly altered terms of reference.

CHAPTER XII

THE INFRASTRUCTURE PROGRAMME

DURING the 1950s the word 'supranational' was increasingly employed in connexion with the movement to unite Europe. The formation of the European Coal and Steel Community, with its special powers, was a landmark achievement. Franco-German co-operation in this endeavour, and that of Italy and the Benelux countries, was a significant first step toward European integration. The idea of a European Economic Community which would embrace Britain and the other countries which came to form the European Free Trade Association captured the interest of the entire world.

Unfortunately European co-operation in military and political affairs in the 1950s was neither so widespread nor so successful. The proposed European Defence Community (EDC), which might have brought some supranational control over military integration, was stillborn. Even if it had proved possible to arrive at an acceptable treaty, the feasibility of an effective defence community was uncertain. Notwithstanding this, the demise of EDC closed the door to any truly effective politico-military supranationalism in Europe. The nadir of politico-military co-operation in the 1950s was reached in 1956 with the Suez débâcle, which among other things symbolized the effort of former European Great Powers to retain their freedom of politico-military action. Thereafter, at least for Britain, interdependence with the United States became the watchword.

Thus, in political and military affairs the idea of supranationalism was more a symbol of something hoped for than a description of things achieved. However, the emergence of NATO, which relied upon varying degrees of economic and political cohesiveness for its survival, makes it appropriate to examine that aspect of the Alliance which came nearest to supranationalism.

NATO and supranationality should be examined for two

reasons. First, without a successful NATO—economically as well as militarily—European economic recovery and unity could not have been achieved so quickly and so well. Second, it is significant that, within NATO, nationalistic tendencies were most effectively overcome in economic affairs. It was well recognized in the 1950s that any success NATO might have in becoming a truly international organization had to come as much through economic co-operation as through various politico-military arrangements. Co-operation was indeed constantly stressed in all spheres of NATO economic activity, and it advanced considerably—for example, through the joint work of the OEEC and the International Staff/Secretariat (above, Ch. X).

Although integration was an elusive goal, the student of international administration who looks for pragmatic or evolutionary signs pointing towards supranationalism can take some heart, for, of the Alliance's two primary economic functions—the Annual Review and the Infrastructure Programme—infrastructure showed definite signs of supranationalism.

The word 'infrastructure' came into the NATO lexicon from French.[1] It was defined for NATO purposes as the 'static items of capital expenditure required to give the material backing for operational plans necessary to enable the higher command to function and the various forces to operate with efficiency'.[2] Lord Ismay gave the word a more exact definition:

[1] A distinction must be made between 'common infrastructure' and 'national infrastructure'. Lord Ismay defined the two terms: 'Installations which are set up for the maintenance and training of *national* forces in time of peace, and for the defence of the homeland in time of war, are called "national infrastructure". They are of course paid for out of national budgets. Installations which are set up at the request of NATO international Commanders for the maintenance and training of NATO international forces in time of peace, and for their effective operation in time of war, are called "common infrastructure". They are paid for collectively by member governments.' (*The Five Years*, p. 114, his emphasis.) The present Chapter deals only with common infrastructure because national infrastructure did not come within the range of the International Staff/Secretariat's activities.

[2] This was the official Standing Group definition as of Sept. 1950. (NATO Press Release, 1 Dec. 1952.)

. . . a generic term to denote all those fixed installations which are necessary for the effective deployment and operations of modern armed forces, for example, airfields, signals communications, military headquarters, fuel tanks and pipelines, radar warning and navigational aid stations, port installations, and so forth.[3]

The Infrastructure Branch of the Production and Logistics Division derived its origins from WUDO. The major contribution of the WUDO phase of the Infrastructure Programme was that all the participating nations (the Benelux countries, Britain, and France) agreed to share in the cost of projects which, owing to the dictates of geography, could be located in only a few of the countries concerned. Thus cost-sharing, the heart of any supranational endeavour, evolved from WUDO. But agreement on a cost-sharing formula did not come easily. It was difficult for nations to see that what might appear as an economic advantage to one nation, owing to the installations construction carried out in that nation under infrastructure contracts, was in fact to the advantage of all. If one recalls the difficulty the United States government had in the early 1950s in breaking away from the 'equal share' concept of the budgets for the three military services, then one gains some measure of the problem.

In WUDO during 1949 the construction of certain installations was planned—specifically, 30 airfields, one headquarters, and about 34 signal communications projects—but member countries had not given the actual authorization to begin the work. In January 1950 the Finance Ministers of WUDO at a meeting in Paris, primarily at the suggestion of the United Kingdom which was reluctant to become too economically enmeshed in Europe, decided not to authorize the necessary funds. Fortunately, however, the decision was reversed at a combined meeting of the Foreign, Defence, and Finance Ministers of WUDO held in April 1950 in Brussels. As the story went:

. . . on the night before the meeting opened, it was learned that the British would not insist on maintaining the Paris decisions and when the Infrastructure programme came up for discussions in the Council, the United Kingdom Defence Minister, Mr. E.

[3] *The Five Years*, p. 114.

Shinwell, announced that the United Kingdom realised that the burden of the proposed Infrastructure programme would fall disproportionately heavily upon his country's Continental Allies in view of the operational requirements for the airfields and tele-communications to be located in those countries. He said the United Kingdom would be prepared to contribute a reasonable sum towards the cost of the programme, on the condition that it was reduced to the essential minimum.[4]

This authorization became known as the 'first slice', and was the only one entirely undertaken by WUDO. It was, however, no more than a commitment to support the projects— the actual formula by which costs would be shared, and the ceilings on costs were not worked out. The planning of the 'second slice' was begun by WUDO but was taken over by NATO after SHAPE came into existence in June 1951. SHAPE's recommendations were submitted to the NATO Council Deputies, which appointed a Council Committee to report on the feasibility of financing the projects proposed: namely, the building of 13 new airfields, 8 extensions, and 53 signals communications projects, the total cost of which would be £79,000,000.[5] In this committee, called the Infra-structure Committee, the financial negotiations to arrive at an equitable method of cost-sharing took place.

Mijnh. G. O. J. van Tets of The Netherlands, former Chair-man of the Infrastructure Payments and Progress Committee, says of the difficulties which the Committee encountered:

At first, attempts were made to arrive at a cost-sharing by the application of certain basic principles agreed in advance.

Many nations favoured the criterion of 'capacity-to-pay', which could be calculated on the basis of the statistics on the Gross National Production. These figures could to some extent be adjusted to take into account the income per head of the population in each

---

[4] G. O. J. van Tets, 'The Birth and Significance of Common Infra-structure', *The Fifteen Nations*, II, Sept. 1956, p. 51. Mijnh van Tets was the first Chairman of the Infrastructure Payments and Progress Committee. The non-participation of the U.S. and Canada at this time was in part due to their already having large foreign aid programmes to the WUDO countries.

[5] *The Five Years*, p. 115. NATO continued WUDO's practice of carrying infrastructure accounts in pounds sterling.

country, the economic benefit to host countries as a result of the installations built on their territory, and other relevant factors. Such factors were of great importance in the cost-sharing. While a considerable proportion of the work to be executed under a slice was, for instance, located in France, the French budget could not possibly bear more than a fraction of the cost, unless this were to be met at the expense of other portions of the defence effort. On the basis of the Gross National Production Statistics, French capacity to pay would be less than one-tenth of the total, that of the United States well over 70%.

One should add to this the effect of adjustments by taking into account *per capita* national income and realise that income per head of the population in the United States is roughly three times as high as that in some of the richer European countries. . . . It is clear that the capacity-to-pay formula would have resulted in a very high share for the U.S. who were already granting a large amount of aid to NATO nations in other fields.

Some, therefore, favoured the 'user nations' criterion. The cost of airfields, for instance, would be shared in accordance with the number of squadrons deployed by each nation in the area concerned, the telecommunications on the basis of the number of military personnel to be similarly deployed. Such a formula, however, was not acceptable to other nations. Apart from leaving a number of problems unsolved because no accurate calculations could be made on the basis suggested, it would have meant that the United States, Canada and the United Kingdom—which have the greatest capacity to pay—would only share to the extent of the units they deployed on the continent of Europe, while the continental countries would by the very nature of things in view of their geographical location deploy practically all their units in that area.

When it became clear that no formula could be worked out on the basis of the application of certain basic criteria, advantage was taken of the presence of all the Defence and Finance Ministers in Ottawa to agree to the sharing of the cost of the programme on the basis of negotiation.[6]

The second slice was therefore negotiated at Ottawa in September 1951, with the United States and Canada joining the five Powers of WUDO which had financed the first slice. The Ottawa meeting of the Council was a very significant event, for it was at this time that NATO came to grips with the problem of how to finance the entire Alliance. Earlier, a system of

[6] van Tets, p. 54.

common funding had been considered whereby the Alliance would have been empowered to direct its own financial future, not only in infrastructure but also in such areas as arms standardization and procurement. However, the idea had lost most of its vitality by 1951 owing to the inability of the member nations to devise a common stocktaking or budgetary system to serve their purposes, and also to their unwillingness to delegate to NATO discretionary authority in economics and finance. Until 1952, as mentioned earlier, there was no NATO civilian administrative machinery which could be called an international bureaucracy: administration was conducted through various committees and working groups composed of representatives of the member nations largely on an *ad hoc* basis.

As explained earlier (*above* Chapter X), the TCC was established at Ottawa to resolve this situation and was empowered to bring order to NATO's finances and to make recommendations for strengthening its administrative machinery. Among other things the TCC frankly recognized that no mathematical formula based on assumptions for sharing infrastructure costs could be worked out which would eliminate at least an appearance of inequity among the member nations. From September 1951 until the Lisbon meeting the TCC attempted to arrive at a solution to this problem.

During this time the Infrastructure Programme had grown apace. The third slice, submitted by SHAPE early in 1952, consisted of 53 new airfields, 27 extensions of airfields already under construction, about 58 additional schemes for improving communications facilities, and the construction of 10 new headquarters.[7] The third slice was shared by ten countries for, since some of the new installations were to be built in Denmark, Italy, and Norway, these three countries consented to participate in the Programme. By the time of the fourth slice in December 1952 all the NATO nations except Iceland were

---

[7] The second slice ultimately came to £124·76 million; the third slice to £183·22 million. The first three slices, formulated and applied before estimates and cost controls for the Programme had been worked out, were not finally settled until 1956, when retroactive ceilings were put on them. (Interview with Dr. H. West-Burnham, 28 Aug. 1959.)

sharing in the cost. The fourth slice, set at £297,000,000 in the first place, was reduced by the Supreme Commanders to £182,000,000 by retaining only those items which they foresaw would be needed by 1954. The Council further reduced this figure to £80,000,000 by directing the military planners to defer, until after the completion of the first Annual Review, estimates for all projects which did not need to be started immediately. The enduring problem at this time was to find a proper formula according to which the 'slices' of the Programme could be paid for by the member countries. It was recognized that, although common funding was not politically or economically feasible as a method of rearming all NATO nations (the United States for instance insisted on retaining a bilateral rather than a multilateral aid programme), it was a necessity if infrastructure projects were to be carried out as a co-operative endeavour.

To escape from the impasse which existed between its meetings in December 1952 and April 1953 and which had blocked all NATO financial activities, the Council authorized the Secretary-General to propose a cost-sharing formula for paying infrastructure costs, stipulating that the fifth and sixth slices should be paid for in the same proportions as had been set down for the fourth slice. After the failure to reach agreement through multilateral negotiation, Lord Ismay accordingly offered a formula. He described the incident thus:

They dumped the whole problem in my lap, so I called in three assistant secretaries-general, and each of us drew up our own list of what we thought the percentage of sharing should be, and then we averaged them out. I couldn't for the life of me possibly say on what basis I acted, except that I tried to take into account all sorts of things like the ability to pay and whether the building would be going on in a country so that it would benefit from the construction and the money spent.

Then we got into the Council meeting in April of 1953, and everybody around the table thought it was a jolly good distribution except for his own, which they thought was too high. Anyway, we went round the table and finally got agreement of each to take what was given within 1·8 per cent of the total, and then we simply divided up that 1·8 per cent among the fourteen, and that's all there was to it. That's why all the shares are in those funny percentage amounts.[8]

The Council had agreed that cost-sharing should be handled independently of the geographical distribution of the infrastructure projects: that is, without any nation knowing in advance what facilities would be jointly constructed in its territory. To have done otherwise would have opened the door to endless wrangling over who should pay how much for which projects. By 1956 the entire programme added up to over £700,000,000 in commitments. Fortunately for Lord Ismay the problem of the cost-sharing formula for this huge sum had been solved successfully, if not too tidily mathematically.

The execution of the Programme—that is, the various 'slices'—was carried out under the supervision of the Infrastructure Committee. The Committee did not have its own staff until early in 1952. Initially, serious consideration was given to the proposal that SHAPE should carry out the work because the installations were being constructed for the military forces. The civilian technicians, mostly civil engineers, who were to be given the task of co-ordinating and supervising the accomplishment of the projects, would thus have been on the military and not the civilian side of NATO. One government even suggested that military technicians should be used, and said that since it had civil engineers who were part of its military forces, it could provide them for the rest of NATO. Obviously, acceptance of its offer would have given this country an overwhelming influence in infrastructure matters.

After some discussion the Council decided to use civilian technicians and to incorporate them into the International Staff/Secretariat as the Infrastructure Section of the Production and Logistics Division. The Section became the agent of the Infrastructure Committee.[9] This decision to assign the infra-

[8] Anne M. Warburton and John B. Wood, p. 31; *New York Herald-Tribune*, 8 May 1953. For a breakdown of the percentage, see NATO Press Release, 24 Apr. 1953.

[9] The decision to place the infrastructure functions in the Production and Logistics Division was made upon the recommendation of Mr. William Batt in his 1952 O&M survey of the Division. Mr. Batt's reasoning was that logistics being the provision of supply and material, it was logical that this should include permanent installations.

structure function to the civilian International Staff/Secretariat, and thus to make it independent of the military staff, was of some significance. It demonstrated, for example, that the military authorities were subject to civilian control and that the civilian infrastructure staff would not be subject to military supervision. In general, the principle was laid down in 1952 that non-military matters would be handled by the civilian authorities of NATO.

Mr. Basil Wedd, a Canadian engineer who had had experience in NATO defence production activities, was brought in as Executive Officer to the Committee to supervise the administration of funds. His duties were to travel about to inspect the construction projects, to co-ordinate matters between the various agencies involved and the International Staff/Secretariat, to head the Infrastructure Section, and to provide the secretariat for the infrastructure committees. The working groups for signals, airfields, and petrol, oil and lubricants (POL), which had been created before the International Staff/Secretariat and which consisted of national representatives, were brought into the section. The civilian technicians were organized in the same subject areas as the working groups, but they now became part of the infrastructure staff and thus international civil servants. Thus, at the operating level, infrastructure matters were likely to be regarded as of a technical rather than a political nature.

Another body, set up in 1951 as a subcommittee of the Infrastructure Committee, to supervise the financial controls over the expenditure of funds, was the Payments and Progress Committee (P & P). It became a full-fledged Council Committee in 1952, with Mijnh. van Tets serving as its first Chairman. The two Committees divided their labour in the following way: the Infrastructure Committee made the basic policy decisions and the P & P Committee supervised their implementation.

In 1953, when Mr. Wedd resigned from his position as Executive officer, the Assistant Secretary-General for Production and Logistics, Mr. Lowell Weicker, wanted to replace him with another Canadian engineer but he was unable to obtain the services of the man he had in mind. He then asked the American Permanent Representative to the Council,

Mr. William Draper, to nominate a replacement.[10] Mr. Eugene Merrill, an American civil engineer with broad experience in private and government activities, was nominated. Immediately before his appointment to NATO he had been a Commissioner of the Federal Communications Commission. Earlier he had served with the United States occupation administration in Germany. Mr. Weicker sent a memorandum to Lord Ismay recommending Mr. Merrill and suggesting that he be given the title of Director of Infrastructure. Lord Ismay agreed with the appointment, but suggested that the title should be 'Comptroller'. In British administrative parlance the term 'comptroller' is a variation of 'controller', meaning, according to the *Concise Oxford Dictionary*, 'one who controls the expenditure of funds'.[11] In other words Lord Ismay viewed the post as one which should be occupied by a person with a financial as well as an engineering background. As it turned out, the title of 'Controller for Infrastructure', was adopted and the American engineer occupied the post for the remainder of Lord Ismay's period in office.

It is interesting to note that the Management Survey Team which examined the International Staff/Secretariat in 1956 recommended the creation of a new Division under an Assistant Secretary-General for Infrastructure and for Emergency Planning. '[He] would be responsible for the major common financial projects of the Alliance. Substantial amounts of money are involved in this work as well as judgements of major political and economic importance, deserving attention at a high level in the Secretariat'.[12]

The suggestion that a new Division should be created was received with reservation. Mr. Eugene Merrill, the Controller for Infrastructure thought that the Infrastructure Programme did not warrant Division status because, in relation to the overall purposes and functions of the Alliance, it was not

[10] In 1952 the Council had redesignated the Deputies as Permanent Representatives.

[11] 4th ed., 1951. The first chairman of the Infrastructure Committee, Mr. C. E. F. Gough of the U.K., had recommended that a financial expert with the title of 'comptroller' be appointed.

[12] NATO Management Survey Team, General Report, 1 May 1956, par. 27(e).

important enough.[13] Apparently Lord Ismay and the Council agreed with this opinion for the recommendation was never carried out. In any event, from the outset there was some confusion as to the exact nature of the Controller's duties— whether the emphasis should be on the financial rather than on the engineering aspects of the Programme. In practice Mr. Merrill performed both functions until 1957, using his Deputy for general co-ordination activities and for supervision of the Branch during his absence.[14]

When the Chairman of the Infrastructure Committee, a representative of the United Kingdom, was recalled in September 1953, according to custom he recommended that his national successor should be made Chairman also. However, Mr. Weicker, the Assistant Secretary-General for Production and Logistics, suggested to Lord Ismay that Mr. Merrill should be nominated for the position. Lord Ismay agreed, and after some hesitation the Committee accepted the nomination. This was the first time a member of the International Staff/Secretariat had been nominated for the chairmanship of a Council Committee, and the hesitation was not any personal reflection on Mr. Merrill. A question of principle was involved. Specifically, should the Controller participate actively both in the formulation of policy and in its execution? In addition, opposition arose because some of the delegations wished to nominate one of their representatives for the Chair.

When the Committee agreed to the nomination it created a precedent which was followed increasingly as the line between the purely political and the technical became more difficult to draw. Other Council Committees which were chaired by officers

[13] Interview with Mr. Merrill, 26 Aug. 1959.

[14] The Management Survey Team had recommended that: 'On the assumption that the Assistant Secretary-General will normally act as Chairman of these two committees [Infrastructure and P & P] and that the recommended Executive Director will devote most of his time to the active direction of the work of the Division, the Team recommends the suppression of the deputy's post in the division. The title of Executive Director is recommended as being more descriptive of the wide range of engineering, administrative and financial work of the post than is the present title of Controller'. (General Report, Annex I, par. 59.) This separation of functions of the Controller was never carried out.

of the International Staff/Secretariat were the Annual Review Committee, which was chaired first by the Deputy Secretary-General and then by the Assistant Secretary-General for Economics and Finance, and the Defence Production Committee which was chaired by the Assistant Secretary-General for Production and Logistics. When the Committee of Political Advisers was approved late in 1956 the Assistant Secretary-General for Political Affairs was made Chairman. He also became Chairman of the Information Committee after M. Spaak became Secretary-General.

For Mr. Merrill, from the chairmanship of the Infrastructure Committee to that of the P & P Committee was a short step. Mijnh. van Tets's recall early in 1954 resulted in Mr. Merrill's assuming that position as well; he retained it throughout Lord Ismay's tenure of office. An argument advanced in favour of this arrangement was that the close relationship necessary between the two Committees—of which one formulated and the other supervised the execution of infrastructure policy—could best be preserved by having the same person head both Committees. Mr. Merrill also suggested that his chairmanship of the P & P Committee would counteract a tendency of the technical representatives, who were part of the International Staff/Secretariat, to look directly to the P&P for guidance in infrastructure budgetary matters rather than to the Controller.[15] The membership of the two Committees was virtually the same; they merely 'changed hats' for different sittings. With everyone working in close proximity the Controller felt that he could make sure that duplication and overlapping of duties was avoided. Some of the delegations, however, thought that the Controller would exercise too much influence and would control initiatives excessively by virtue of his dual role, and that, as Controller, his only mandate from the Council was to keep the two committees informed of the work of his Branch.

When the Controller was appointed the Infrastructure Section was retitled the Infrastructure Branch. Under the Controller were his Deputy, a Secretariat Section (including Budget and Control), and five Technical Sections: POL, Naval,

<hr />

[15] Interview with Mr. Merrill, 26 Aug. 1959.

Signals, Airfields, and Construction. By 1956 the Infrastructure Committee secretariat had been placed in the Office of the Executive Secretary, the Budget and Control Section had become the budget and analysis section, working under the P & P Committee; and a Programme Control Officer had been appointed to head a Programme Control Section. The Construction and Naval Sections were later incorporated into one section, reducing the total number of Sections to five.[16]

The technicians who worked in the Technical Sections had offices in the Palais de Chaillot, but much of their time was spent in travelling in order to inspect and report on the progress of the projects. They were instructed to:

(*a*) provide technical reports, assistance and advice in respect to the preparation, costing and screening of infrastructure programmes; (*b*) provide technical reports, assistance and advice on requests submitted by host nations for authorisation to commit funds; (*c*) offer to the host countries technical assistance and advice, interpretation of approved standards for construction and, when required, issue technical details and specifications, in accordance with approved standards; (*d*) provide for the exchange of technical information on methods of construction within NATO, with a view to achieving economies and improving construction; (*e*) make field inspections of the technical aspects of infrastructure projects in accordance with approved NATO infrastructure inspection procedures; (*f*) make recommendations to the Infrastructure Committees on methods which might facilitate the work of these Committees, effect economies and improve technical quality and rate of progress of construction; (*g*) on behalf of the Infrastructure Committees, co-ordinate the need for and collect such reports, technical data and other information as may be required by the Committee and the infrastructure staff to carry out their functions, from NATO countries, the Standing Group, NATO commands and other sources and assist the Committees in ensuring that unnecessary reports, etc., are not called for; (*h*) maintain contact on technical matters with NATO countries and NATO commands; (*i*) refer matters of policy raised by national or NATO military authorities concerning infrastructure to the appropriate Infrastructure Committee.[17]

[16] See Charts on pp. 244–5 for illustration of how the infrastructure activities fit into the Production and Logistics Division.
[17] NATO Doc. C-M(54)13.

Some consideration was given to placing the technicians at offices in the field, but the disadvantages of this course seemed to outweigh the advantages. In general it was felt that to station officials of the International Staff/Secretariat permanently in a member country would not be appropriate. This attitude was in line with the NATO policy that a programme must be carried out within a country by that country's government and not by agents of the International Staff/Secretariat.[18] They could co-ordinate programmes and suggest ideas, but their execution was accomplished in the member countries by the appropriate national agency.

The work of the secretariat side of the Infrastructure Branch also engendered some discussion. At the outset the secretariat was placed exclusively within the Branch's purview, instead of being attached to the Executive Secretary's Office as were the secretariats of most of the Council Committees. It was organized into four units: a financial unit, which served as the records-keeping agency; the secretariat to the P & P Committee; the secretariat to the Infrastructure Committee; and the secretariat to the various working groups. These units made up the Budget and Control Section until 1956 when, as pointed out above, this Section became the Budget and Analysis Section working under the P & P Committee.

Except for the detachment of Programme Control from the Section, the change was made to conform to the general rule, based on a recommendation of the 1956 Management Survey Team, that the secretariats of all policy-formulating Council Committees should be placed within the office of the Executive Secretary. The secretariat to the Infrastructure Committee was thus transferred to the Executive Secretary's Office.[19] On the other hand, the P & P Committee's secretariat, which served a policy-executing committee, was retained as part of the Budget and Analysis Section.

The Infrastructure Committee secretariat drafted the papers of the Committee and its working parties and submitted memoranda which encouraged the discussion of infrastructure

[18] In contrast, the UN was authorized to set up UN public relations offices in its member countries.

[19] Also a special subcommittee to the Infrastructure Committee was set up in 1956 to work out financial problems.

questions. The secretariat provided secretaries to the various committees and working parties, and prepared maps, charts, reports, and similar data of financial and construction progress.

The Controller was the dominating spirit of the Branch. He spent about 25 per cent of his time travelling in the member countries in order to gain an impression of the technicians' work, to inspect construction projects, to obtain or disseminate the latest thinking about the projects and the latest objectives, and to receive the comments and recommendations of governments. Both he and the technicians were careful to work through the delegations or the host governments rather than directly with the contractors. He spent about 10 per cent of his time at the military Commands in order to learn their plans and to tell them of the progress of the projects. As Chairman of the Infrastructure Committee he met the Committee for about half a day a week, and as Chairman of the P & P Committee he met them for an average of one day a week.[20]

The Controller's activities centred on the work of his two Committees much more than on the work of the Council. The Council had such confidence in the work of the Infrastructure and P & P Committees that it delegated almost complete responsibility to these Committees to act on behalf of the Council in infrastructure matters.

The procedure by which the work of the Infrastructure Branch was accomplished was as follows. After the military Commands had drawn up their detailed estimates and specifications for the slice of the Programme under consideration, the Infrastructure Committee was responsible for reviewing and screening the submission on behalf of the Council to ensure that the estimates gave the lowest possible figure to obtain the standards required. The relationship of the military planners to the civilian technicians at the pre-Council approval stage was set forth by Lord Ismay:

The first step is for Subordinate Commanders to submit to their Supreme Commanders proposals for infrastructure in their commands. The next step is for the Supreme Commanders to co-ordinate these plans and to satisfy themselves that the installations proposed are militarily essential to support the forces which have been agreed in the Annual Review and that they are for common use, in accordance with the established criteria. In the course of preparing their programmes Supreme Commanders draw upon the advice of the technicians of the International Staff. The programme is then passed to the Standing Group and to the Infrastructure Committee of the North Atlantic Council. The Standing Group examines it from the standpoint of military necessity and urgency and submits its comments to the Military Committee. The Infrastructure Committee examines it from the financial and technical point of view, and verifies that the projects are in fact for common use and therefore qualify for common financing. The final reports from the Military Committee and the Infrastructure Committee are then placed before the Council and considered simultaneously.[21]

When a project had been approved, responsibility for its execution rested with the host country. The bidding for contracts was handled by the host government, with the International Staff/Secretariat and the P & P Committee only reviewing the procedure. The host government was required to consider all bids according to a system of international competitive bidding, 'the underlying idea being that since thirteen NATO countries contribute towards the cost of a project, they should all have a chance to benefit from the economic advantages which result from its construction'.[22] The only stipulation as regards the choice of contractor was that the contract should be awarded to the lowest bidder consistent with the standards set. This system of open competitive bidding was similar to national practice, and Lord Ismay in discussing the infrastructure procedures found direct analogy between NATO's practice and that which governments observe in budgeting for and constructing fixed installations. The P & P Committee authorized the financing of the project and reimbursed the host government as the project was being completed according to the cost-sharing agreement.

The military Commands established criteria which governed the procurement and construction of works after their approval by the Infrastructure Committee. The NATO infrastructure staff gave technical guidance that countries were required to follow in the design and execution of works. The appropriate

[21] *The Five Years*, pp. 119–20.   [22] ibid.

infrastructure technicians verified plans and specifications and assisted in the inspection of the projects to ensure that what had been approved by the Council and the Infrastructure Committee had in fact been done. The final decision on the acceptability of a project rested with the Infrastructure Committee. Payments were authorized by the P & P Committee only after a project's acceptance. This is another example of the control exercised by the civilian elements in NATO.

Infrastructure accounts were checked by a NATO International Board of Auditors. The auditors were private accountants employed by NATO. They were responsible to the Council in much the same way as the General Accounting Office was responsible to the United States Congress. This ensured the proper use of funds just as the inspections by the International Staff/Secretariat and the military Commands ensured that construction was according to specifications and cost estimates. It was deemed especially important that there should be no irregularities because this was the only major NATO activity for which the nations had pooled their economic resources; it would have been singularly unfortunate if any single member country or any national contractor appeared to have gained an advantage literally at the expense of other nations. This unhappy situation was successfully avoided.

The host country, needless to say, was consulted continuously in the planning period and could even initiate a plan for a project which would then go to the military authorities. Altogether the two Committees, the International Staff/Secretariat, the military authorities, and the host government cooperated to bring the various infrastructure projects to fruition.

The major parts of the Programme fell into the categories of signals communications, airfields, naval (construction of docks and harbours), and POL (pipeline systems). The signals communications projects were first initiated by WUDO, for it was early recognized that in Western Europe, with eight different languages, linguistic and communications diversification could prove disastrous to prompt and effective international command. 'Put briefly, the requirement was for the production of agreed allied communication procedures, for the standardization of equipment or (where this could not be made) for the means of connecting otherwise incompatible equipment, for the standardization of training and for the installation of communication facilities for the military command.'[23]

NATO's communications agencies came under the Standing Group rather than under the International Staff/Secretariat. They were the NATO Communications Electronics Board, the Communication Electronics Co-ordinating Section, and the Regional Communication Electronics Agencies. Under the last were placed the European Military Communications Co-ordination Committee (EMCC), the European Long Lines Agency (ELLA), the European Radio Frequency Agency (ERFA), the European Crypto Security Agency (ECSA), and the European Naval Communication Agency (ENCA). In communications activities the general policy was to use those civilian facilities already in existence, and then to augment and extend them to meet military needs if necessary. Furthermore, this need had to be a NATO need and not a national military one.

Almost half of the first slice was earmarked for signals communications projects. The specifications set down by NATO were those which had been adopted by the European Consultative Committee for Telecommunications of the United Nations at Geneva. In 1957, in line with the increased emphasis on air warning, an Air Experimental Centre was established at The Hague, under the direction of SHAPE, to keep abreast of the latest developments in air warning techniques. This Centre was financed by the United States.

By far the greatest construction effort undertaken in infrastructure was that of new air and army installations. By mid-1956, 136 airfields had been either constructed or modernized for the use of NATO forces. Three types of airfields were constructed—tactical, maritime, and air training. The maritime and air training fields accounted for about 10 per cent of the airfield construction programme.

[23] Brigadier Cole, 'Signal Communications in NATO', *The Fifteen Nations*, II, Sept. 1956, p. 61. More than three-quarters of infrastructure funds, over the years 1952–7, were devoted to airfields, signals communications, and POL. The naval, land training, navigational and radar warning stations construction projects took up the remaining quarter. (*The Five Years*, p. 124.)

For land forces, training grounds were built which enabled tank and infantry or armoured divisional training. NATO built the necessary installations on land furnished by the host country. The relationship between the host country and NATO in regard to the provision of installations was as follows:

As a general rule, it can be said, everything provided out of international funds is fixed and not movable, with water and electricity being the responsibility of the host country up to the airfield boundaries, after which NATO provides the facilities for the use of the major utilities.[24]

The user nation furnished personnel accommodations, such as barracks, hospitals, messes, recreation rooms, and chapels, on the principle that every nation was responsible for the logistic requirements of its own forces.[25] In fact the user country was free to add in any way to the minimum facilities, subject only to the qualification that the additional installations conformed to NATO standards and specifications and that the user country paid for them. The United States and Canada were most often the user countries, and the United States, Canada, and the German Federal Republic were the three countries that most often required facilities beyond the minimum standards. Agreement was reached through bilateral negotiations between the user and the host country on the costs required over and above the minimum, and then the user country made a lump-sum payment to the host country for the construction of the additional facilities.[26]

The requirement that the host country must provide the land was not as easy to comply with as it might look at first glance. For one thing, the requisitioning of land for airfields tended to fall on two nations, France and The Netherlands, and most of the major training areas were situated in the German Federal Republic. For another, the domestic political impact of

[24] NATO Press Release, 1 Dec. 1952.

[25] ibid. For land training facilities, NATO built the minimum of barracks, kitchens, first aid posts, utility services, and roads. The host country took the roads and utilities up to the training area. The military Commands provided the tanks and guns.

[26] The U.S. took four years to negotiate the cost of an airfield with NATO and France. (Interview with Mr. Merrill, 28 Aug. 1959.)

dispossessing local citizens of their land could prove embarrassing. Lord Ismay cited an example to illustrate some of the political implications of requisitioning land:

[Lord Ismay] said that to build an airfield in Alsace the French Government had to dispossess 40 farmers on very rich land where there were hops, tobacco and geese for pate de fois gras. 'The site happened to be in the constituency of one of the members of the French Government, so you will understand the complications.' Lord Ismay did not mention the Minister by name. He is M. Pflimlin, Minister of State in charge of the Council of Europe. Fortunately for himself and NATO, he is no longer Minister for Agriculture—a portfolio he held in eight previous Governments.[27]

Naval base construction started in 1954; it emphasized storage facilities for naval fuel and ammunition. In addition dry docks, repair facilities, piers and breakwaters were built where it could be established that the need was directly related to NATO. No construction was undertaken for the exclusive national use of a member country. However, if the military need was not immediate, the host country could lease out the facilities to commercial enterprises, thereby assisting to defray the expenses, provided that NATO could regain them immediately when necessary. A chain of navigational aid stations was built in the Eastern Atlantic for the Supreme Commander Atlantic's forces.

The fourth major part of the Infrastructure Programme, POL, was designed to meet the need arising out of the enormously high rate of fuel consumption of modern military forces, especially jet aircraft. NATO constructed an extensive pipeline system to provide the quantity and quality of fuel needed as expeditiously and inexpensively as possible. The first POL project was approved in December 1953; by 1956, 5,821 miles of pipelines had been laid, including storage facilities for more than 1,836,000 cubic metres of fuel.[28] The host countries were Norway, Denmark, Belgium, Luxembourg, France, Italy, Greece, Turkey, The Netherlands, and the German Federal Republic.

---

[27] *Daily Telegraph*, 14 Oct. 1952; *New York Herald-Tribune*, 9 Oct. 1952.
[28] 'Pipe-lines are Europe's Life-Lines', *The Fifteen Nations*, II, Sept. 1956, p. 91.

By 1957 a NATO Pipeline Committee was established to arrange for the operation and maintenance of the pipeline system. A Pipeline Operating Agency was set up which was made independent of the International Staff/Secretariat. It was a semi-private company which employed civilians and served civilian as well as military needs. Financially speaking, it was more of a commercial enterprise than a government-type one.[29] The tendency to assign certain functions to semi-autonomous agencies which were initially developed by the International Staff/Secretariat created a third dimension to NATO's international administration, the first two being the 'staff' (planning and programming), and the 'secretariat' functions.[30] This third dimension needs further study as a new phenomenon in international administration.

The Infrastructure Programme was a considerable advance in international co-operation. With NATO's failure to devise a general supranational budgeting system, and therefore to institute common funding, this area alone reflects supranational co-operation. It rested on one motive—necessity. It is interesting to note that traditional diplomatic negotiation did not produce sufficient consensus to find a cost-sharing formula, and so Lord Ismay, as a 'disinterested broker', was handed the problem.

As Secretary-General Lord Ismay acknowledged the important role of the United States in infrastructure—indeed in the whole of logistics—by appointing Americans to the top posts. It was often said in NATO that Lord Ismay did not concern himself too deeply with this aspect of the International Staff/Secretariat, for it was highly technical. Once the cost-sharing formula had been worked out and the key appointments made, administrative initiative passed to the international civil servants, and especially to Mr. Merrill, who could deal directly and intimately with his Council Committees by virtue of his role as their Chairman.

Although in its early stages the Programme showed signs of being dominated by the military side of NATO, after the

[29] Interview with Mr. Merrill, 28 Aug. 1959; *The North Atlantic Treaty Organization* (Paris, 1957), p. 72.

[30] E.g. the NATO Maintenance and Supply Service Agency, described in Ch. XI.

principle of civilian control was laid down, close co-operation developed between the military planners and the civilian technicians. Some tension always existed, for the civilians tended to dampen the enthusiasm of the military people. Since Americans were assigned to important civilian and military infrastructure posts, sometimes the discussions appeared to be more 'in the family' than in an international body. On the other hand many of the civilian technicians came from other nations, and of course the Programme could be carried out only in and with the Continental nations.

It was at first assumed that the Infrastructure Programme would be self-liquidating, that is, once the fixed installations were built the work would be finished. But changing technology and weapons systems even during Lord Ismay's tenure of office proved this assumption to be wrong. But, as procedures have become established and confidence has grown, the uniqueness of the venture has lost some of its impact. This is unfortunate in some ways for the Programme proved that supranationalism can be introduced into an otherwise multinational international organization and can be made to work without impinging on the freedom of diplomatic manoeuvre of member nations in other areas. The achievements of the Infrastructure Programme can be summarized as follows:

The co-operation of the . . . NATO governments has been largely responsible for the success of the infrastructure programme to date. Potential waste or duplication of effort has been virtually avoided due to an established procedure of screening, by experts, item by item authorisation by committees of the Council, joint civilian and military inspections and final auditing, in full co-operation with the military establishment. The comprehensive system of budgetary control assures that essential military requirements are met with minimum expense to the Allies, and in turn, the co-operation of member governments in forwarding each project has assured that standards, established through the NATO mechanism are met. The principle of opening infrastructure construction contracts to international competitive bidding has also tended to reduce cost, improve quality and implement the objectives of Article 2 of the North Atlantic Treaty.[31]

[31] NATO Press Release, No. 54–26.

PART V

CONCLUSIONS

'Administration is an art, not a science.'
A. Loveday

CONCLUSIONS

THE major conclusion of this study is that, where the traditions and precepts of administration have not been firmly implanted and endowed with their own authority, a tendency arises for them to give way to the interplay of interests and personalities. In international administration this situation is complicated by the fact that it is the combination of personalities from both a national and a 'non-national' administrative milieu, and national interests, that influences the nature of administration. For the International Staff/Secretariat, the circumstance that the first Secretary-General belonged to the British Cabinet Secretariat tradition affected both the political nature of his role and the administrative nature of the Organization he headed.

As its name implies, the International Staff/Secretariat executed policy according to two basically dissimilar concepts of international administration. One concept, which was favoured by Lord Ismay, emphasized the co-ordination of a range of multinational committees and working groups by a central international secretariat. These committees and working groups would be composed of representatives of the national delegations. Only the secretariat would be 'internationalized'. The other concept was the so-called 'functional' or staff approach to international administration. According to this concept policy would be carried out by technicians and specialists assigned directly to the international body. They could be formed into operational agencies which would be responsible for ongoing activities. A secretariat, if one were needed, would be made an integral part of the respective operational sections it served, rather than standing apart from them. This concept was favoured by the United States and France. The result, in the case of the International Staff/Secretariat, was an increasingly uncomfortable compromise.

In practice the so-called operating agencies, instead of being really engaged in the development and execution of programmes which could be administered by the International

Staff/Secretariat in the member countries, served more as channels for the collection and exchange of information which would be useful to the member countries in devising ways of meeting the major political, economic, and military requirements of the Alliance. The execution of all programmes (with the exception of the Infrastructure Programme) rested with the member nations themselves.

Lord Ismay gave primary internal administrative (or 'housekeeping') authority to his Executive Secretary, whom he regarded as a kind of chief-of-staff. The Executive Secretary was also Secretary to the Council and had under him the secretaries to the various Council Committees. The Council gave sporadic and limited operational authority to the functional Divisions into which the International Staff/Secretariat was organized and which in part had their own secretariats. In his personal role the Secretary-General directed the greater part of his energies to smoothing out the political problems of the Alliance and to creating a feeling of *esprit de corps* among those who worked in the International Staff/Secretariat. He also gave a lot of attention to projecting an image before the world of the Office of Secretary-General as the focus of the Alliance.

However, as the International Staff/Secretariat and the national delegations gained experience in working together on common problems and gained confidence in one another, the International Staff/Secretariat was increasingly allowed to participate in policy-making. An example of this trend was the increasing use made of senior officers of the International Staff/Secretariat as Chairmen of Council Committees. In the early days these Committees were chaired by a representative of a delegation; later on they were chaired by the officer in the International Staff/Secretariat who had primary responsibility for the functional area involved. As experience accumulated, there was also a tendency either to reduce matters of a political nature to a routine administrative responsibility which could be handled by the International Staff/Secretariat, or else to deny to the International Staff/Secretariat authority to carry out a programme which involved political considerations.

The Annual Review function of the Economics and Finance Division, for instance, posed a tremendous challenge to the

International Staff/Secretariat in the early years because the Alliance's political authorities had not agreed on the extent to which certain information-gathering and evaluatory methods could be applied, or should be allowed to influence national domestic budget policies, which were of course based on domestic political considerations as well as on economic or financial ones. As these decisions were gradually made, the Annual Review became more or less a routine operation which demanded less and less attention from the Council and less special effort from the International Staff/Secretariat.

An opposite result occurred in the defence production activities of the Alliance. There, political considerations dictated that the operational methods proposed—standardizing of equipment specifications, mass purchasing, and rationalizing of production—could not be accepted. Given this situation, the Production and Logistics Division, except in certain limited instances, was never more than a vehicle for facilitating national planning efforts. It became less of an ongoing operational activity than a secretariat-within-a-secretariat, serving a constellation of working groups. The only part of the Division which did not develop in this way was the Infrastructure Branch. In this case a clear-cut political decision, resting upon military necessity, was made. If there were to be troops-in-being the facilities with which to house and supply them had to be built and paid for. The equipment they were to use had to be supplied with fuels, lubricants, and maintenance facilities. Once the political decision to create forces-in-being had been made in 1951 (which was followed by the decision to form an International Staff/Secretariat), then the question of method, i.e. administration, became relevant. Procedures of common-funding, specifications standardization, open-bidding, international inspection and auditing, were worked out and applied. This is a clear case of functionalism in international administration.

In public relations and information, the political environment in the member nations prevented any uniform application of NATO-wide projects. The question of administrative method never became a major matter. The only relevant question was whether certain information or public relations projects were acceptable to certain member governments, and if so, to what extent. Execution of the projects was entirely dependent upon the attitude and internal administrative arrangements of each member nation.

Housekeeping administration was entirely at the political mercy of the Council, as it is in most international organizations. The Secretary-General, in his capacity as the chief Administrative agent of the Council, had operational authority. Serving a primarily military-security organization, the International Staff/Secretariat was denied the right to use an outside Administrative Tribunal to resolve disputes involving conditions of employment or working conditions in general. Very little room was left between the Council and the Secretary-General in which the Staff Association could manoeuvre. This is not to imply that the Secretary-General or the Council were insensitive to such matters. One of the significant facts revealed in this study is the concern of the Secretary-General and the Council to create a suitable environment for its career international civil servants. In this respect the use of outside Groups of Experts with free access to appropriate people and information and the open encouragement given by the Council and the Administration to the Staff Association to express itself through its Staff Committee on matters of personnel administration are noteworthy precedents. During the years of Lord Ismay's leadership, the administrative liberalism about which Alexander Loveday spoke in his book, *Reflections on International Administration*, was put into practice to the maximum extent possible. If Lord Ismay experienced only qualified success in furthering the interests of his International Staff/Secretariat, this was due not to a reluctance on his part, but to the necessity of working with a multinational governing body in which the rule of unanimity prevailed. This was a political problem which was especially relevant where money was involved, and, in most instances, issues would be—and had to be—expressed in financial terms. In summary, the Staff Committee's efforts on behalf of its 'clientele' were strongly conditioned by its dependence upon the goodwill and forbearance first of the Secretary-General and then of the Council.

It is small wonder, then, when all the considerations enumerated above are taken into account, that Lord Ismay viewed his role as being first and foremost of a political nature. He had fifteen masters to serve, and an organization under him which was not homogeneous in either structure or mission. The Secretary-General had to rely upon diplomacy first and administration second to achieve his aims.

Turning to Lord Ismay's external role, there is no doubt that during his tenure of office he generated greater understanding of what NATO was and what it did. He tried actively to influence world public opinion. But in this respect he was confronted by an ambiguous situation. He could, it is true, make public speeches and public appearances as often as he wished. But he was limited either to making generalizations about the defensive nature of the Alliance, or to giving dry descriptions of its history and workings. He could not engage publicly in discussions of policy unless he had a mandate from the Council to do so, and there was only limited co-ordination of national foreign policies between 1952 and 1957. Some observers have said that a Secretary-General should try to form an Alliance position and to lead out in political matters. But to do so would mean either implicitly or explicitly criticizing at one time or another the foreign policies of various member countries. There is no surer way for an international civil servant to find his effectiveness nullified than to engage publicly in an argument with one of the 'governing countries' of his international organization. This thought was always uppermost in Lord Ismay's calculations as he tried to influence the policies of the member nations constructively. His lasting success and the success of the International Staff/Secretariat lay in building up NATO's prestige as much as possible, in performing all possible functions in the best possible manner, and in attempting to reduce disagreements and misunderstandings in NATO to the minimum.

Lord Ismay's greatest contribution was the creation of an international climate in which political decisions could be taken by the Council with the least friction. In the political realm, his role was one of 'playing-down'—finding the common denominator among varied and sometimes conflicting interests. In the realms of public relations and administration, his role was one of 'playing-up'—pouring content into such general conceptions as 'Atlantic Community', 'equitable sharing of the defence burden', and 'an Alliance for Peace'. Great quantities of tact, patience, determination, and optimism were required to overcome the temptations towards frustration, cynicism, and discouragement. Lord Ismay was the servant of the Council and the leader of the International Staff/Secretariat in the highest sense of both functions. He created the habit of working together and bequeathed it as a precious legacy to his successors.

SELECT BIBLIOGRAPHY

I. Books

Ball, M. Margaret. *N.A.T.O. and the European Movement* (London, 1959).

Beckett, Sir W. E. *The North Atlantic Treaty, the Brussels Treaty, and the Charter of the U.N.* The Library of World Affairs, 12 (London, 1950).

Beishline, John R. *Military Management for National Defense* (Harrisburg, 1949).

Beloff, Max. *Europe and the Europeans* (London, 1957).

Critchley, T. A. *The Civil Service Today* (London, 1951).

Ehrman, John. *Cabinet Government and War 1890–1940* (Cambridge, 1958).

Hankey, Lord. *Diplomacy by Conference* (London, 1946).

Howard-Ellis, C. *The Origin Structure and Working of the League of Nations* (London, 1928).

Ismay, Lord. *NATO: The First Five Years, 1949–1954* (Paris, 1956).

Jennings, Sir W. Ivor. *Cabinet Government*, 2nd ed. (Cambridge, 1951).

Keith, A. B. *The British Cabinet System*, ed. N. H. Gibbs (London, 1952).

Lie, Trygve. *In the Cause of Peace* (New York, 1954).

Loveday, Alexander. *Reflections on International Administration* (Oxford, 1956).

Moore, Ben T. *NATO and the Future of Europe* (New York, 1958).

Nicolson, Harold. *The Evolution of Diplomatic Method* (London, 1954).

Ranshofen-Wertheimer, Egon F. *The International Secretariat* (Washington, 1945).

Reuter, P. *Institutions internationales* (Paris, 1955).

Ritchie, Ronald S. *NATO: The Economics of an Alliance* (Toronto, 1956).

Robertson, A. H. *European Institutions* (London, 1959).

— *The Council of Europe* (London, 1956).

Robson, William A. *The Civil Service in Britain and France* (London, 1956).

Roll, Eric. *The Combined Food Board: A Study in Wartime International Planning* (Stanford, 1956).

Rosen, S. McKee. *The Combined Boards of the Second World War* (New York, 1951).

Salter, Sir Arthur. *Allied Shipping Control* (London, 1921).

Schwebel, Stephen M. *The Secretary-General of the United Nations* (Cambridge, 1952).

Scitovsky, Tibor. *Economic Theory and Western European Integration* (London, 1958).

Scott, F. R. *The World's Civil Service* (New York, 1954).

Walters, F. P. *A History of the League of Nations*, Vols. I and II (London, 1952).

Wheare, K. C. *Government by Committee* (Oxford, 1955).

Willson, F. M. G. *The Organization of British Central Government, 1914–1956*, ed. D. N. Chester (London, 1957).

Young, T. C. *International Civil Service: Principles and Problems* (Brussels, 1958).

Yu, Wangteh. *The English Cabinet System* (London, 1939).

Zimmern, Sir Alfred. *The League of Nations and The Rule of Law 1918–1935* (London, 1936).

II. Pamphlets

Alliance for Peace, The First Five Years of NATO (London, 1954).

Anderson, Rt. Hon. Sir John. *The Machinery of Government*, Romanes Lecture (Oxford, 1946).

Atlantic Alliance. NATO's Role in the Free World (London, R.I.I.A., 1954).

Bridges, Sir Edward (Lord). *Portrait of a Profession: the Civil Service Tradition*, Rede lecture (Cambridge, 1950).

Collective Defence under the Brussels and NATO Treaties (London, H.M.S.O., 1950).

Defence in the Cold War (London, R.I.I.A., 1950).

Economic Aspects of North Atlantic Security (New York, Committee for Economic Development, 1951).

General Guidance for NATO Groups of Experts (Paris, NATO, 1955).

Gibbs, N. H. *The Origins of Imperial Defence*, Inaugural Lecture (Oxford, 1955).

Hankey, Lord. *The Development of the Higher Control of the Machinery of Government*, Haldane Memorial Lecture (London, 1942).

Hankey, Lord. *The Science and Art of Government*, Romanes Lecture (Oxford, 1951).

Patterson, G. and E. Furniss. *NATO, A Critical Appraisal*, A Symposium held at Princeton University (Princeton, 1957).

The International Secretariat of the Future (London, R.I.I.A., 1944).

United Kingdom Administration and International Organizations (London, R.I.I.A., 1951).

Warburton, A. M. and J. B. Wood. *Paying for NATO* (London, 1956).

Weeks, Lt.-Gen. Sir Ronald M. *Organization and Equipment for War*, Lees Knowles Lecture (Cambridge, 1950).

III. JOURNAL ARTICLES

Gaudemet, P. M. 'Le fonctionnaire européen.—Notion.—Role. Condition juridique', *La fonction publique européenne* (November, 1955).

Harrison, R. J. P. 'The Organization of the Cabinet Secretariat', *O & M Bulletin* (December 1951).

Jacob, Lt.-General Sir Ian. 'The High Level Conduct and Direction of World War II', *Journal of the Royal United Services Institution* (1956).

Jenks, C. Wilfred. 'Some Problems of an International Civil Service', *Public Administration Review*, Vol. III, No. 2 (1943).

Katz, Milton. 'A Case Study in International Organization', *Harvard Business Review* (Autumn 1946).

Stone, Donald C. 'The Application of Scientific Management Principles to International Administration', *American Political Science Review* (October 1948).

IV. VARIOUS NATO DOCUMENTS (as cited)

INDEX

(t) = table, (n) = note